Paula R. Worthington

TAX POLICY AND THE ECONOMY 2

edited by **Lawrence H. Summers**

National Bureau of Economic Research
The MIT Press, Cambridge, Massachusetts

Send orders and business correspondence to:
The MIT Press
55 Hayward Street
Cambridge, MA 02142

In the United Kingdom, continental Europe, and the Middle East and Africa, send orders and business correspondence to:
The MIT Press Ltd.
126 Buckingham Palace Road
London SW1W 9SD England

ISSN: 0892-8649
ISBN: hardcover 0-262-19272-1
       paperback 0-262-69121-3

Copyright Information
Permission to photocopy articles for internal or personal use, or the internal or personal use of specific clients, is granted by the copyright owner for users registered with the Copyright Clearance Center (CCC) Transactional Reporting Service, provided that the fee of $5.00 per copy is paid directly to CCC, 27 Congress St., Salem, MA 01970. The fee code for users of the Transactional Reporting Service is: 0892-8649/88 $5.00. For those organizations that have been granted a photocopy license with CCC, a separate system of payment has been arranged.

© 1988 by The National Bureau of Economic Research and The Massachusetts Institute of Technology.

NATIONAL BUREAU OF ECONOMIC RESEARCH

Officers:
Richard N. Rosett, *Chairman*
George T. Conklin, Jr., *Vice Chairman*
Martin Feldstein, *President and Chief Executive Officer*
Geoffrey Carliner, *Executive Director*
Charles A. Walworth, *Treasurer*
Sam Parker, *Director of Finance and Administration*

Directors at Large:

John H. Biggs	Martin Feldstein	Robert T. Parry
Andrew Brimmer	David L. Grove	Peter G. Peterson
Carl F. Christ	George Hatsopoulos	Robert V. Roosa
George T. Conklin, Jr.	Franklin A. Lindsay	Richard N. Rosett
Kathleen B. Cooper	Paul W. McCracken	Bert Seidman
Jean A. Crockett	Geoffrey H. Moore	Eli Shapiro
George C. Eads	Michael H. Moskow	Harold Shapiro
Morton Ehrlich	James J. O'Leary	Donald S. Wasserman

Directors by University Appointment:

Charles H. Berry, *Princeton*
James Duesenberry, *Harvard*
Ann F. Friedlaender, *Massachusetts Institute of Technology*
Jonathan Hughes, *Northwestern*
Saul Hymans, *Michigan*
J. C. LaForce, *California, Los Angeles*
Marjorie McElroy, *Duke*
Merton J. Peck, *Yale*
James L. Pierce, *California, Berkeley*
Andrew Postlewaite, *Pennsylvania*
Nathan Rosenberg, *Stanford*
James Simler, *Minnesota*
William S. Vickrey, *Columbia*
Burton A. Weisbrod, *Wisconsin*
Arnold Zellner, *Chicago*

Directors by Appointment of Other Organizations:

Richard Easterlin, *Economic History Association*
Edgar Fiedler, *National Association of Business Economists*
Robert S. Hamada, *American Finance Association*
Robert C. Holland, *Committee for Economic Development*
James Houck, *American Agricultural Economics Association*
David Kendrick, *American Economic Association*
Eric Kruger, *The Conference Board*
Rudolph A. Oswald, *American Federation of Labor and Congress of Industrial Organizations*
Douglas D. Purvis, *Canadian Economics Association*
Dudley Wallace, *American Statistical Association*
Charles A. Walworth, *American Institute of Certified Public Accountants*

Directors Emeriti:

Moses Abramovitz	Frank W. Fetter	George B. Roberts
Emilio G. Collado	Thomas D. Flynn	Willard L. Thorp
Solomon Fabricant	Gottfried Haberler	

Since this volume is a record of conference proceedings, it has been exempted from the rules governing critical review of manuscripts by the Board of Directors of the National Bureau (resolution adopted 8 June 1948, as revised 21 November 1949 and 20 April 1968).

CONTENTS

Introduction: *Lawrence H. Summers* vii

Acknowledgments xi

BUDGET DEFICITS AND THE BALANCE OF TRADE 1
B. Douglas Bernheim

TAXATION AND U.S. MULTINATIONAL INVESTMENT 33
James R. Hines, Jr.

TAX NEUTRALITY AND INTANGIBLE CAPITAL 63
Don Fullerton and Andrew B. Lyon

DO WE COLLECT ANY REVENUE FROM TAXING CAPITAL INCOME? 89
Roger H. Gordon and Joel Slemrod

DID ERTA RAISE THE SHARE OF TAXES PAID BY UPPER-INCOME TAXPAYERS? WILL TRA86 BE A REPEAT? 131
Lawrence B. Lindsey

PENSION BACKLOADING, IMPLICIT WAGE TAXES, AND WORK DISINCENTIVES 161
Laurence J. Kotlikoff and David A. Wise

INTRODUCTION

Lawrence H. Summers
Harvard University and NBER

The 1980s have already witnessed four major tax reform bills. Tax reform has commanded the attention of policymakers, the media, and the public. Although the 1986 Tax Reform Act will not take full effect for some time, attention is already turning to further efforts to alter the tax system. Many observers see the need for revenue increases in light of continuing federal deficits. Others use the need for reforms to address the adverse incentive effects of existing provisions or to introduce new incentives into the tax system. The only confident prediction one can make is that tax policy debates will be with us for years to come.

Economic research can make an important contribution to tax policy debates. It can quantify the effect of potential tax changes on economic behavior, and it can isolate the many indirect effects of tax policies on economic efficiency and on the distribution of income. All too often, however, the results of research by economists on tax policy issues are not presented in a way that is accessible to policymakers, attorneys, business people, and others involved in the formulation of tax policy.

In an effort to communicate research results, the NBER has initiated a series of conferences and publications on "Tax Policy and the Economy." This volume is the second in the series. Like its predecessor, its content is nontechnical and directed not only toward academics but also toward the much broader tax policy community. In keeping with the NBER's standard practice, the papers included here provide information and analysis that can enlighten tax policy debates but do not make specific policy recommendations. In the remainder of this introduction, I will describe and draw some connections between the six studies presented in this volume.

Traditionally, international taxation has been an arcane subspecialty among tax lawyers, and international considerations have played only a subsidiary role in shaping American tax policies. This is changing in light of the increasing internationalization of the world economy. Some $200 billion of foreign exchange are traded each day. Multinational corporations account for more than two-thirds of American trade. Close to one-third of

American exports pass between American multinationals and their subsidiaries. This volume contains two studies directed at international issues: Douglas Bernheim's "Budget Deficits and the Balance of Trade" examines the impact of changes in the overall level of taxation on the trade balance, and James R. Hines's "Taxation and U.S. Multinational Investment" examines the impact of specific tax provisions on the foreign direct investment decisions of U.S. companies.

Bernheim's chapter uses information on budget and trade deficits for the United States and its five leading trading partners—Japan, West Germany, Canada, the United Kingdom, and Mexico—to evaluate the impact of changes in budget deficits on trade deficits. He examines both the effects of changes in budget deficits within individual countries and of differences across countries in budget deficits. Bernheim concludes that "the evidence corroborates the view that fiscal deficits significantly contribute to the deterioration of the current account. Indeed, it appears that U.S. budget deficits have been responsible for roughly one-third of the U.S. trade deficit in recent years."

As I have already stressed, U.S. trade patterns are shaped to a significant extent by the behavior of multinational corporations. Hines's study seeks to assess the impact of the 1986 Tax Reform Act on the incentives faced by multinational corporations. Hines begins by reviewing historical information on the effects of taxes on multinational corporations as a prelude to considering the effects of the 1986 Act. He finds that particularly in the case of countries with substantial investment incentives, U.S. taxes have generally worked to discourage investment. He argues, however, that the 1986 Act "all but relieves most U.S. multinationals of U.S. tax obligations on their foreign income." He suggests that this will make foreign investment decisions of U.S. companies much more dependent on foreign tax rules and much less dependent on American tax policies.

Discussions of the need to "level the playing field" by designing a more neutral tax system played an important part in debates surrounding the 1986 Tax Reform Act. Supporters of the Act stressed the importance of eliminating incentives that allegedly favored certain types of investment at the expense of others, and the potential desirability of reducing statutory corporate and individual tax rates. The chapter by Don Fullerton and Andrew Lyon on "Tax Neutrality and Intangible Capital" and that by Roger Gordon and Joel Slemrod "Do We Collect Any Revenue From Taxing Capital Income" contribute to our understanding of the distorting effects of various tax provisions.

Fullerton and Lyon note that previous analyses have concentrated on the effects of taxes on physical investments in new plants and equipment. They argue that intangible investments in research and development, advertising, marketing, or worker training are also of substantial importance, and so it is necessary to consider neutrality toward these investments in evaluating tax policies. They note that since firms are permitted to "expense" outlays for intangibles, the tax system is biased in favor of the firms, and the authors attempt to evaluate the magnitude of this bias. After painstakingly deriving estimates of the stock of intangible capital, Fullerton and Lyon reconsider the effects of the 1986 Act on economic efficiency. They find that the Act increases production efficiency, but they note that the efficiency effects of eliminating the investment tax credit are reduced or possibly eliminated once intangible capital is taken into consideration.

Gordon and Slemrod focus on the problem of "tax arbitrage" in connection with the taxation of interest income. Tax arbitrage arises when interest deductions are taken at a higher tax rate than the rate at which interest income is taxed. For example, tax arbitrage occurs when an untaxed pension fund buys the bonds of a profitable corporation that deducts interest. They find that because of the importance of tax arbitrage, "taxing real rather than nominal interest would have raised tax revenues by $25.7 billion in 1983." A further finding is that exempting financial assets and liabilities from taxes and taxing only cash flows from real capital would have raised tax revenues by $9.1 billion. However, Gordon and Slemrod note that such a hypothetical reform would benefit high-bracket taxpayers at the expense of those in lower tax brackets.

The final two chapters explore aspects of the taxation of individual income. Lawrence Lindsey's "Did ERTA Raise the Share of Taxes Paid by Upper-Income Taxpayers? Will TRA86 be a Repeat?" examines the impact of changes in tax rates on tax collections. Among his other findings, Lindsey highlights the fact that the amount of wage and salary income showing up on the returns of high-bracket taxpayers rose sharply following the implementation of ERTA. Partially as a result of this change, tax collections from top-bracket taxpayers actually rose following the reduction in the top rate from 70 to 50 percent. Lindsey suggests that the increase in wages and salaries probably resulted from some combination of a shift in compensation away from fringe benefits and deferred payments toward wages and salaries, and some increase in labor supply. Lindsey's analysis suggests that reduced top rates contained in the 1986 Act will result in a significant increase in the wage and salary income of top-bracket taxpayers. However, he believes that this effect is likely to be more than offset by decreases in capital gains tax collections due to increased capital gains tax rates.

The chapter by Laurence Kotlikoff and David Wise, "Pension Backloading, Implicit Wage Taxes, and Work Disincentives," examines aspects of the impact of private pensions on the behavior of older workers. Because pension arrangements are substantially influenced by tax rules, this is a subject of some importance for tax policy design. Kotlikoff and Wise find that despite ERISA regulations appearing to mandate that benefit accruals occur smoothly over time, many private pension plans cause workers' benefits to be very sensitive to the length of their working life. Kotlikoff and Wise find that many pension plans give very substantial incentives for early retirements, that these incentives are much greater than those created by Social Security, and that they have an important impact in inducing earlier retirement by the workers who are affected.

ACKNOWLEDGMENTS

The authors and I are indebted to the people who made this volume and the conference on which it is based possible. NBER President Martin Feldstein and NBER Executive Director Geoffrey Carliner have wholeheartedly supported this effort to communicate the results of economic policy research to a wide audience from the outset. Deborah Mankiw administered this project with great skill and good cheer. There would be no volume without her efforts. Kirsten Foss Davis and Emery Brisson did their usual outstanding job of handling conference logistics. Tom Curtiss, Deborah Nicholson, and Vicki Rogers cheerfully typed and retyped the manuscripts here with endless patience. Finally I am grateful to the authors of the papers presented here for their thoughtful contributions.

Lawrence H. Summers

BUDGET DEFICITS AND THE BALANCE OF TRADE

B. Douglas Bernheim
Stanford University and NBER

The object of this chapter is to identify historical relationships between fiscal policy and the current account for the United States and five of its major trading partners. I attempt to provide some measures of the extent to which variations in budget deficits explain variations in current account balances, both across time and across countries. Overall, the evidence corroborates the view that fiscal deficits significantly contribute to a deterioration of the current account. Indeed, it appears that U.S. budget deficits have been responsible for roughly one-third of the U.S. trade deficit in recent years.

1. INTRODUCTION

In recent years, the U.S. economy has been characterized by soaring federal deficits and deteriorating trade balances. Many analysts suspect that these features are closely, and perhaps even causally, related. Indeed, national income accounting identities guarantee that budget deficits must create either an excess of private saving over investment or an excess of imports over exports. Standard economic reasoning suggests that government borrowing decreases the domestic supply of funds available to finance new investment, which leads to an inflow of funds from overseas. An offsetting

---

This paper was prepared for the NBER conference "Tax Policy and the Economy" held in Washington, D.C. on November 17, 1987. I would like to thank Ronald I. McKinnon, Robert Staiger, and Lawrence Summers for helpful comments. Any opinions expressed here are mine and should not be attributed to any other individual or institution.

adjustment to the current account is then required to reestablish international account balance. In short, budget deficits may well produce trade deficits.

This observation raises a number of questions concerning the effects of alternative fiscal policies. To what extent can one attribute the current U.S. trade deficit to budget deficits? How might legislation such as the Gramm-Rudman-Hollings Act affect the balance of payments? Is fiscal policy an effective tool for influencing patterns of international trade?

The object of this chapter is to identify historical relationships between fiscal policy and the current account for the United States and five of its major trading partners. I attempt to provide some measures of the extent to which variations in budget deficits explain variations in current account balances, both across time and across countries. The reader should bear in mind that even a strong empirical correlation between these two variables does not necessarily indicate a causal relationship—the fact that budget and trade deficits have moved together in the past does not guarantee that the current account will respond in the same way to future fiscal policy innovations. Nevertheless, a robust empirical pattern would signal the existence of some systematic underlying relationship and, in the context of sound economic arguments, would lend support to the hypothesis that fiscal deficits cause the balance of payments to deteriorate.

To the extent historical experience provides a reliable guide for policy, my analysis of U.S. time series suggests that a $1 increase in government budget deficits leads to roughly a $0.30 rise in the current account deficit. I obtain similar figures for Canada, the United Kingdom, and West Germany, as well as from an overall cross-country comparison. For Mexico, the historical relationship between trade deficits and budget deficits suggests that this effect is significantly larger, perhaps $0.80 to a dollar. In contrast, for Japan the data appear inconsistent with the view that budget deficits significantly affect the current account balance. This may well reflect the stringent controls that the Japanese have traditionally placed on international trade and flows of capital.

Overall, the evidence corroborates the view that fiscal deficits significantly contribute to a deterioration of the current account. Indeed, it appears that U.S. budget deficits have been responsible for roughly one-third of the U.S. trade deficit in recent years. Accordingly, the implementation of the Gramm-Rudman-Hollings deficit reduction provisions could dramatically improve the U.S. balance of trade.

The chapter is organized as follows. In section 2, I discuss the link between budget deficits and trade deficits and describe the factors that determine the quantitative importance of this link. Section 3 describes the data used in subsequent sections. I conduct an international comparison in section 4. Section 5 is devoted to the U.S. experience. The remaining five countries are considered in successive subsections of section 6. Finally, section 7 summarizes and reviews my findings in the context of other evidence on the effects of government budget deficits.

2. THE LINK BETWEEN BUDGET DEFICITS AND TRADE

To clarify the relationship between fiscal deficits and the balance of trade, it is helpful to begin with some national income accounting identities. First, individuals dispose of income (Y) either as consumption (C), saving (S), or taxes (T):

$$Y = C + S + T. \qquad (1)$$

Second, income must arise from either the domestic sale of consumption goods (C), investment goods (I), governmental goods (G), or the net sale of goods to foreign agents (exports, X, minus imports, M):

$$Y = C + I + G + (X - M). \qquad (2)$$

Combining equations (1) and (2), we obtain

$$C + S + T = C + I + G + (X - M),$$

which simplifies to

$$T - G = (X - M) + (I - S). \qquad (3)$$

In words, equation (3) states that the government budget surplus is equal to the trade surplus plus the excess of investment over private saving. Suppose then that the government fixes spending (G), and cuts taxes (T), thereby creating a deficit. Equation (3) indicates that, as a result, either the trade surplus ($X - M$) must decline or the excess of investment over saving ($I - S$) must decline, or both. Note that this conclusion follows directly from accounting and does not depend on any behavioral theories.

Nevertheless, whether the impact of budget deficits falls on $X - M$ or $I - S$ is an open question. Indeed, there are two important conditions under which fiscal policy would only affect $I - S$ and leave net exports unchanged. The first condition would arise if world capital markets were completely nonexistent. In that case, all investment would have to be financed domestically. Accordingly, private saving would always equal the sum of investment and government borrowing. An increase in the deficit would necessarily produce a commensurate increase in $S - I$, and $X - M$ would remain unchanged. The second condition would arise if taxpayers did not believe that higher disposable income resulting from fiscal deficits constitutes an increase in available resources. If people understand that deficits merely postpone taxes, and if they expect to pay the postponed tax at some point in the future, then they may respond to a tax cut by saving all incremental disposable income toward the future liability. Accordingly, saving would rise by exactly the amount of the deficit—any change in T (with G fixed) would alter S, and leave I, X, and M unchanged.

The empirical relevance of both these conditions is highly controversial. The efficiency of world capital markets has been debated by Harberger (1978,1980), Feldstein and Horioka (1980), and Feldstein (1983). More recently, Frankel (1986), Sachs (1981), Obstfeld (1986), and Summers (1986a) have made significant contributions in this area. It now appears that international capital markets are integrated to a very large extent, and that this integration is in some ways imperfect. The extent to which individuals anticipate and save for future tax liabilities has also received a great deal of attention in recent years, with most of the discussion focusing on Barro's (1974) notion of "Ricardian equivalence." In Bernheim (1987), I reviewed the existing theory and evidence concerning the doctrine that fiscal deficits are economically irrelevant, and concluded that this doctrine is not at all descriptive of the U.S. economy.

Since it seems that neither of the two conditions described above holds in practice, we may conclude that budget deficits almost certainly affect the balance of payments. I have mentioned these conditions not because I take them to be empirically plausible, but because they help us to identify the factors that will determine the magnitude of the impact of fiscal policy on trade deficits. If one believes that international capital markets are well integrated and that taxpayers tend to consume out of disposable income, then one is naturally led to the conclusion that this impact must be quite large.

It is useful to trace the economic links between budget deficits and trade in some detail. The standard story (see Branson (1985)) works as follows. When the government cuts taxes (holding spending constant), taxpayers respond by increasing consumption. If the economy is initially in a state of full employment, national saving must fall. Domestic funds are then insufficient to cover all profitable investment opportunities (at current interest rates) plus government borrowing. This imbalance between the supply and demand for funds places upward pressure on interest rates. Higher rates lead to less investment and more saving, but this redresses only a portion of the imbalance. Attracted by the availability of more profitable investment opportunities, foreign investors increase their supply of financial capital to the United States. To accommodate this shift in the international capital account, it is necessary to have an offsetting change in the current account. Specifically, investments in the United States require foreign capitalists to acquire U.S. currency. The resulting increase in the demand for dollars drives the value of the dollar up, making it more attractive for U.S. consumers to purchase imports and less attractive for foreign consumers to purchase U.S. exports.

Alternatively, if the economy is not initially in a state of full employment, then tax cuts may stimulate production. This would cause both national income and private saving to rise. Accordingly, national saving may decline much less than in a fully employed economy. The effect of budget deficits on trade deficits is therefore likely to be smaller in the presence of unemployed resources.

Finally, budget deficits may stimulate investment by raising the return to capital. This could occur through two channels. First, in the presence of unemployed resources, deficits may augment aggregate demand, thus generating higher returns to investment. Second, deficits permit the reduction of taxes on capital income, which raises the after-tax rate of return. In either case, the effect is to widen the gap between investment and national saving. International account balance then requires a larger increase in the current account deficit.

Although there has been a great deal of empirical work on the efficiency of international capital markets and the effect of government budget deficits on national saving, there has been almost no effort to measure the impact of fiscal policy on the balance of trade. Two exceptions are Milne (1977) and Summers (1986b). Milne studied time series data from thirty-eight countries for the period 1960–1975. Her strategy was simply to regress the current account deficit on the government budget deficit for each of the thirty-eight countries. This strategy produced mixed findings. Unfortunately, in considering so many countries, Milne was unable to analyze the data from any country in great detail and therefore failed to consider factors other than fiscal deficits that might have influenced trade deficits in systematic ways. As we shall see, the apparent absence of a systematic relationship between fiscal policy and trade can often be explained upon more careful analysis of the data. Although Summer's (1986b) findings corroborate the view that budget deficits depress the current account balance, his analysis was confined to the United States.

My strategy here is to employ a relatively small sample of countries: the United States and its five largest trading partners (as measured by U.S. exports). For each country, I analyze the historical relationship between budget deficits and current account balances, paying careful attention to third factors that might have influenced patterns of trade in any particular year.

3. DATA

I focus on the experiences of the United States and its five largest trading partners (as measured by U.S. exports)—Canada, the United Kingdom, West Germany, Japan, and Mexico—during the twenty-five-year period from 1960 to 1984. With a few exceptions (noted below), the data are drawn from the OECD National Accounts.

The first variable employed here is net saving for the general government. The OECD defines net government saving as the sum of direct and indirect taxes, the operating surplus of government enterprises, property income, and transfers received minus the sum of final consumption expenditures, payment of interest, rent, and royalties, subsidies, and transfers made. The general government includes the central government, social security funds, and all provincial, state, and/or local governments. I use this variable as my measure of the government's budget surplus (the negative of its deficit).

Although the OECD's measure of net government saving is appropriate for accounting purposes, it is in some ways deficient for studying economic behavior. For example, the OECD does not correct government deficits for the inflationary erosion of the value of outstanding debt that occurs during inflationary periods (see Eisner (1986) for a discussion). I have made no attempt to remedy this problem. The reader should therefore bear in mind that the relationship between budget deficits and trade deficits might be somewhat obscured during inflationary periods.

The OECD also provides a measure of each country's current account surplus, denominated in domestic currency. My primary objective is to determine the extent to which variations in the budget surplus variable can explain variations in this measure of the current account.

Throughout this investigation, I treat the budget surplus variable as exogenous. In essence, I assume that budgets are determined independently of the current account balance. This assumption is almost certainly descriptive of the recent U.S. experience, but more generally its validity is debatable. In particular, Summers (1986a) has argued that governments systematically use fiscal policy tools in an effort to maintain approximate current account balance. If this is true, then endogenous fiscal responses will tend to create a negative correlation between the budget surplus and current account surplus. By assuming that budgets are determined exogenously, my analysis will therefore tend to *understate* the true relationship between these variables.

It is also important to realize that budget surpluses and trade deficits may move together for entirely spurious reasons. It is therefore necessary to control for a number of third factors. First of all, since most macroeconomic time series tend to grow over time, both variables must be scaled relative to gross domestic product (GDP). Henceforth, I will use BSUR to denote the ratio of the budget surplus to gross domestic product (also obtained from the OECD National Accounts), and CAS to denote the ratio of the current account surplus to GDP. Second, budget deficits, saving, and investment (and hence the current account) all tend to move in systematic ways over the course of the business cycle. Rather than use cyclically adjusted variables, I control for business cycle effects by including current and lagged values of real GDP growth (henceforth denoted GROW) in regression equations explaining the current account surplus. Finally, budget deficits are systematically correlated with government consumption. Higher government consumption should tend to depress national saving, leading to larger current account deficits. I control for this effect by including the OECD's measure of government consumption (henceforth denoted GOV) as an additional explanatory variable in some of the reported regressions.

Unfortunately, OECD data is not available for Mexico. Since Mexico is the only developing country among the five largest U.S. trading partners, its experience is of particular interest. As an alternative data source, I use information collected by the International Monetary Fund (IMF), published in the IMF's *International financial statistics* and *Government financial statistics*. There are several drawbacks to using this data. First, the IMF's methods of accounting and sources of data differ from those of the OECD. This raises the possibility that systematic differences may produce spurious results for cross-country comparisons. Second, IMF data on the net saving of local governments in Mexico is not available after 1982. Since local governments save (or borrow) very little relative to the central government, I chose to use central government net saving as my measure of the Mexican budget deficit rather than to sacrifice the most recent years of data. Third, IMF data on government finances in Mexico are not available at all prior to 1972. My analysis of Mexico is therefore confined to a much shorter time span.

In the case of Canada, I also employ data on bilateral trade relations with the United States. I obtain this data from the IMF's *Direction of trade statistics*. The IMF measures the bilateral trade surplus in U.S. dollars; I express it as a fraction of U.S. GDP (henceforth, I refer to this variable as BTS).

In analyzing these data, it is essential to bear in mind that these variables are not the sole determinants of the trade deficit. Many other factors play a significant role and may explain apparently anomalous fluctuations in the current account. For the time period considered here, it is particularly important to think about the effects of three kinds of events.

First, from 1971 to 1973 international currency markets were in a period of great flux. The collapse of the Bretton Woods system of fixed exchange rates in 1971 and the intervening turmoil before its eventual replacement with a system of floating exchange rates in 1973 undoubtedly disturbed previous patterns of trade. Indeed, it is arguable that the sample period considered here should be divided into two subperiods in order to allow for systematically different fiscal effects under fixed- and floating-exchange-rate regimes.

Second, the 1970s witnessed two enormous shifts in relative prices and the terms of trade, which were brought about by large increases in the price of oil. The first oil crisis occurred at the end of 1973; oil prices remained abnormally high for 1974 and 1975. The second oil crisis was touched off by the Iranian revolution in 1979. Oil prices rose sharply and remained at very high levels through 1981. After 1981, the price of oil declined somewhat but remained significantly above its precrisis level. During these periods, deteriorations in the balance of trade for oil-importing countries (and improvements for oil-exporting countries) are probably attributable to the oil crises rather than to fiscal policy. One must also bear in mind that some countries, such as the United Kingdom, switched from oil-importing to oil-exporting status between the two crises. Finally, the first oil crisis precipitated a significant recession throughout the Western world. Since this had a large impact on saving and the profitability of investment, it may have affected the current account balance in systematic ways.

Third, the United States began to run extremely large budget deficits beginning in 1982. It is important to bear in mind that the current account balance of each country should depend not only on its own budget deficit but also on the budget deficits of its trading partners. In essence, it is the *relative* size of budget deficits that determines which countries will import capital and which will import goods. Thus, U.S. fiscal policy may well have significantly affected the balance of payments for other countries. This is particularly important in the cases of Canada and Mexico, since these countries conduct disproportionately large fractions of their trade with the United States.

4. AN INTERNATIONAL COMPARISON

If fiscal policy plays a significant role in determining the balance of payments, then we should observe a significant relationship between these variables, both over time and across countries. I will therefore begin my

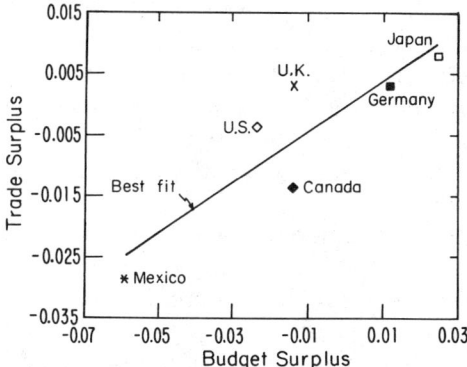

FIGURE 1. *Cross-Country Comparison Ten-Year Averages, 1975–1984*

analysis of the data by comparing budget deficits and trade deficits, averaged over a substantial time interval, for the six countries in my sample.

As one averages over longer time periods, one finds less variation in the current account surplus across countries. Accordingly, I have arbitrarily chosen to study the most recent ten-year period in my sample (1975–1984). For each country I compute ten-year averages of the BSUR and CAS and plot the resulting averages in a scatter diagram (Figure 1).

Note that there appears to be a strong positive relationship between budget surpluses and trade surpluses across countries. The line marked "best fit" represents the best linear approximation to this relationship (as determined by ordinary least squares regression). The slope of this line is 0.412, which indicates that a $1 increase in the budget deficit is associated with a $0.41 rise in the trade deficit. Despite the fact that there are very few data points (only four degrees of freedom), this coefficient is estimated quite precisely; its standard error is 0.108.

Note that the United Kingdom deviates from the best-fit regression line more than any of the other countries. In light of the fact that the United Kingdom became a major oil exporter in the late 1970s, just in time to benefit from the second oil crisis, it is hardly surprising that its current account shows an abnormally large surplus.

It is also noteworthy that Japan has both the highest government budget surplus and the largest current account surplus over this ten-year period. This fact is often obscured by official government statistics, which in recent years have shown the Japanese government running a substantial deficit. It is essential to realize that Japan and the United States follow very different accounting conventions when constructing their national income accounts (see, e.g., Boskin and Roberts (1986)). For example, the Japanese do not include their social security system as part of the budget of the central government. This particular omission is extremely important, because the Japanese have accumulated substantial resources in social security trust funds over the last several years. Thus, when one employs the OECD accounts for the consolidated government, the Japanese government appears as a large net saver.

In contrast to Japan, Mexico has the largest budget deficit and the largest current account deficit over this ten-year period. As the only developing country in this sample, Mexico's economic problems were different from those of the other five countries, particularly during the 1980s. Specifically, a foreign debt crisis led to the virtual suspension of foreign credit; simultaneously, the IMF imposed an austerity program on the Mexican government. Had foreign credit not been suspended, Mexico would have undoubtedly continued to run very large current account deficits after 1981, and the relationship in Figure 1 would have been all the more pronounced. Nevertheless, one might simply regard the Mexican experience as atypical and argue that it should not be included in the cross-country comparison. If one omits Mexico, a relationship between the budget surplus and current account surplus is still evident, although the slope of the least squares regression line falls to 0.276 (with a standard error of 0.174).

Unfortunately, the empirical pattern noted above may be produced by spurious factors. For example, there may be cultural differences in attitudes toward saving. In countries with high private saving rates, the government may be fiscally conservative, whereas in other countries extravagance may characterize both the public and private sectors. Unless investment opportunities vary systematically with these same predispositions, countries with high public and private saving will also run large current account surpluses (see equation (3)). Thus, a positive correlation between budget surpluses and trade surpluses does not necessarily indicate causality. It is therefore necessary to explore the variation in fiscal policy and current account balances over time as well as across countries.

5. THE U.S. EXPERIENCE

I will begin with an analysis of the U.S. time series. In Figure 2, I plot both the U.S. budget surplus and current account surplus (as a percentage of GDP) against time. One immediately notes a general coherence between the two series. Both have been trending down gradually throughout the twenty-five-year sample period. The shorter-term movements in these series are also often coincident (e.g., between 1978 and 1979 or between

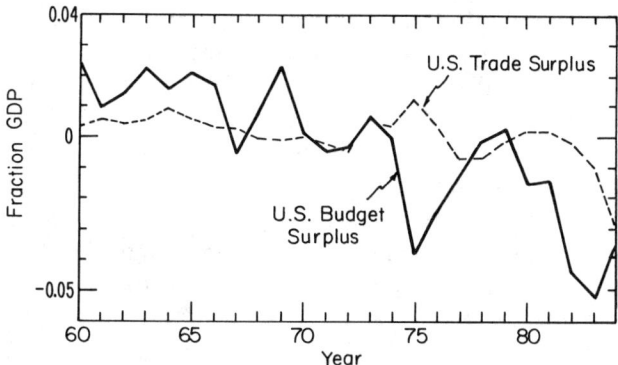

FIGURE 2. *U.S. Time Series 1960–1984*

1981 and 1983), although there are some significant exceptions (most notably between 1974 and 1976, when the two series moved sharply in opposite directions).

It is much easier to see the historical relationship between these two series by plotting the trade surplus against the budget surplus in a scatter diagram (see Figure 3). This diagram reveals that the series are highly correlated. In fact, with few exceptions the data points seem to line up extremely well. The two exceptions are 1975, during which the current

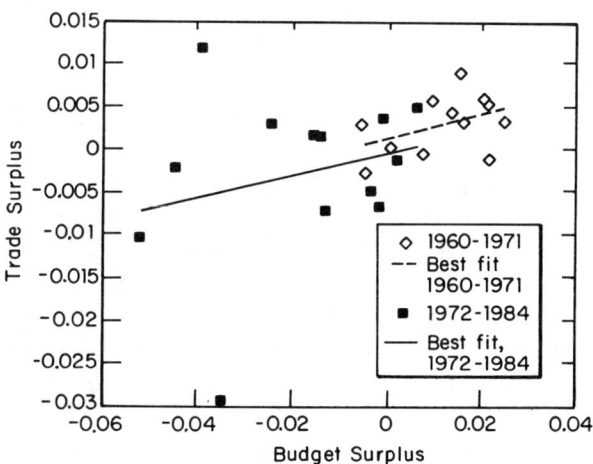

FIGURE 3. *Scatter Plot for United States 1960–1984*

account surplus was abnormally high, and 1984, in which it was abnormally low. 1975 must be considered atypical because trade patterns were undoubtedly disturbed by the first oil crisis, and many countries were experiencing recessions. The large current account surplus may have been due to the slow pace of the U.S. recovery—poor profitability may have caused U.S. capitalists to seek investment opportunities abroad, causing an offsetting movement in the current account (see equation (3)). The budget deficit during these two exceptional years was roughly the same, about 3.5 percent of GDP. Thus, the outliers roughly offset each other, and their inclusion does not much affect one's overall impression of the relationship between budget deficits and trade deficits.

It is possible to quantify the significance of this relationship through linear regression. Specifically, the slope of the line that represents the best fit to the data points in Figure 3 is 0.161. This coefficient has a standard error of 0.069, which indicates that, with 95 percent probability, the true slope lies between about 0.02 and 0.30. A coefficient of 0.161 should be interpreted as indicating that a $1 increase in the budget deficit is associated with a contemporaneous $0.16 increase in the current account deficit.

I have noted in section 3 that a variety of unusual events took place after 1971 (significant changes in the system of international exchange, two oil crises, and large U.S. deficits). One must therefore wonder whether the relationship considered here remained stable throughout the sample period. I investigate this issue by dividing the sample period into two roughly equal segments: 1960–1971 and 1972–1984. In Figure 3, I have differentiated between data points associated with each of these periods. Note that the two subperiods have very different characteristics: before 1972 the United States generally had budget surpluses and healthy current account balances; in later years, deficits were the rule. It is therefore particularly striking that the relationship between fiscal policy and the current account remained essentially unchanged across the two subperiods.

In Figure 3, I have plotted least squares regression lines for 1960 to 1971 and 1972 to 1984 separately. Note that these lines have almost exactly the same slopes. The regression line for 1972 to 1984 is slightly lower, perhaps reflecting a decline of the U.S. saving rate (independent of fiscal policy effects). However, the impact of budget deficits on the current account balance has remained stable over time. It is also possible that the relationship observed in Figure 3 is due to spurious factors that I have not yet considered. One possibility is that both fiscal policy and current account balance vary systematically over the business cycle. To control for business cycle effects, I regressed the current account variable (CAS) on the current budget surplus (BSUR), and current and lagged values of real GDP growth (GROW). In general, this strengthened the empirical relationship. For example, with a single lagged value of GROW, I obtained

$$\text{CAS} = 0.0095 + 0.303 \times \text{BSUR} - 0.0015 \times \text{GROW} - 0.0011 \times \text{GROW}(-1) + \varepsilon$$
$$(0.0032) \quad (0.080) \qquad\qquad (0.0005) \qquad\qquad (0.0006)$$

$$R^2 = 0.469$$

where GROW(−1) indicates the value of GROW from the previous year, ε reflects unexplained variation, and standard errors are given in parentheses. After we correct for cyclical variation, the observed relationship between budget deficits and trade deficits is almost twice as large (the coefficient of BSUR rises from 0.161 to 0.303). It is, of course, possible that the current and lagged values of GROW control incompletely for business cycle effects. It is therefore noteworthy that the inclusion of additional lagged variables (GROW(−2) and GROW(−3)) reduces the coefficient of BSUR only slightly.

As mentioned in section 3, a positive correlation between budget deficits and current account balances might also reflect variations in government spending. To test for this possibility, I added the OECD's measure of government consumption (GOV) to the list of explanatory variables. As expected, the coefficient of GOV turned out to be negative (indicating that government consumption contributes to the current account deficit). Somewhat surprisingly, the coefficient of BSUR actually increased slightly (for example, in a specification that included BSUR, GROW, GROW(−1), and GOV, the estimated coefficient of BSUR was 0.324 with a standard error of 0.082).

Figure 3 and the preceding regression results make a strong case for the existence of an empirical relationship between budget deficits and trade deficits, but it is conceivable that this analysis of contemporaneous movements overlooks a significant portion of the story. If, for example, international capital markets are imperfect, then the effects of fiscal policy on international trade may show up only after a lag. That is, capital may flow across national borders in response to differential rates of profit, but it may do so somewhat slowly.

Figure 1 tends to corroborate this conjecture. Generally, it appears that movements in the current account have followed changes in the budget deficit by one or two years. In fact, from 1974 on, the two series appear to track each other extremely well when one shifts the budget surplus forward by two years. In Figure 4, I have plotted the trade surplus against the budget surplus lagged one year. Note that the relationship between these variables is now more striking, and even the outliers in 1975 and 1984

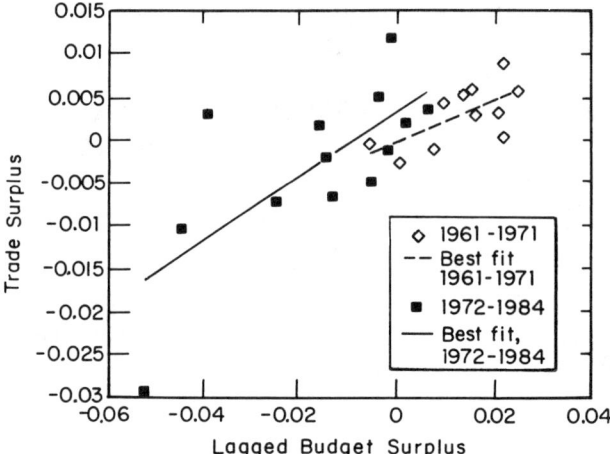

FIGURE 4. *Scatter Plot for United States 1961–1984*

appear less extreme. Indeed, the slope of the regression line in Figure 4 is 0.274. The standard error of this coefficient is 0.057, which indicates that, with 95 percent probability, the true slope lies between 0.16 and 0.39. Thus, the lagged effect is not only larger but is also estimated more precisely than the concurrent effect.

Again we ask whether this relationship has been stable over the entire sample period. Accordingly, in Figure 4 I have distinguished between data points from each of the two subperiods defined above (note, however, that the earlier period must now begin in 1961 in order to accommodate the need for a lagged value of the budget surplus). Both regression lines are clearly downward sloped, although the line for 1972 to 1984 is somewhat steeper. Given the variation around the regression line after 1971, this difference cannot be considered terribly significant.

In light of Figure 4, it is appropriate to study the temporal nature of the relationship between budget deficits and trade deficits more carefully. To determine the precise pattern of these effects, I estimated a regression equation explaining the current account surplus as a linear function of the current budget surplus and the budget surpluses for the previous four years. This procedure necessitated dropping the first four years of data. In order to conserve on valuable degrees of freedom, I placed a restriction on the pattern of coefficients (specifically, I required the lagged coefficients to evolve as a third-degree polynomial). The results were not terribly sensitive to the presence of cyclical variables; I report results based on a specification that includes GROW and GROW(-1). I have plotted the estimated coeffi-

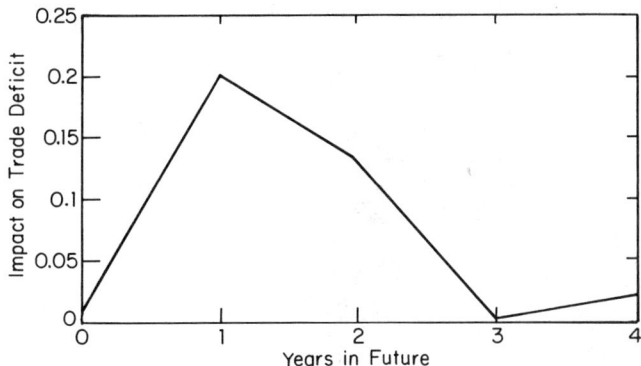

FIGURE 5. *The Effect of Budget Deficits on Subsequent Trade Deficits*

cients in Figure 5. One interprets this figure as follows. When one controls for previous fiscal policy, there is little if any concurrent relationship between budget deficits and trade deficits. Most of the impact of the budget deficit is felt one year later, and a substantial effect follows after two years. Note that the coefficients for budget deficits three and four years in the past are essentially zero (I should emphasize that I did not constrain the fourth lagged coefficient to equal zero)—all of the effects of fiscal policy on trade are felt within two years. By summing the coefficients for the current and lagged budget variables, I obtain an estimate of the total effect that a sustained deficit policy would eventually have on the current account balance. The sum of these coefficients is 0.366, with a standard error of 0.117 (this indicates that, with 95 percent probability, the true sum of these coefficients lies between 0.13 and 0.60). Thus, a permanent increase in the annual budget deficit of $1 is associated with a permanent $0.366 increase in the annual trade deficit.

I also estimated a specification that included all of the explanatory variables described above—a polynomial distributed lag on BSUR, GROW, GROW(-1), and GOV. This specification has the advantage of controlling for both cyclical effects and government spending while simultaneously allowing for lagged fiscal effects. It is therefore noteworthy that this procedure generated the most striking results: the coefficients on the current and lagged values of BSUR summed to 0.628, with a standard deviation of 0.107.

In summary, the data for the United States indicate that there is a strong, stable relationship between the budget deficit and the trade deficit. Once one allows for the fact that international capital markets may adjust slowly,

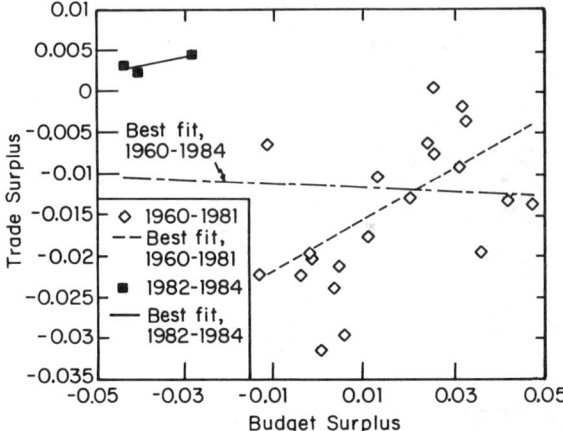

FIGURE 6. *Scatter Plot for Canada 1960–1984*

the total effect estimated from U.S. data is roughly comparable to that obtained from the international comparison.

6. THE EXPERIENCES OF OTHER COUNTRIES

In this section I analyze time series data from the five largest U.S. trading partners (measured by U.S. exports) in order to determine whether trade deficits are systematically related to budget deficits.

6.1 Canada

In Figure 6, I plot the Canadian trade surplus against the Canadian budget surplus in a scatter diagram. Taken as whole, the data do not appear to reveal any clear pattern. Indeed, the best-fit regression line for the entire period is slightly downward sloping. This is anomalous, because a downward slope would imply that budget deficits actually improve the balance of trade. On the other hand, the coefficient is very small and statistically indistinguishable from zero.

The absence of a clear pattern may simply reflect the influences of various third factors. If it is known that such factors led to atypical behavior in specific years, then one should minimize the importance of those years when searching for systematic relationships.

In the case of Canada, there are three years in which behavior was almost certainly atypical: 1982, 1983, and 1984. I have already mentioned in section 3 that the U.S. began to run very large budget deficits in 1982. Since Canadian trade is dominated by the United States (for example, in 1986

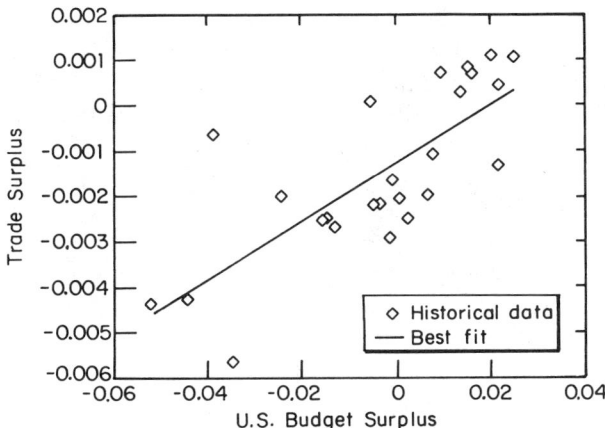

FIGURE 7. *Bilateral Trade Balance between United States and Canada 1960–1984*

three-fourths of all Canadian exports were destined for the United States), one would naturally expect the Canadian current account balance to be very sensitive to U.S. fiscal policy. Indeed, as noted in Figure 6, these three years witnessed abnormally high current account surpluses (they correspond to the three outliers in the upper left-hand corner of the diagram). It is therefore possible that the favorable current account balances beginning in 1982 simply reflect the effects of U.S. budget deficits.

To investigate this hypothesis, I analyze time series data on bilateral trade between the United States and Canada. In Figure 7, I plot the bilateral trade surplus for the United States (as a fraction of U.S. GDP) against the U.S. budget deficit. Note that the data show a clear relationship between the variables of interest. The only significant outliers are, as in section 5, 1975 and 1984. The large U.S. bilateral trade deficits with Canada in 1982 and 1983 are not at all abnormal, given the U.S. fiscal policy in those years.

The question remains: can the effects of U.S. fiscal policy on bilateral trade explain the three outliers in Figure 6? To answer this question, I measure the effect of U.S. budget deficits on bilateral trade by computing the least squares regression line for the data points in Figure 7. I find that a $1 budget deficit is associated with a $0.064 increase in the bilateral trade deficit for the United States. This coefficient has a standard error of $0.011, which indicates that it is estimated very precisely.

There are, of course, several problems with this measure of U.S. fiscal policy effects. First, bilateral trade between the United States and Canada should be affected by U.S. budget surpluses and by Canadian budget surpluses. To the extent fiscal policies are correlated across countries, a simple regression of the bilateral balance on the U.S. budget surplus will confound the effects of U.S. and Canadian policy. It is therefore necessary to control for the Canadian budget surplus. Second, as before, systematic variation over the business cycle may produce a spurious correlation between the variables of interest. Accordingly, I regress the bilateral trade surplus as a fraction of U.S. GDP (BTS) on the U.S. budget surplus (BSURUS), the Canadian budget surplus (BSURC), and current and lagged values of the real GDP growth rates for the United States and Canada (GROWUS and GROWC, respectively). I obtain the following estimates:

$$\text{BTS} = -0.0003 + 0.085 \times \text{BSURUS} + 0.004 \times \text{BSURC} + 0.0001 \times \text{GROWUS}$$
$$\phantom{\text{BTS} = }(0.001) \quad (0.024) \phantom{\times \text{BSURUS}} \quad (0.026) \phantom{\times \text{BSURC}} \quad (0.0002)$$

$$\phantom{\text{BTS} =} - 0.0004 \times \text{GROWUS}(-1) - 0.0002 \times \text{GROWC} + 0.0002 \times \text{GROWC}(-1)$$
$$\phantom{\text{BTS} = }(0.0002) \phantom{\times \text{GROWUS}(-1)} \quad (0.0003) \phantom{\times \text{GROWC}} \quad (0.0002)$$

$$R^2 = 0.662$$

Note that, after controlling for Canadian fiscal policy and business fluctuations, I find an even larger effect of U.S. budget deficits on the bilateral trade surplus ($0.085 on the dollar rather than $0.064). The only anomalous result is that BSURC is positive. Note, however, that this coefficient is dwarfed by its standard error, so that one cannot reject the possibility that it is negative with any degree of statistical confidence. Indeed, one can only conclude that, with 95 percent probability, the true coefficient lies between −0.048 and 0.056. These values may appear small in absolute value: since U.S.–Canadian trade is larger relative to total trade for Canada than it is for the United States, one would expect a $1 increase in the Canadian budget deficit to have a larger effect on bilateral trade than would a $1 increase in the U.S. budget deficit. However, one must bear in mind that the Canadian budget surplus is measured relative to Canadian GDP, and all other variables are measured relative to U.S. GDP. Since U.S. GDP is roughly eleven times as large as Canadian GDP, a coefficient of, say, −0.02 would imply that a $1 increase in the Canadian budget deficit would increase net imports from the United States by about $0.22. Thus, plausible fiscal effects are within one standard deviation of the estimated coefficient. The data simply do not allow us to distinguish between interesting hypotheses concerning the impact of Canadian budget deficits. Also if one allows for lagged fiscal effects by incorporating polynomial distributed lags on the budget surplus variables, the estimated cumulative effect of the Canadian budget surplus becomes negative, although its standard error remains quite large (the measured cumulative effect of U.S. budget surpluses rises to more than $0.11 on the dollar).

What do these estimates imply about the effects of U.S. budget deficits in the early 1980s? Prior to 1982, the U.S. budget deficit for the most part remained below 2 percent of GDP; from 1982 to 1984, it increased to 4 or 5 percent of GDP. Accordingly, the change in U.S. fiscal policy probably caused the bilateral U.S. trade deficit with Canada to rise by about 0.25 percent of U.S. GDP. This is equivalent to about 2.8 percent of Canadian GDP.

Now return to Figure 6. Note that I have plotted least squares regression lines for each of two subperiods: 1960–1981 and 1982–1984. Observe also that the vertical distance between the leftmost tip of the former and the rightmost tip of the latter is about 0.03 (3 percent of Canadian GDP). The arguments in the preceding paragraph therefore establish that U.S. fiscal policy can account for virtually all of the favorable shift in the Canadian balance of payments between the first and second subperiods.

Since it is possible to account reasonably well for the three outliers in the manner described above, it seems likely that one would obtain the best measure of the relationship between Canadian budget deficits and trade deficits by focusing on the period 1960 to 1981. It is therefore noteworthy that the slope of the regression line for this subperiod is 0.310, with a standard error of 0.109. This is virtually identical to the effect obtained for the United States in section 5. Note that the regression line for 1982 to 1984 also has a positive slope. The relationship simply appears to have shifted upward. Unfortunately, it is impossible to estimate this slope precisely with only three data points, so this conclusion is extremely tenuous.

Once again, it is desirable to improve this estimate by controlling for the effects of business cycle fluctuations. Accordingly, I regress the Canadian current account surplus (CAS) on the Canadian budget surplus (BSUR), and current and lagged values of real GDP growth for Canada (GROW) for the sample period 1960 to 1981. The estimated coefficients are

$$CAS = -0.019 + 0.310 \times BSUR + 0.0001 \times GROW - 0.0001 \times GROW(-1) + \varepsilon$$
$$\quad\;\, (0.008) \quad (0.169) \qquad\quad (0.0012) \qquad\qquad (0.0013)$$

$$R^2 = 0.289$$

Thus, the inclusion of cyclical variables has virtually no impact on the estimated coefficient of BSUR (although its standard error does rise). The addition of GROW(−2) to the list of explanatory variables reduces the coefficient of BSUR slightly; the addition of GROW(−2) and GROW(−3) raises it to 0.418, with a standard error of 0.202.

Similarly, one should control for the potentially spurious effects of government consumption. For each of the specifications mentioned above, the addition of Canadian government consumption (GOV) as an explanatory variable reduces the measured effect of budget deficits only slightly, by approximately $0.02 to $0.03 on the dollar.

As with the United States, it is also desirable to examine the timing of Canadian fiscal effects. To do so, I follow the procedure outlined in section 5, adding four lagged values of the Canadian budget surplus and conserving degrees of freedom by requiring the corresponding coefficients to evolve as a third-degree polynomial. This procedure yields cumulative fiscal effects that are larger than the contemporaneous effects discussed above (for example, with GROW and GROW(−1) the cumulative effect of BSUR is 0.424). Unfortunately, the standard errors increase significantly (to 0.263 for the coefficient of BSUR in the specification mentioned above). In addition, the pattern of lagged coefficients is peculiar. The contemporaneous coefficient is, in general, very close to the cumulative effect, which suggests that most of the impact is felt immediately. However, although the cumulative lagged effect is typically close to zero, coefficients on individual terms vary substantially. This evidence is somewhat ambiguous, but I am inclined to conclude that Canadian fiscal effects are primarily contemporaneous. This contrasts sharply with the U.S. experience.

One possible explanation for this difference is that the U.S. and Canadian capital markets are very highly integrated, and the U. S. economy is roughly eleven times as large as that of Canada. When saving falls short of investment in Canada, funds from the United States can easily make up the difference. Conversely, when Canadian saving exceeds investment, the U.S. can easily absorb the residual. Furthermore, due to the high degree of integration, this happens very quickly. On the other hand, when saving is either high or low relative to investment in the United States, Canada is simply too small to supply or absorb the residual funds. Instead, the rest of the world must play that role. Since U.S. capital markets are generally less well integrated with those of countries other than Canada, this tends to occur after a lag.

In summary, when analyzing data on Canadian trade, one must explicitly allow for the important roles played by the United States and its fiscal policy. Having done this, it is evident that there is a significant relationship between the budget deficit and the trade deficit in Canada, and that the magnitude of fiscal policy effects are roughly the same as in the United States.

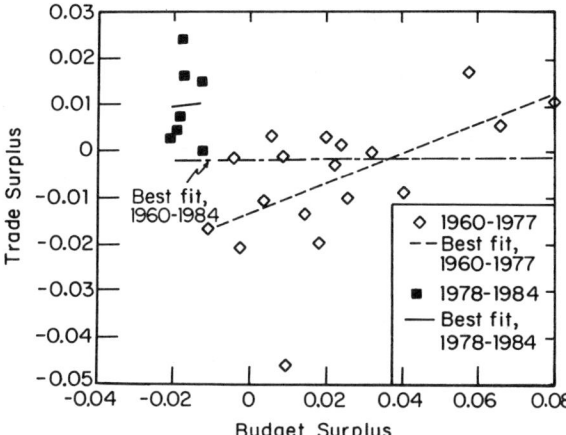

FIGURE 8. *Scatter Plot for the United Kingdom 1960–1984*

6.2 The United Kingdom

In Figure 8, I plot the British trade surplus against the British budget surplus in a scatter diagram. As with Canada, the data do not initially appear to reveal any clear pattern. Indeed, the least squares regression line is flat, raising the possibility that one of the two conditions discussed in section 2 holds for the United Kingdom.

Upon closer inspection, systematic patterns are evident. As before, my strategy is to identify years in which, on the basis of other information about the British economy, one would have expected to find atypical behavior. In the case of the United Kingdom, there are some obvious candidates. In particular, there were three developments in the late 1970s that could well have changed the basic structural relationship between current account surpluses and budget deficits in Great Britain. The first development was that Britain began to pump oil in the North Sea and thus became a major oil exporter. The second development was the oil crisis of 1979, which, combined with the first development, vastly improved Britain's terms of trade. The third and final development was the election of Thatcher's conservative government. For reasons entirely unrelated to the factors that improved Britain's current account, Thatcher attempted to stimulate Britain's economy by reducing taxes. Although the resulting deficits coincided with current account surpluses, it seems highly likely that these surpluses occurred for independent reasons, and would have been much larger in the absence of the deficits.

In view of these developments, it is natural to divide the sample into two subperiods: 1960–1977 and 1978–1984. During the first subperiod, there is a clear relationship between fiscal policy and the balance of trade. Indeed, the least squares regression line has a slope of 0.326, with a standard error of 0.121. Thus, a $1 increase in the budget deficit is associated with a $0.326 increase in the trade deficit. This result coincides almost exactly with those obtained for the United States and Canada, and is only slightly below the estimate based upon my comparison of ten-year averages across the six countries in my sample.

It is once again desirable to attempt to control for third factors that might have produced a spurious correlation between British trade and fiscal policy. Following the strategy used in earlier sections, I control for business cycle fluctuations by regressing the British current account surplus (CAS) on the British budget surplus (BSUR), along with the current and lagged values of real GDP growth (GROW) for the period 1960 to 1977. The estimated coefficients are

$$CAS = -0.013 + 0.322 \times BSUR - 0.0008 \times GROW + 0.0006 \times GROW(-1) + \varepsilon$$
$$(0.006)\ \ (0.119) \ (0.0009) \ (0.0009)$$

$$R^2 = 0.445$$

The inclusion of additional cyclical variables (lagged values of GROW) actually increases the measured coefficient of BSUR and reduces its standard error. For example, when one adds GROW(−2) and GROW(−3) to the list of explanatory variables, the coefficient rises to 0.369, with a standard deviation of 0.090.

I have also estimated several specifications in which I controlled for government consumption (GOV), as well as for cyclical effects. As with Canada, the impact of including GOV was to reduce slightly the measured impact of budget deficits on the current account balance (in this case, by approximately $0.06 on the dollar). The coefficient of BSUR remained significant at conventional levels of confidence.

It is desirable to examine the importance of lagged fiscal effects as in the preceding sections; however, this is impossible for Great Britain. The inclusion of four lags would require me to drop the first four years of data. Since I have truncated the sample at 1977, this leaves only fourteen data points. Estimation of an intercept as well as coefficients for fiscal variables (current and lagged values of BSUR) and cyclical variables (current and lagged values of GROW) would leave only seven degrees of freedom. In practice, the residual variation in the data is insufficient to identify this set of coefficients with any precision.

So far, I have confined attention to 1960 to 1977. Returning to Figure 8, note that the least squares regression line for 1978 to 1984 also slopes downward, but the slope coefficient is very small and estimated very imprecisely. During this period there simply was not very much variation in the ratio of budget deficits to GDP, so recent experience in the United Kingdom can tell us little about the effects of fiscal policy. Variation in the current account balance undoubtedly arose from other sources, such as movements in the price of oil.

In summary, Britain exhibits a clear relationship between budget deficits and trade deficits through 1977. The magnitude of these fiscal policy effects appears to be roughly the same as for the United States and Canada, and is only slightly lower than the figure obtained from an international comparison. Due to developments in the late 1970s, Britain began to run large budget deficits along with current account surpluses for completely unrelated reasons. Variation in British fiscal policy since 1977 is insufficient to allow precise measurement of fiscal effects.

6.3 West Germany

In Figure 9 I plot the German trade surplus against the German budget surplus in a scatter diagram. To the extent there is a significant relationship between fiscal policy and trade, it is obscured by the degree of variation in the current account balance. Although the least squares regression line for Germany is slightly upward sloping, it appears that many other lines would fit the data almost equally well. More formally, the slope coefficient

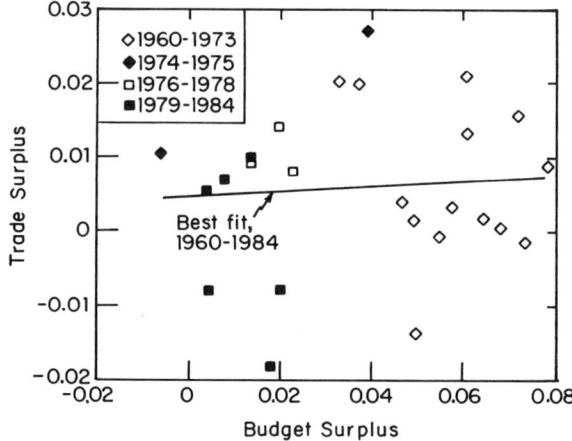

FIGURE 9. *Scatter Plot for Germany 1960–1984*

is 0.0185, with a standard deviation of 0.0872. Thus, the data are consistent with the hypothesis that there is no systematic relationship between the budget surplus and the trade surplus. However, the data are also consistent with the hypothesis that a $1 increase in the budget deficit causes the trade deficit to rise by nearly $0.20. Evidently, the variation in the German current account balance arising from third factors is too large to allow us to differentiate between the various hypotheses of interest.

As in the preceding sections, one can use other information to identify years in which the behavior of the German current account might be considered atypical. The most plausible candidates are years in which the German economy suffered from the effects of the two oil crises. In Figure 9 I have separately identified data points from each of four subperiods: 1960–1973, 1974, and 1975 (the first oil crisis), 1976–1978 (the period between the oil crises), and 1979–1984 (the second oil crisis and its aftermath). It is possible to account for some of the current account variation in this way. For example, German trade deficits were concentrated in the years 1979–1981, at the height of the second oil crisis. This is understandable, since Germany imports most of its primary materials. One apparent anomaly is that Germany ran its largest current account surplus in 1975, during the first oil crisis. This is probably because the crisis induced a recession, and German investment was very slow to recover. In the meantime, savings flowed to other countries, producing a large current account surplus in response. Nevertheless, even after allowing for atypical behavior in the oil crisis years, no clear pattern emerges.

It is also possible that cyclical variation in the budget deficit and current account balance obscures an underlying relationship between these two variables. Following the strategy adopted in earlier sections, I control for business cycle effects by regressing the current account surplus (CAS) on the budget surplus (BSUR), and current and lagged values of real GDP growth (GROW). The estimated coefficients are

$$CAS = 0.0057 + 0.189 \times BSUR - 0.0005 \times GROW - 0.0016 \times GROW(-1) + \varepsilon$$
$$(0.0041) \quad (0.166) \quad\quad\quad (0.0011) \quad\quad\quad\quad (0.0012)$$

$$R^2 = 0.083$$

Note that the coefficient of BSUR increases substantially to 0.189. Its standard error is still relatively large, but the movement in this coefficient suggests that cyclical fluctuations bias the coefficient of BSUR downward. Although I have noted a similar bias in previous sections, the effect here is far larger and hence much more important. The direction of this bias should not be surprising: during booms, rising income generates increased tax revenues and hence reduces deficits; at the same time the demand for imports rises with disposable income, contributing to a deterioration of the balance of payments.

Since cyclical fluctuations are evidently very important for West Germany, it is important to determine whether a single lagged value of GROW fully controls for factors that induce the spurious correlation. Accordingly, I also estimate specifications in which I include additional lagged values of GROW as explanatory variables. The addition of GROW(−2) raises the estimated coefficient of BSUR to 0.330 (with a standard deviation of 0.205); the addition of both GROW(−2) and GROW(−3) raises the coefficient to 0.547 (with a standard error of 0.240). Note that this last coefficient is statistically significant at conventional levels of confidence. Thus, as one controls more completely for business fluctuations, the observed relationship between budget deficits and trade deficits becomes stronger.

As in previous sections, it is also important to control for the effects of government spending. The addition of the government consumption variable (GOV) to the specifications discussed above causes the coefficient of BSUR to decline slightly (e.g., by $0.02, $0.06, and $0.09 on the dollar, respectively, for the specifications with one, two, and three lagged values of GROW). The overall relationship between budget deficits and trade deficits remains quantitatively large.

Finally, it is useful to explore the effects of fiscal policy on German trade patterns through time. I follow the strategy adopted in previous sections, adding four lagged values of the budget surplus as explanatory variables and constraining the lagged coefficients to evolve as a polynomial distributed lag. The estimated cumulative effect of BSUR on CAS is much larger than the contemporaneous effect discussed above: with one lagged value of GROW, it is 0.542 (with a standard deviation of 0.181); with two lagged values of GROW, it is 0.603 (with a standard deviation of 0.221). However, as with Canada, the pattern of lagged coefficients is somewhat peculiar—the coefficient on the current value of BSUR is virtually equal to the cumulative effect, and coefficients on the lagged variables vary between fairly large positive and negative numbers, with no apparent pattern. Although this evidence is somewhat ambiguous, I am inclined to conclude that West German fiscal effects are primarily contemporaneous.

In summary, business fluctuations appear to obscure a systematic relationship between budget deficits and trade deficits in West Germany. When one controls for such effects, the impact of fiscal policy on the current account appears to be as large, if not larger, for West Germany as it is for the countries considered in previous sections.

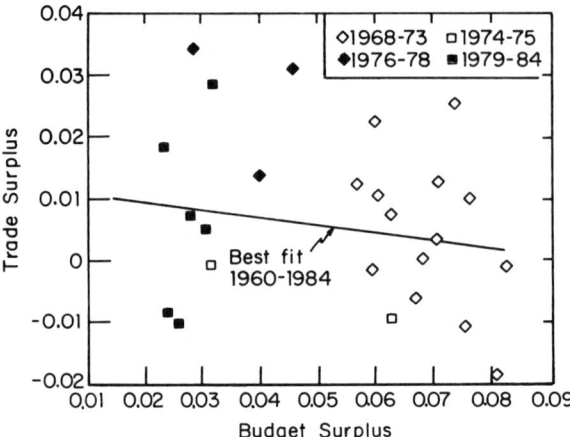

FIGURE 10. *Scatter Plot for Japan 1960–1984*

6.4 Japan

In Figure 10 I plot the Japanese trade surplus against the Japanese budget surplus in a scatter diagram. The data appear to rule out the existence of a significant positive relationship between these two variables. The slope coefficient of the least squares regression line is −0.125, with a standard error of 0.109. This estimate is inconsistent with the view that Japanese budget surplus significantly contributes to Japanese trade surpluses.

Unlike Germany, the Japanese government takes a strongly interventionist role with respect to international trade. Japan has traditionally regulated imports, exports, and capital flows. The absence of a strong relationship in Figure 10 may reflect the relative importance of these other interventionist policies in determining the Japanese current account balance.

Once again one can attempt to account for the lack of a clear relationship by using other information to identify years in which behavior was probably atypical. However, as with Germany, this effort meets with very little success. In Figure 10 I have separately identified data points for each of the subperiods described in section 6.3. As expected, one sees deteriorating current account balances during periods of high oil prices (1974, 1975, and 1979–1981), reflecting Japan's status as a major oil importer. Yet no clear pattern emerges even when these years are deleted.

In view of my results concerning West Germany, it is extremely important to control for the effects of business cycles. Yet even when one regresses the Japanese current account surplus on the Japanese budget surplus and current and lagged values of real GDP growth, fiscal effects of the sort observed in previous sections fail to materialize. In all specifications, the coefficient of BSUR remains negative, although it is never significant at conventional levels of statistical confidence. The addition of a government consumption variable (GOV) does not alter this conclusion, nor does the estimation of polynomial distributed lags.

We can gain some insight into the Japanese experience by referring again to Figure 10. This diagram reveals a cleavage between a large group of high budget surplus years (in which surpluses ranged from about 6 to 8 percent of GDP) and a large group of low budget surplus years (in which surpluses ranged from about 2 to about 4 percent of GDP). As it happens, the first group of points represent the years 1960–1974, and the second group represent 1975–1984. Apparently, high prices for primary goods during the first oil crisis forced the Japanese government to reduce its budget surpluses, and since then Japan has never reestablished its previous levels of fiscal restraint. Note that within each of these subperiods the variation in budget deficits is very small relative to the variation in the Japanese current account balance. Thus, within-period movements in these variables are insufficient to establish the magnitude of fiscal effects. The slope of the regression line is primarily determined by differences in averages before and after the cleavage. Because the late 1970s and early 1980s differed in a large number of important respects from the 1960s and early 1970s, this observation casts doubt on the validity of the finding that fiscal effects are insignificant in Japan. It does not, however, establish that the data support the existence of large fiscal effects.

In summary, the data for Japan appear to support the view that budget deficits do not cause significant deterioration of the current account. Nevertheless, this finding is primarily derived from a comparison of the average Japanese experience before and after 1975, and may reflect spurious factors.

6.5 Mexico

In Figure 11 I plot the Mexican trade surplus against the Mexican budget surplus in a scatter diagram. As with Canada, the United Kingdom, and West Germany, the data do not, as a whole, reveal any clear pattern. In fact, the least squares regression line for the entire period is absolutely flat. This appears to suggest that budget deficits have no effect on trade, and that Mexico satisfies one of the two conditions discussed in section 2.

Upon closer inspection, one quickly sees that this conclusion is unfounded. Other information strongly suggests that the events of the early 1980s was extremely atypical, and that the Mexican current account balance was primarily determined by spurious third factors. In particular, Mexico

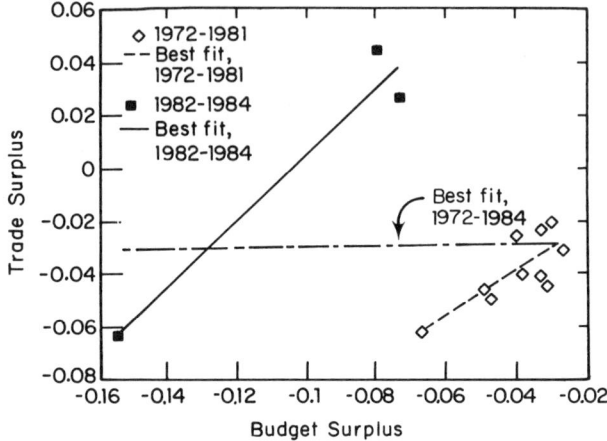

FIGURE 11. *Scatter Plot for Mexico 1972–1984*

experienced a foreign debt crisis in 1982. This led to a virtual suspension of foreign credit and to the adoption of a rather severe austerity program. The resulting sharp decline of capital inflows produced a dramatic improvement in the Mexican current account, completely independently of any ordinary economic influences. At the same time it was generally believed that the Mexican government would be tempted to monetize a substantial fraction of its outstanding debt. This expectation undoubtedly resulted in a devaluation of the Mexican currency, which led to a further improvement in the current account. Thus, fears of monetization may have produced a spurious relationship between budget deficits and the current account surplus during a period in which net exports were already artificially high.

Not surprisingly, the data points corresponding to 1982, 1983, and 1984 appear as extreme outliers in Figure 11. The remaining points are closely grouped together and give clear evidence of a strong positive relationship between the Mexican budget deficit and trade deficit. The slope of the least squares regression line for this subperiod is 0.853. Although it is estimated somewhat imprecisely (a standard error of 0.251), one can nevertheless conclude that the slope of the true relationship lies between 0.35 and 1.35. Note that even the lower end of this range exceeds the point estimates for the United States and Canada.

As in the preceding sections, it is desirable to control for the effects of business cycle fluctuations. A regression of the Mexican current account surplus (CAS) on the Mexican budget surplus (BSUR) and current and lagged values of real GDP growth (GROW) yields the following coefficients:

$$\text{CAS} = 0.002 + 0.749 \times \text{BSUR} + 0.0001 \times \text{GROW} - 0.0016 \times \text{GROW}(-1) + \varepsilon$$
$$(0.017) \quad (0.302) \qquad\qquad (0.0018) \qquad\qquad\qquad (0.0017)$$

$$R^2 = 0.653$$

Although the inclusion of proxies for the business cycle somewhat reduces the coefficient of BSUR, the estimated fiscal effect remains extremely large. This conclusion holds up when one adds GROW(−2) and GROW(−3) to the list of explanatory variables.

As with Canada, the United Kingdom, and West Germany, the inclusion of a measure of government consumption (GOV) reduces the estimated fiscal effect. In a regression of CAS on BSUR, GROW, GROW(−1), and GOV, the coefficient of BSUR was 0.557, with a standard error of 0.257. Despite this reduction, the coefficient remains quite large.

Because data on Mexico are unavailable before 1972, the Mexican time series is extremely short. It is therefore impossible to determine the lagged effects of fiscal policies through the estimation of polynomial distributed lags.

Why should the effect of fiscal policy be so much larger in Mexico than in the United States or Canada ? Recall from the discussion in section 2 that the magnitude of the fiscal effect depends in large part upon the extent to which consumers spend out of increases in disposable income. For a relatively poor country like Mexico, this propensity to consume may be extremely high. Indeed, many consumers may save nothing at all. As a result, a $1 tax cut may cause consumption to rise (and national saving to fall) by nearly $1. Foreign funds are required to make up the difference, and the current account adjusts accordingly.

Turning to the data for the early 1980s, note finally that the least squares regression line for 1982 to 1984 is roughly parallel to the line for 1960 to 1981. As with Canada, the relationship between the budget surplus and trade surplus simply seems to have shifted upward toward a more favorable balance of payments, although once again it is impossible to draw any clear inferences on the basis of three data points.

In summary, the Mexican economy exhibited a strong and clear relationship between the budget deficit and the current account through 1981. Quantitatively, the effects of fiscal policy on patterns of trade were significantly larger for Mexico than for any of the other countries considered. After 1981 these effects were obscured by the Mexican debt crisis.

7. CONCLUSIONS

Analysis of time series data for six countries reveals a robust and significant link between fiscal policy and trade deficits. For the United States, Canada, the United Kingdom, and West Germany, a $1 increase in the budget deficit is associated with roughly a $0.30 decline in the current account surplus. A cross-country comparison produces a slightly higher figure ($0.40). Fiscal effects are substantially larger for Mexico (perhaps as much as $0.85 on the dollar). No fiscal effects are evident for Japan, but this evidence is very weak.

At this point there is a very large empirical literature on the economic effects of government budget deficits. It is useful to review these findings in the context of this literature in order to produce a coherent view of fiscal policy. I recently reviewed this literature (see Bernheim (1987)) and reached the following conclusions. First, a number of studies have identified a strong positive relationship between fiscal deficits and private consumption. This finding is extremely robust. Generally, most studies estimate that the effect of increasing the deficit by $1 is to raise private consumption by about $0.30. Second, the evidence on the relationship between budget deficits and the interest rate is extremely mixed. No one has yet made a compelling empirical case for the view that budget deficits significantly raise interest rates.

Both of these conclusions are consistent with my current findings. If we suppose that international capital markets work reasonably well (and recall that there is an independent body of research that, on balance, supports this view), then budget deficits should not alter domestic investment. In fact, interest rates will be largely determined in the world capital market. It is therefore not at all surprising that various economists have been unable to identify a robust empirical relationship between fiscal policy and interest rates. On the other hand, government borrowing does depress national saving. If we take this effect to be $0.30 on the dollar (as suggested in the preceding paragraph) and suppose that investment remains fixed, we are led to the conclusion that a $1 increase in the budget deficit attracts $0.30 of investment funds from abroad, creating an offsetting $0.30 movement in the current account. This is exactly the magnitude of the effect that I have estimated here.

Only one anomaly remains. In a recent paper, Evans (1986) has argued that there is no empirical relationship between budget deficits and exchange rates. This is troublesome because the economic mechanism described in section 2 hypothesized that the current account would deteriorate in response to an appreciation of the domestic currency.

Evans's results are, however, contradicted by Feldstein (1986), who finds that the value of the dollar rises significantly in response to budget deficits.

REFERENCES

Barro, Robert J. 1974. Are government bonds net wealth? *Journal of Political Economy* 82.

Bernheim, B. Douglas. 1987. Ricardian equivalence: an evaluation of theory and evidence. *NBER Macroeconomics Annual* 2. Forthcoming.

Boskin, Michael J., and John M. Roberts. 1986. A closer look at saving rates in the United States and Japan. Stanford University, mimeo.

Branson, William H. 1985. Causes of appreciation and volatility of the dollar. In *The U.S. dollar—recent developments, outlook and policy options*, symposium sponsored by the Federal Reserve Bank of Kansas City.

Eisner, Robert. 1986. *How real is the federal deficit?* New York: The Free Press.

Evans, Paul. 1986. Is the dollar high because of large budget deficits? *Journal of Monetary Economics* 18: 227–49.

Feldstein, Martin. 1983. Domestic saving and international capital movements in the long run and the short run, *European Economic Review* 21: 129–51.

———. 1986. The budget deficit and the dollar. NBER Working Paper no. 1898.

Feldstein, Martin, and Charles Horioka. 1980. Domestic saving and international capital flows. *Economic Journal* 90: 314–29.

Frankel, Jeffrey. 1986. International capital mobility and crowding-out in the U.S. economy: Imperfect integration of financial markets or goods markets? In *How open is the U.S. economy?*, ed. R. W. Hafer. Lexington Books: Lexington, Mass.

Harberger, A. C. 1978. Perspectives on capital and technology in less developed countries. In *Contemporary economic analysis*, eds. M. J. Artis and A. R. Nobay. London.

———. 1980. Vignettes on the world capital market. *American Economic Review* 70: 331–37.

Helliwell, John. 1987. Some comparative macroeconomics of the United States, Japan, and Canada. University of British Columbia, mimeo.

Milne, Elizabeth S. 1977. The fiscal approach to the balance of payments. *Economic Notes* 6: 889–908.

Obstfeld, Maurice. 1986. Capital mobility in the world economy: Theory and measurement. *Carnegie-Rochester Conference Series on Public Policy* 24: 55–104.

Sachs, Jeffrey D. 1981. The current account and macroeconomic adjustment in the 1970s. *Brookings Papers on Economic Activity* 12: 201–68.

Summers, Lawrence H. 1986a. Tax policy and international competitiveness. Harvard Institute of Economic Research Discussion Paper no. 1256.

———. 1986b. Debt problems and macroeconomic policies. Harvard Institute of Economic Research Discussion Paper no. 1272.

TAXATION AND U.S. MULTINATIONAL INVESTMENT

James R. Hines, Jr.
Princeton University and NBER

In 1985, nonbank U.S. multinational companies employed 24.5 million workers, had worldwide sales of almost $3.5 trillion, and net income of $150 billion on assets of $4.2 trillion. The foreign (non-U.S.) affiliates of these companies had 6.4 million employees, $900 billion of those sales, and $43 billion of net income, with assets of $838 billion. United States multinationals accounted for roughly three-quarters of total American merchandise exports in 1985 and half of total imports, with approximately 40 percent of each category arising from transfers within U.S. multinationals between American parent firms and their own foreign affiliates.[1] And 1985 is widely regarded as a sluggish year for U.S. multinationals.

By any measure, U.S. multinationals play an important role in the world economy. Yet multinational corporations operate in economic and legal environments that are often extremely complex and subject to abrupt changes. Volatility in exchange rates is one recent example of such changes; the U.S. Tax Reform Act of 1986 (TRA) is another. The recent U.S. tax change seems likely to have a considerable effect on the net earnings U.S. multinationals can expect to get abroad.

This paper was prepared for presentation at the NBER Tax Policy and the Economy Conference, Washington, D. C., November 1987. I am grateful to Mark Gersovitz, Gene Grossman, David Hartman, Joosung Jun, Scott Newlon, James Poterba, Harvey Rosen, Lawrence Summers, and especially Daniel Frisch for helpful comments and to David Andres and Joseph Marucci of Price Waterhouse-Princeton for data they provided.

[1] Data on U.S. multinationals in 1985 is reported in Brereton (1987).

This chapter analyzes the impact of the U.S. tax system on overseas investments of U.S. multinationals. The TRA is just the most recent in a series of significant changes over the last twenty-five years in the U.S. tax law that applies to the foreign earnings of U.S. companies. The issue of U.S. tax incentives for overseas investments arises time and again in policy debates in the United States, as the goals of domestic employment and competitiveness in foreign markets compete with each other for legislative support. There is a widely held view that the U.S. tax system encourages American companies to invest excessively abroad, thereby depriving this country of capital, jobs, and productivity growth. However desirable it may be to encourage U.S. companies to invest their capital abroad, there appears to be little in the way of hard analysis of current and past incentives provided by the U.S. tax system. This chapter argues that the U.S. tax system has served to discourage foreign investment by U.S. multinationals more than is widely believed, but that the TRA has substantially reduced this negative incentive.

Section 1 examines some of the striking effects that foreign country tax systems have had on U.S. multinational activity. Section 2 describes the method by which the United States taxes the foreign income of its multinationals, and some of the theoretical implications of this system. Section 3 presents and analyzes recent data on U.S. and foreign tax collections from U.S. multinationals. Section 4 examines the financial behavior of U.S. multinationals and its tax consequences. Section 5 presents new estimates of effective tax rates on U.S. multinational investments in selected countries and considers recent investment behavior in the light of these estimates. Section 6 is the conclusion.

1. TAX HAVENS AND MULTINATIONAL ACTIVITY

Foreign countries are free to choose whatever tax regimes they want to impose on multinationals operating within their boundaries. Not surprisingly, tax rates vary widely from one country to another. In addition, many countries have signed bilateral tax treaties with other countries providing for mutual special tax treatment of the income from each others' multinational investments.

Tax havens are countries with very low rates of taxation of foreign investment. The governments of these countries are presumably willing to sacrifice some potential tax revenue in return for the employment, technology, and capital that foreign multinationals can provide. For U.S. firms investing overseas, the most important tax havens include the Bahamas, the Netherlands Antilles, Bermuda, Panama, Hong Kong, Liberia, Luxembourg, and Switzerland. By offering very low tax rates to induce foreign

TABLE 1
Tax Havens and U.S. Multinationals, 1982

Country	Foreign source taxable income	GNP	MNC income % of GNP	Current year foreign taxes	Average tax rate (%)
Bahamas	$ 2,222	$ 840	264.5	$ 40	1.8
Netherlands Antilles	1,152	1,370	84.1	196	17.0
Bermuda	552	790	69.9	3	0.5
Panama	1,259	4,060	31.0	239	19.0
All countries	57,059	—	0.8	21,998	38.6

Note: Dollar amounts are millions of current (1982) dollars.
Source: U.S. Department of the Treasury (1985).

investment, these countries provide a simple illustration of the ability of taxes to affect economic behavior.

Table 1 reports the taxable activity of U.S. multinationals in tax havens in 1982. A quick glance at the level of U.S. multinational earnings in the Bahamas, the Netherlands Antilles, Bermuda, and Panama is enough to suggest the conclusion that *something*, most likely favorable tax treatment, is inducing U.S. multinationals to concentrate an inordinate share of their income production in tax havens.[2] And since (as will be discussed shortly) the tax law discourages U.S. multinationals with operations in low-tax countries from taking actions that make their foreign source income taxable, the *true* foreign source income generated in these tax havens is quite likely to be greater than the reported figures.

The common wisdom in government and industry circles is that U.S. multinationals have over the last twenty years become increasingly adept at planning their overseas investment and financing activity in order to minimize tax obligations. All other things equal, one obvious way to avoid taxes is to locate as much foreign income production as possible in tax havens. Of course, there may be more geographical discretion in some industries than in others. Table 2 explores recent trends in tax haven activity of U.S. multinationals. The tax haven fraction of worldwide pretax earnings of the controlled foreign corporations of U.S. multinationals rose from 11 to 20 percent over the period 1968–1982. As the table suggests, this use rise is largely attributable to a greater fraction of U.S. multinational profits coming from the wholesale trade and finance, insurance, and real

[2] Strictly speaking, U.S. multinationals *report* inordinate earnings in tax havens. How much of these profits is the product of tax-avoiding accounting tricks is impossible to gauge.

TABLE 2
Growth of Tax Haven Activity By Controlled Foreign Corporations of U.S. Multinationals 1968–1982

		Earnings before tax of CFCs		
Industry of CFCs	Year	In tax havens	In all countries	In tax havens (%)
All industries	1968	$855	$7,744	11.0
	1972	1,972	15,356	12.8
	1980	6,681	47,622	14.0
	1982	7,405	36,696	20.2
Finance, insurance, and real estate	1968	109	358	30.4
	1972	422	1,190	35.5
	1980	2,048	4,822	42.5
Wholesale trade	1968	285	1,323	21.5
	1972	731	2,141	34.1
	1980	2,220	9,890	22.4
Services	1968	34	117	19.2
	1972	113	589	19.2
	1980	365	1,841	19.8
Other industries	1968	427	5,886	7.3
	1972	706	1,436	6.2
	1980	2,048	31,069	6.6

Note: Dollar amounts are millions of current dollars. The following constitute the tax havens: the Bahamas, the Netherlands Antilles, Bermuda, Panama, Hong Kong, Liberia, Luxembourg, and Switzerland.

Source: States (1986–1987). Detailed industry earnings are not available by country for 1982.

estate industries, which have proclivities for tax haven locations. Indeed, the rising importance of these industries may in part be due to their ability to locate in low-tax countries.

The casual evidence from tax havens is consistent with the view that foreign tax systems influence the investment decisions of U.S. multinationals, and that this influence is growing. For those interested in American tax policy, the next question is to what extent the U.S. tax code affects the overseas investment decisions of our multinationals. In order to address that question, it is necessary to consider in detail some of the provisions of the code as they affect the taxation of foreign source income.

2. THE TAX SYSTEM

The tax treatment of income generated by overseas investments of U.S. multinational corporations is extremely complicated. This section contains a brief description of some of its primary features. To begin with, the United States uses a "residence" standard to tax its corporations, which means that U.S. corporations owe tax to the U.S. Treasury on all of their worldwide income, wherever earned. (The alternative system would be one of "territorial" taxation, under which the U.S. would tax only that corporate income actually earned in the United States and would not tax at all the offshore earnings of U.S. corporations. A number of European countries, including France and the Netherlands, use territorial-type tax systems.)

Thus, when U.S. multinationals earn profits in other countries, they owe U.S. taxes on these profits. In addition, U.S. multinationals are typically required to pay income and other taxes to the foreign countries in which they operate. Being subject to the tax authorities of not only their home country (the United States) but also their host countries (e.g., West Germany), ordinary treatment of the profits earned abroad by U.S. multinationals would subject them to double taxation. In order to prevent the same profits from being taxed twice, the U.S. tax system permits firms to receive a credit for income taxes paid to other governments. Under the credit system, U.S. multinationals first pay their foreign taxes and then calculate the taxes they would owe to the U.S. government based on their (pretax) worldwide income just as if all of their income were earned domestically in the United States. The income taxes paid to foreign governments are then credited toward payment of U.S. taxes, so that taxes otherwise owed the U.S. Treasury are reduced dollar for dollar by taxes paid to other governments. The practical operation of this credit can be anything but straightforward, however.

To take a simple example, suppose that a U.S. manufacturing firm has a branch in a foreign country that imposes a 20 percent tax on corporate profits. Assume the effective tax rate on U.S. corporations to be 34 percent. Upon earning $100 through the foreign branch, the firm will owe $20 to the foreign government and $14 ($100 $\times$ 0.34 $-$ $20) to the U.S. government. This calculation assumes the absence of a number of important real-world complications (discussed later).

United States corporations investing overseas generally can choose from among several forms of legal organization for these investments, an option that complicates tax analysis, since this choice may have dramatic tax consequences. The primary decision facing a U.S. multinational is whether to organize its foreign operation as a branch or as a controlled foreign corporation (CFC).[3] Branch operations are considered by U.S. law to be

---

[3] United States multinationals can also organize their foreign affiliates with less than 50 percent U.S. ownership, thereby not qualifying as CFCs, but since there are reasons not to do

integral components of the domestic U.S. corporation, so branch profits, losses, deductions, taxes paid, and other financial activities are all treated as if performed by the U.S. corporation. Not so with CFCs, which are legally separate entities, incorporated in host countries (e.g., West Germany), and are more than 50 percent owned by U.S. shareholders, each of which has at least 10% of the stock.[4] Host countries often impose somewhat different tax and legal requirements on CFCs than they do on branch operations of U.S. multinationals. But the U.S. tax system treats CFCs very differently than it does foreign branches of U.S. companies.

The most important tax distinction between foreign branches and CFCs is that the United States taxes profits of the CFCs of U.S. multinationals only when CFCs send profits back to their U.S. parent companies. Legally, CFCs are entirely separate entities from the U.S. parent companies that own them, and it is only the U.S. parents that, strictly speaking, have tax obligations to the U.S. government. A U.S. parent is considered to earn income on its CFC investment only when that income is returned to the U.S. (with some exceptions). Thus, if a 100 percent American-owned CFC operates in Japan and runs up large profits there but does not pay out any dividends to the American corporation that owns its stock, then no U.S. tax liability is generated that year. Of course, U.S. taxes on those profits may have to be paid at some point in the future, if and when the profits are ultimately repatriated to the U.S. parent corporation.

When U.S. parent companies receive dividends from their CFCs, they calculate the U.S. taxes they owe based on the income they receive *plus* the foreign taxes credited to this income.[5] The tax credit system is designed to treat repatriated CFC income in the same way that an equal amount of branch income would be treated. One legal complication is that when a foreign government taxes branch income, it is the U.S. corporation that

---

so and they typically use CFCs, the analysis in this paper assumes all nonbranch overseas operations of U.S. multinationals to be CFCs.

[4] One question that naturally arises is, what are the consequences of less than 50 percent U.S. ownership of a foreign corporation? If an individual corporation owns less than 10 percent of foreign corporation, then it is not entitled to use the foreign tax credit when it receives taxable dividends in the United States. On the other hand, the Subpart F restrictions apply only to corporations that qualify as CFCs. Of course, there are a number of nontax reasons why a corporation might want more than 50 percent control of a foreign subsidiary. And the foreign corporation would presumably be less inclined to follow financial policies aimed at minimizing U.S. taxes of its shareholders if American firms own less than half the shares. In practice, in 1985 more than 75 percent of the U.S. share of earnings and assets of foreign corporation were located in majority-owned foreign affiliates, which includes foreign branches and a subset of all CFCs (see Brereton (1987)).

[5] The 85 percent exclusion rule, which provides that U.S. corporations are taxed on only 15 percent of the dividends they receive on their corporate stock holdings, does not apply to dividends received from foreign corporations.

officially pays the tax, whereas income tax paid by a CFC to a foreign government is, strictly speaking, paid by the CFC, not the U.S. corporation that owns the CFC. To handle this situation, the law provides that when the U.S. parent calculates the U.S. taxes it owes on dividends received from a CFC, the taxes paid to the foreign government by the CFC on *this* income are "deemed paid" by the U.S. parent and thereby can be added to the foreign tax credit the U.S. parent gets for foreign taxes paid on branch income.

When a U.S. parent corporation receives dividends from a CFC, the U.S. parent must determine the appropriate foreign tax credit (FTC) allowable on this income. Foreign tax credits have several sources, the most important being foreign withholding taxes and foreign income taxes. Many countries impose withholding taxes on CFC dividends remitted to U.S. parents, and U.S. corporations are allowed to credit these taxes toward their U.S. tax payments.[6] It is trickier to calculate the allowable tax credit for the income taxes paid by the CFC. The basic method is to calculate the fraction of the *current year's* after-tax CFC income represented by the dividend, and multiply that fraction by the foreign taxes paid by the CFC to arrive at the foreign taxes the U.S. parent can credit toward its U.S. taxes. Table 3 illustrates this procedure for a simple example.

In this example, a U.S. parent corporation is assumed to own 75 percent of a foreign corporation that in the current year earns $5,000 in profits. The foreign income tax rate is assumed to be 20 percent, so the CFC pays foreign income tax of $1,000 and has $4,000 in after-tax profits. Assume the foreign corporation to pay out 60 percent of its after-tax profits as dividends, and that the foreign government imposes a 10 percent withholding tax on dividends sent to foreign shareholders. Since the American parent is entitled to 75 percent of the dividends paid out, it gets $1,800 minus the 10 percent withholding tax, or $1,620.

In calculating its U.S. tax liability, the U.S. parent is allowed to take a tax credit for the $180 withholding tax paid on its dividend, plus a fraction of the $1,000 paid this year by the CFC in income taxes. The fraction is determined by the ratio of the parent's pre-withholding-tax dividend ($1,800) to the CFC's after-tax income ($4,000), in this case 45%. Thus, the U.S. parent gets a tax credit of $450 for "deemed paid" income taxes plus $180 for withholding taxes. But the U.S. parent is also required to "gross up" the dividend it receives from the CFC by the amount of the foreign

---

[6] Strictly speaking, though they never actually see the money, the U.S. parent corporations pay these withholding taxes out of the dividends they would have received from their CFCs. Foreign governments require the CFCs to be withholding agents for these payments. As a result, the U.S. parents get full tax credits for the withholding taxes, and the foreign governments can lean on CFCs located in their countries to ensure that taxes are paid.

TABLE 3
Illustrative Computation—U.S. Tax Liability from Repatriated CFC Profits

(1)	Pretax earnings of CFC	$5,000
(2)	Foreign income tax at 20 percent	1,000
(3)	Net earnings and profits: (1) − (2)	4,000
(4)	Dividend paid to all shareholders: 60% of (3), by assumption	2,400
(5)	Dividend paid to U.S. parent company: 75% of (4), by assumption	1,800
(6)	Foreign withholding tax at 10%: 10% of (5)	180
(7)	Net dividend received in U.S.: (5) − (6)	1,620
	Foreign creditable taxes:	
	Direct credit for withholding tax	180
	Deemed paid credit for subsidiary's income tax:	
	[(5)/(3)] × (2)	450
(8)	Total creditable taxes	630
	Includable as U.S. income:	
	Dividend received	1,800
	Foreign deemed paid tax	450
(9)	Total grossed-up foreign dividend	2,250
(10)	U.S. tax due: 34% of (9)	765
(11)	Foreign tax credit	630
(12)	Net payment due U.S. government: (10) − (11)	135

Note: This table presents the end-of-year tax calculation for a U.S. parent company that owns 75 percent of a foreign corporation. The foreign income tax rate is assumed to be 20 percent, the foreign government imposes a 10 percent withholding tax on dividends paid to U.S. shareholders, and the foreign corporation pays out 60 percent of its after-tax earnings as dividends.

taxes deemed paid, so the U.S. tax liability is based on $2,250 of foreign income. At a U.S. tax rate of 34 percent, the U.S. parent owes $765 in U.S. taxes, but it can subtract $630 in FTCs from this amount to yield a net payment due the U.S. government of $135.

2.1 Some Complications

Although the FTC can be a strong palliative for the burden of foreign taxes, there are limits to the credit's applicability. For example, the FTC can be claimed only for income taxes; other types of taxes paid (or deemed paid) to foreign governments can generally be deducted like other business expenses but are not eligible for the credit. The distinction between foreign income taxes and other types of foreign taxes is, for this reason, important, but the distinction is sometimes murky. The law is designed to prevent U.S. multinationals from obtaining a U.S. tax credit for paying user fees disguised as foreign income taxes, but in practice it seems that the law disallows FTCs whenever the foreign taxes do not resemble U.S. corporate income taxes.[7] On the other hand, withholding taxes on dividend remittances generally qualify as creditable income taxes, since they are attributed to be "in lieu of" income taxes that foreigners would have paid to their own governments had *they* been the shareholders.

In addition, there is an overall limit to the FTC: the law stipulates that a firm cannot apply more FTCs toward its U.S. tax liability than the total of its foreign source income times the *average* U.S. tax rate it pays. The FTC limitation is designed to enforce the restriction that FTCs cannot be used to offset taxes due on domestic U.S. income. That part of foreign taxes paid at a rate higher than the U.S. rate cannot be used as a tax credit in the current year. Since 1976, the U.S. government has required U.S. multinationals to average their worldwide foreign income and foreign taxes for purposes of calculating taxes and credits. This requirement limits the ability of U.S. firms to reduce their taxable income through foreign losses, but it allows firms to get credits for taxes paid in high-tax foreign countries by averaging with operations in low-tax countries. The slight nonlinearity of the U.S. corporate tax rate also affects the FTC limit, since the limit is based on average rather than marginal rates. Under the pre-TRA the U.S. corporate tax rate started at 15 percent and became 46 percent only once a corporation had income of $100,000; furthermore, capital gains were taxed at 28 percent. Hence, a corporation that had much of its income in capital gains or that had low profits (or better yet, losses) would have an average tax rate below 46 percent and could credit only those foreign taxes that did not exceed this rate.

The structure of the FTC mechanism means that tax timing issues loom large for some U.S. multinationals, particularly those with substantial variations in foreign and domestic income. If a U.S. multinational cannot use all of its FTCs currently, it is permitted to carry them back up to two years or forward up to five years to reduce U.S. tax obligations on eligible foreign source income. Indeed, there is a significant inventory of unused FTCs that U.S. corporations carry forward each year.[8]

Another complication arises when CFCs pay out dividends exceeding their current year's income. In that event, the excess of current dividends over current income is attributed to previous years' undistributed incomes in reverse order, last year first. Firms are required, in other words, to keep

---

[7] For example, certain foreign oil income taxes based on "posted price" rather than market revenues were disqualified as income taxes. McDaniel and Ault (1981) contains a discussion of this issue.

[8] For example, U.S. corporations carried accumulated FTCs of $17.5 billion forward into 1982 while acquiring an additional $20.7 billion credit that year. Only $18.9 billion of those FTCs could be used in 1982, the bulk of the difference presumably eligible to be carried forward into future years. (See Barlow (1986) for 1982 data.)

inventories of each year's income and dividends, reducing the inventories in last-in–first-out fashion as future dividends exceed future earnings. Given this accounting system, it is in the interest of U.S. multinationals that do not bump up against the FTC limit to receive dividends selectively from those of their CFCs having higher-than-average foreign tax years. Indeed, CFCs may reduce their overall tax burdens by taking actions that raise their average foreign tax burdens but at the same time increase their variability so that dividends can be paid in high-tax years. Industry sources suggest that firms make widespread use of this so-called "rhythm method" of paying dividends. The TRA limited (but did not eliminate) the ability of U.S. corporations to profit from year-to-year fluctuations in their CFCs' average foreign tax rates by providing that all post-1986 CFC earnings and foreign taxes be pooled to construct a multiple-year average foreign tax rate for purposes of calculating the indirect FTC.

Confident in the ability of U.S. corporations to exploit opportunities for tax avoidance, the U.S. Congress has written into the law a number of provisions that trigger tax obligations of U.S. parent companies for certain actions taken by their CFCs. The most important such provisions are the Subpart F rules, which were adopted in 1962. These rules attempt to discourage U.S. parents of CFCs from indefinitely delaying the repatriation of CFC income if minimizing U.S. taxes were the goal behind their no-dividend strategy.

The Subpart F rules provide that certain types of CFC expenditures or investments will be treated as if they were dividend payments to the U.S. parent, and hence will increase the U.S. tax obligation of the parent company. The most important category of these financial activities is passive investments. Thus, the profits of a U.S. multinational's French CFC are not taxable by the U.S. if reinvested in the French business, but the same profits if invested by the nonbank CFC in French bonds earn interest that *is* taxable in the United States as earned.

The Subpart F rules generally prevent nonfinancial CFCs from making financial investments in lieu of returning dividends to the United States. Besides passive investment income, Subpart F requires CFC investments in U.S. property and insurance of U.S. risks to be taxable as if the money were repatriated to the U.S. parent. Various earnings by CFCs in countries outside their host country trigger Subpart F tax liabilities, as do foreign illegal payments and income earned in countries that engage in certain illegal boycotts. Once the U.S. parent incurs a tax liability through Subpart F, however, the Subpart F income can be repatriated to the United States without any further U.S. tax consequences.

The taxation of foreign source income raises issues that are not present or are less important to domestic business taxation. For example, the allocation of income between countries can have very large tax consequences for U.S. multinationals. It is generally in the interest of multinationals to earn their income in low-tax jurisdictions. (Although, once earned, multinationals have incentives to attribute income to high-tax sources for FTC purposes.) Thus it might be tempting for U.S. multinationals to sell intermediate products to their foreign affiliates located in tax havens, at bargain prices, and to locate the head office and as many companywide fixed expenditures as possible in high-tax countries. But U.S. law generally requires firms to use market prices (or the equivalent) for intracompany transfers and to allocate fixed costs according to formulas based on criteria such as sales and assets. The law also restricts even the tax location of some assets; for example, income earned by Americans in outer space or in Antarctica is taxed as though earned on the ground in the United States.[9]

Other features of the tax law applying to foreign source income include much less generous investment incentives than those given to domestic capital until the recent tax reform. Foreign investments are not eligible for the investment tax credit and must be depreciated for tax purposes over long lifetimes. Special rules apply to foreign oil and gas income, and there are special recapture provisions that recoup in subsequent years tax losses that are usually associated with those industries. More generally, the TRA requires various baskets of foreign earning sources to keep separate accounts in hopes of preventing high foreign tax income, such as that derived from petroleum, from pooling tax credits with low foreign tax income from other sources. Other significant changes included in the tax reform include the introduction of functional currencies for foreign affiliates. Before passage of the TRA, the law was unclear over the appropriate way to treat for tax purposes changes in the value of foreign affiliates resulting from exchange rate movements. Under current law, each foreign affiliate chooses (usually) one functional currency and earns taxable income only for transactions in that currency.

2.2 Implications for Investment Behavior

The most striking features of U.S. taxation of multinational income are the provisions for credit and deferral. From a static and purely self-interested perspective, it may be hard to understand why the U.S. government permits a tax credit for foreign taxes paid. Taking the tax systems of foreign governments as given, foreign taxes paid by U.S. companies are costs of doing business and nothing more. As such, one might expect the U.S. government to permit a U.S. tax deduction for foreign taxes paid; but a credit goes beyond that. The FTC mitigates the double taxation of U.S.

---

[9] Special rules apply to communications satellites.

multinationals on their foreign earnings but does so by allowing foreign governments to extract tax revenues from U.S. companies without fear of excessively discouraging U.S. investment within their borders, since the cost is borne largely by the U.S. Treasury. In fact, even a tax deduction for foreign taxes paid might represent too generous a policy, since if American capital as a whole has market power overseas the U.S. government could create rents by taxing multinational investments (relative to allowing a deduction), restricting the quantity of American investments and raising their returns. But neither of these alternatives—a tax deduction for foreign taxes paid or only a partial deduction (or tax)—may make sense if other countries are thereby encouraged to adopt similar policies in taxing the U.S. investments of their own multinationals. All countries can be worse off in a worldwide regime of heavy double taxation of multinational income. The FTC is probably best understood as a measure designed to preserve an international political equilibrium of limited multinational taxes.

The deferral of U.S. taxes on unrepatriated CFC income further encourages U.S. investment abroad. By reinvesting their foreign CFC earnings in active investments in foreign host countries, where tax rates are lower than the U.S. tax rate, U.S. multinationals can effectively earn interest abroad on what would have been taxes due to the U.S. government. Even though U.S. taxes are ultimately due on all foreign earnings, firms are generally better off by delaying their U.S. tax payments. Hence deferral has two consequences: it may encourage initial equity investments by U.S. parents in their foreign CFCs, since the returns are lightly taxed, and CFCs have particularly strong incentives to invest out of retained earnings, since those funds are subject to U.S. tax if not reinvested.

The deferral of U.S. taxes is widely thought to have substantial effects on CFC investment behavior. Horst (1977) argues that deferral lowers (in the case of a U.S. tax rate that is higher than foreign taxes) the effective tax rate on CFC investments to a weighted average of U.S. and foreign tax rates, with weights determined by the CFC's (fixed) dividend payout ratio. Hartman (1985) argues that deferral is even more powerful than that: he claims that the reinvestment decisions of mature CFCs will be completely unaffected by U.S. tax considerations. Newlon (1987) arrives at the same conclusion, using a model that includes the full range of financial options available to the multinational firm. In the Hartman and Newlon models the U.S. tax system can affect only the initial equity investments of U.S. multinationals overseas. Once firms have sufficient retained earnings abroad, they finance their own investments out of these earnings as if the U.S. tax rate on this income were zero. Assuming foreign tax rates to be lower than U.S. rates, CFCs of U.S. multinationals will therefore reinvest their earnings to a greater degree than would those companies in the United States. Hartman (1981), Frisch and Hartman (1983), and Boskin and Gale (1987) tested whether domestic tax variables affect foreign investment by U.S. multinationals out of retained earnings and found no significant effect. But these regressions encounter difficulties acknowledged by the authors, and in section 5 explores channels through which U.S. taxes affect CFC reinvestment decisions that the earlier studies do not incorporate.

United States companies are not the only entities whose behavior is likely to be affected by U.S. provisions for taxing the foreign income of U.S. multinationals. Foreign governments may respond, or threaten to respond, in a retaliatory fashion to aggressive U.S. tax increases. The worldwide averaging provision of the U.S. tax code may encourage some high-tax countries to raise their taxes on U.S. multinationals in order to free ride off other, low-tax, countries where U.S. multinationals generate income. In addition, foreign governments have incentives to design their tax systems to show a high rate of income tax that is eligible for the U.S. FTC. As Gersovitz (1987) argues, the optimal strategy for a host country often is to tax multinationals at a high rate while offering other direct or indirect investment subsidies, thereby encouraging investment *and* allowing U.S. firms to claim hefty FTCs. Baldwin (1986) reports that indirect subsidies for multinational investment are quite common, including U.S. government subsidies for foreign investment projects in the United States.

3. HOW BIG ARE U.S. TAXES?

Much of the preceding discussion was predicated on the assumption that the U.S. tax rate on foreign source income exceeds foreign tax rates. If the U.S. tax rate exactly equalled foreign tax rates, then the U.S. tax system would raise no revenue from foreign sources and have no effect on the overseas behavior of U.S. multinationals. Unfortunately, it is not easy to construct summary statistics on the difference between U.S. and foreign tax rates, since applicable statutory tax rates as well as depreciation and other provisions vary widely from one country to another.

Table 4 presents some evidence on the relative historic magnitudes of average foreign and U.S. tax rates on foreign source income of U.S. multinationals. Of course, these tax rates represent tax collections as a fraction of realized taxable income and so do not reflect many of the tax incentives that affect investor decisions by encouraging lightly taxed activities and discouraging business activities taxed at full rates. In addition, these figures do not incorporate unreported foreign income of U.S. firms or the incentives generated by the tax system to earn foreign income in ways that are easily hidden from U.S. tax authorities. Still, Table 4

TABLE 4
Average Foreign and U.S. Tax Rates on Realized Foreign Income, 1972–1982

Year	Branch income	Foreign taxes on branches	Average tax rate (%)	CFC income	Foreign taxes on CFCs	Average tax rate (%)	Taxable foreign income of U.S. corporations	FTCs	U.S. average tax rate on current-year foreign income (%)	U.S. average tax rate on all corporate income (%)
1982	$14,572	$5,630	38.6	$36,696	$14,077	38.4	$59,388	$18,932	6.8	36.5
1980	21,871	10,088	46.1	47,621	16,440	34.5	70,541	24,880	17.5	46.6
1978	11,275	5,036	44.7	n.a.	n.a.	n.a.	65,150	26,358	4.6	43.2
1976	6,413	4,146	64.6	23,479	8,630	36.8	55,413	23,547	6.4	46.2
1974	n.a.	n.a.	n.a.	20,938	7,506	35.8	46,770	20,175	19.8	54.4
1972	n.a.	n.a.	n.a.	15,356	5,595	36.4	15,015	5,813	7.2	43.1

Note: The table contains some very minor inconsistencies, since data for some years are available on returns only for those companies with $250 million or more in assets. See the sources.

Source: Author's calculation based on data in U.S. Department of the Treasury (various years), Carson (1986), and Auerbach (1983b).

presents a picture of foreign tax rates that are slightly lower than the average U.S. corporate tax rate. As a result, U.S. taxes have generally been due on foreign income received by U.S. corporations, though at a fairly low average rate.

What does the evidence in Table 4 suggest about the likely effect of U.S. taxes on overseas investments by U.S. multinationals? Since tax collections on foreign source income are positive, it is tempting to infer that firms must pay positive U.S. taxes on repatriated profits, a tax obligation they can defer by continued reinvestment abroad. One difficulty in drawing that conclusion is that, once again, these tax rates reflect average rather than marginal incentives for a firm's foreign investment. In addition, these numbers represent averages across firms and countries. It may be that the CFCs of individual firms located in particular countries face very high or very low effective tax rates on their marginal investments. The TRA, with the reduction in the U.S. corporate tax rate from 46 to 34 percent, is also likely to change the relative sizes of U.S. and foreign tax rates. United States taxes on multinational investment can be expected to diminish in importance; Grubert and Mutti (1987) report Treasury estimates that 70 percent of U.S. manufacturing companies will have excess FTCs.

Even if the U.S. Treasury collected no corporate revenue at all from foreign source income, it would be a mistake to conclude that U.S. taxes have no effect on foreign investment behavior of U.S. multinationals. As discussed in the previous section, the U.S. tax system may induce U.S. multinationals to reduce their U.S. tax liabilities by adjusting the rate at which they pay out dividends, by modifying their use of tax deductions in foreign countries, and by changing the location of overseas investments, all of which have real effects on the after-tax returns available from investments in other countries. Consider the simple case in which a U.S. corporation wants to repatriate some of the income earned by one of its CFCs located in a foreign country with very high taxes. Taken alone, the dividend payment would generate no additional U.S. tax liability, since the associated FTCs exceed the average U.S. taxes that would have to be paid. But by generating foreign tax in excess of the credit limit, this action encourages the same U.S. parent company to repatriate income from CFCs located in low-tax countries, since worldwide averaging permits the U.S. parent to apply the high foreign taxes to the rest of its repatriated income that year and bring the average down to the limit. This technique thereby removes some of the repatriation disincentive for investments in low-tax countries and may contribute to the popularity of tax havens as investment locations. One implication of widespread use of this technique would be average realized foreign tax rates on repatriated income near the U.S.

statutory corporate rate, and low average U.S. tax rates on repatriated income, both of which one observes.

None of this should be taken to minimize the importance of interfirm heterogeneity in applicable marginal tax rates on foreign investments and repatriations to the United States. Some firms carry forward unused FTCs each year, whereas other firms pay substantial taxes on their foreign source income. Although a similar tale can be told of the unused tax credits and deductions of unprofitable domestic U.S. firms going to waste while other U.S. firms face full tax rates (see Auerbach and Poterba (1987)), the rules that apply to foreign source income make it particularly difficult for unused FTCs to find their way into the books of companies that can exploit them. Without tax data on individual firms one cannot know precisely their incentives, but it is still possible to make some general observations about the average tax incentives U.S. firms face. The next question is whether observed behavior is consistent with those incentives.

4. FINANCIAL BEHAVIOR AND TAX INCENTIVES

Because profits earned abroad by the CFCs of U.S. multinationals are not subject to U.S. taxation until received by their U.S. parents, it is to the advantage of these CFCs to delay paying dividends as long as feasible, thereby reducing the present value of the associated U.S. tax obligations. In fact, one well might wonder why CFCs remit dividends to U.S. parents at all, given the tax cost of doing so. A similar question arises in studies of the financial behavior of domestic U.S. corporations, since individuals who own corporate stock are typically taxed much more heavily on the dividends they receive than on their capital gains. Hence, shareholders should prefer their companies to reinvest all their profits, in government bonds if necessary, rather than pay dividends. By reinvesting the profits, the companies would raise the value of their shares and shareholders could take their returns in the form of lower-taxed share appreciation rather than dividends. Or less subtly, corporations can and do return profits to stockholders in lightly taxed form through share repurchases, as Shoven (1987) documents.

In fact, domestic U.S. corporations pay out about one-quarter to one-third of their profits to their shareholders each year in dividends, as indicated in the first column of Table 5. By contrast, column 3 of Table 5 reveals CFCs to payout a significantly higher fraction—almost half—of their annual profits out in dividends each year. The accounting rules underlying these ratios are somewhat arbitrary (see Poterba (1987) for a discussion), but they reveal what appears to be a significant difference in the financial behavior of domestic corporations and their CFCs. In order to

TABLE 5
CFC Dividend Payouts and U.S. Corporate Dividend Payouts

	Dividend payout ratio, all U.S. corporations %	Implicit shareholder tax rate on U.S. dividends %	Dividend payout ratio, CFCs %	Average U.S. tax rate on foreign earnings %
1982	30.6	24.8	64.8	6.8
1980	23.9	30.5	45.3	17.5
1978	22.3	28.7	n.a.	4.6
1976	24.2	28.6	44.2	6.4
1974	28.7	28.2	51.8	19.8
1972	26.8	28.6	52.9	7.2

Note: First and second columns adapted form Poterba (1987).

Sources: Author's calculation based on data in U.S. Department of the Treasury (various) and States (1980–1987). Some CFC data refer only to CFCs whose U.S. parent corporations have assets of at least $250 million.

understand the source of this difference, it helps to explore the reasons why firms pay dividends in the first place. Financial policy is particularly important to the investment decisions of CFCs, since the Subpart F and other rules imply that the tradeoff between dividends and investments in plant and equipment is even stronger for them than it is for domestic firms.

Observers of U.S. corporate financial policy have proposed several explanations for the presence of significant dividend payments despite associated tax costs. The most important of these explanations include the use of dividend payouts by a firm's managers to signal profitability, the willingness of tax-exempt and certain other shareholders to receive dividends rather than accrue capital gains, and the possibility that a reinvested dollar may not raise firm value by a full dollar. The first explanation relies on incompleteness of information flows between firms and their shareholders. By paying dividends, firms reassure their shareholders and the market generally that operations continue to be profitable. By contrast, a reduction in dividends signals pessimistic news about current and future profitability and is likely to depress firm value. Since publicly traded American firms are required to release their financial information to the public, dividends under the signaling interpretation must be conveying information beyond that which firms routinely make available through annual reports, 10–K filings, and the like.[10]

The second explanation for dividend payouts by firms to shareholders is the possibility that tax-exempt shareholders hold the stock of high-payout

[10] Gordon and Malkiel (1981) explore the consequences of this view of dividend behavior.

firms, making those payouts costless from a tax point of view. Then if shareholders would have to incur transactions costs in selling stock, those shareholders would prefer to receive their returns in the form of dividends rather than capital gains. In addition, corporate shareholders can exclude from their taxable income 85 percent of the dividends they receive from domestic corporations, so they generally prefer to receive dividends rather than capital gains.[11]

The third explanation of dividend behavior is the so-called "trapped money" model: once a corporation earns money, it must choose either to pay the money out as a dividend or to reinvest the money. Since corporations are observed to pay some dividends, this model implies that a marginal dollar reinvested in the firm produces the same *after-tax* addition to shareholder value as would the same dollar paid as a dividend. Assuming tax rates on capital gains to be lower than dividend taxes, it must be the case that $1 of marginal investment financed by reinvested earnings is sufficiently unproductive that it raises firm value by less than $1.[12]

Although none of these three models of firm financial policy appear to explain every feature of domestic dividend behavior, it is worth considering how they can be applied to the dividend remittance decisions of CFCs of U.S. multinationals. At first blush, it seems unlikely that information and signaling problems would arise between CFCs and their U.S. multinational parents, since it is all one company and the parent could in principle demand to see detailed financial records, fire foreign managers, and exert control in other ways. Furthermore, the U.S. parent as (in many cases) the only shareholder need not be troubled by temporary changes in share value. But at the same time, one cannot rule out the same kind of agency problems that arise between ordinary corporate shareholders and their firm's managers. Domestic managers of U.S. multinationals inevitably have less information about the financial well-being of foreign affiliates than do their foreign managers, and continued high-dividend payouts provide convincing evidence of the high quality of overseas operations. But this effect seems unlikely to explain payout ratios that exceed even those of domestic corporations.

The second explanation for domestic dividends, the presence of low-tax shareholder clienteles, says little about dividend remittances to heavily taxed multinationals. But the third explanation, that corporate money is

---

[11] Auerbach (1983a) finds some support in data on stock price movements for the hypothesis that low-tax shareholders tend to own stock in firms with high dividend-payout ratios, but even in his estimates these individuals prefer capital gains to dividends.

[12] See Auerbach (1979), Bradford (1981), and King (1977) for the development of this model. Poterba and Summers (1985) do not find support for this theory in their recent examination of U.K. data.

"trapped" within inescapable tax barriers, appears to be very much to the point of multinational financial planning. What can a CFC do with its earnings when there appear to be no profitable foreign investment opportunities? The Subpart F rules prevent passive and other types of internationally invested income from going unrecognized by the U.S. tax system, so dividends to parent companies entail no extra tax cost to the multinational. Of course, these dividends then represent income that the U.S. parent corporation must either reinvest or pay out as dividends to *its* shareholders. The profits of CFCs are thus subject to taxation three times: they are taxed by foreign governments when earned, by the U.S. government when repatriated, and by the U.S. government when distributed ultimately to stockholders. But CFCs cannot avoid indefinitely the last two layers of taxation, and so should be expected to remit dividends in response to declining foreign uses of capital.[13]

Controlled foreign corporations need not pay dividends mechanically, however: the model implies that payout ratios should be sensitive to the associated U.S. tax obligations, and the evidence suggests that they are. Recall from Table 5 that CFC payout ratios are higher than overall U.S. corporate ratios, which is consistent with the lower average U.S. tax rate on CFC dividends than on domestic corporate dividends paid to individual shareholders. In addition, CFC payout ratios vary over time and between CFCs as the U.S. taxes due on CFC dividends vary. Table 6 illustrates the response of payouts to taxes with aggregate CFC data for 1980 and 1982. All other things equal, CFCs facing the highest foreign taxes have incentives to pay dividends at the highest rates, since these dividends may be untaxed by the U.S. government and, indeed, through worldwide averaging these dividends might reduce U.S. taxes due on foreign source income that was lightly taxed by foreign governments. The last column of Table 6 suggests that payout ratios do generally rise with foreign tax rates. This evidence is consistent with other findings that the dividend policies of multinational firms respond to foreign and U.S. tax regimes.

---

[13] One implication of the model is that CFCs that pay dividends should never simultaneously receive equity transfers from their parents. Jun (1987) presents new evidence that more than a quarter of foreign affiliates pay dividends and receive transfers in the same year. But these data do not conclusively reject the theory, since the sample includes branches as well as CFCs, the transfers include debt as well as equity, and the timing of financial operations within the year may be important here. Furthermore, under the current system of worldwide averaging, U.S. parents desire immediate repatriation of profits earned by their CFCs located in countries with taxes higher than U.S. rates, replenishing them if necessary with equity transfers in the same year. The presence of CFCs in high-tax countries may account for Jun's findings.

[14] See, for example, Kopits (1972) and Mutti (1981).

TABLE 6
Analysis of CFC Distributions

	Current earnings and profits before taxes	Foreign income taxes	After-tax foreign profits	Distributions		Current profits distributed as % of after-tax foreign profits (%)
				Total	Out of current earn. & profits	
CFCs of Large U.S. Corporations, 1982 Total with taxes as % of current profits:	$47,617	$14,494	$33,123	$13,559	$9,424	28.5
zero	$5,468	—	$5,468	$1,537	$1,046	19.1
0–10	6,610	$ 257	6,353	1,926	1,365	21.5
10–20	3,812	550	3,262	1,190	692	21.2
20–30	6,154	1,514	4,640	1,344	1,046	22.5
30–40	5,355	1,866	3,489	1,703	1,363	39.1
40–45	4,489	1,910	2,579	1,194	872	33.8
45–50	5,626	2,645	2,981	1,625	1,199	40.2

50–60	4,280	2,305	1,975	1,129	839	42.5
60–80	3,208	2,157	1,051	1,295	666	63.4
80–100	1,389	1,258	131	150	58	44.3
Over 100%	169	280	–111	115	—	—

CFCs of All U.S. Corporations, 1980

Total	$55,795	$16,737	$39,058	$13,199	$9,639	24.7
zero	$ 4,516	—	$ 4,516	$ 991	$ 536	11.9
0–10	7,393	$ 268	7,125	2,358	1,789	25.1
10–20	4,995	741	4,254	1,013	765	18.0
20–30	7,307	1,872	5,435	1,551	1,240	22.8
30–40	10,613	3,699	6,914	2,641	1,817	26.3
40–45	8,667	2,901	5,766	1,288	1,087	18.9
45–50	5,385	2,540	2,845	1,263	1,039	36.5
50–60	4,990	2,677	2,313	1,251	848	36.7
60–80	2,050	1,341	709	455	335	47.2
80–100	762	659	103	166	87	84.5
over 100%	128	188	–60	56		

Note: These data refer only to those CFCs with positive earnings and profits for the current year. Data for 1982 are available only for CFCs of U.S. parent corporations with at least $250 million in assets.

Sources: States (1986–1987) and U.S. Department of the Treasury (1985).

5. EFFECTIVE TAX RATES AND U.S. INVESTMENT ABROAD

The tax incentive for U.S. firms to invest abroad is a subject of major policy interest. As earlier discussion indicates, any individual firm's tax incentives depend on its available tax credit carryforwards, earnings, and tax history against which to carry back deductions and credits, fungibility of current-year dividend repatriations from CFCs in high- and low-tax countries, borrowing opportunities, and a host of other factors. In addition, when new investment opportunities arise, they can be exploited in a number of different forms.

United States multinationals can choose from among three primary methods of investing in foreign countries: branch investments, CFC investments financed out of new transfers of debt or equity from the parent corporation, and CFC investments financed out of retained earnings. Since it is not clear with which of these methods marginal multinational investments take place, it is necessary to analyze the investment tax incentives for all three.

Foreign branch investments are seemingly the most straightforward, since repatriation-timing issues do not arise because branches are taxed currently in the U.S. on all their earnings and profits. As mentioned earlier, the U.S. tax treatment of foreign branches differs from the tax treatment of analogous domestic U.S. investment in that branches must pay taxes to foreign governments at rates possibly higher than U.S. tax rates, and branches are not entitled to some domestic investment incentives such as the investment tax credit and short asset lifetimes for tax depreciation purposes. One big tax advantage that branch organization may offer a U.S. multinational is that foreign branch losses reduce domestic taxable profits dollar for dollar. Since U.S. multinationals are not permitted to use CFC losses to reduce domestic or foreign taxable income, it may be in the interest of firms expecting loss years to organize their foreign operations as branches. It is widely argued that the tax losses associated with oil and natural gas exploration and development motivated U.S. oil companies to form foreign branches rather than CFCs for their overseas operations. Naturally, legal, regulatory, and political considerations also may affect the decision to form a foreign branch rather than a CFC.

New investments financed out of the retained earnings of existing CFCs have the tax advantage of avoiding direct U.S. taxation of either the principal or subsequent profits until profits are repatriated. It is this feature that motivated Hartman (1985) to argue that only the foreign country's tax system affects the marginal incentive for CFCs to invest out of retained earnings. Although Hartman's conclusion is correct for the stylized model he constructs, it is not accurate to conclude that U.S. CFCs with retained earnings face no marginal investment incentives from the U.S. tax code. In particular, the difference between the U.S. definition of foreign earnings and profits and the foreign definition of taxable income generally produces a tax burden on U.S. multinational investment in excess of the foreign effective tax rate.

No two foreign tax systems look exactly alike; however, they typically share the feature that they encourage corporate investment through incentives such as very rapid tax write-off of depreciation charges for new investments. Canada, for example, has very generous investment incentives in the manufacturing industries. When U.S. multinationals make investments through their CFCs, they must calculate their earnings and profits based on "U.S. accounting principles," which provide, among other things, for tax depreciation of investment expenses at slow rates over long depreciable lifetimes. As a result, a new U.S. investment in Canada generates a present value of U.S.-definition earnings and profits that is higher than the present value of Canadian-defined taxable income.

This difference in U.S. and foreign definitions of income, along with the method by which tax credits are computed, means that the U.S. corporate tax rate and U.S. rules for depreciation of foreign property generally combine to discourage even the marginal investments of U.S.-owned CFCs that use retained earnings. The reason the U.S. tax system has this effect is that a new CFC investment will in general change the calculated value of a firm's average foreign tax rate that is used in the tax credit computation. As a result, even though the profits from a new CFC investment may not be themselves subject to U.S. taxation, the accounting rules work in such a way that this investment reduces the FTC the U.S. parent firm is eligible to take on profits from *other* foreign investments made by the same CFC, as long as the tax rate on marginal investments is lower than the average tax rate paid that year. A complete calculation of the true tax incentives for CFC investments should include this effect along with the standard tax incentive provided by foreign law.

By defining foreign income in this way, the U.S. tax law discourages U.S. overseas investments in countries with significantly different income definitions. It is difficult to establish in practice exactly how much of a difference these accounting rules make in the level of reported earnings, but Table 7 provides some suggestion that the difference may be quite substantial. As the table reports, the measured profit margins on sales by CFCs of U.S. multinationals are consistently significantly higher than profit margins of all U.S. corporations. To be sure, these higher profit margins undoubtedly also reflect the different natures of domestic and multinational

TABLE 7
Profit Margins of CFCs and All U.S. Corporations Compared

	Controlled Foreign Corporations			Profit margins of all U.S. corporations (%)
	Business receipts	Current earnings and profits before taxes	Profit margin (%)	
1982	$647.9	$36.7	5.66	3.51
1980	699.0	47.6	6.81	4.17
1976	342.8	23.5	6.85	5.50
1974	281.3	20.9	7.44	5.11
1972	172.4	15.4	8.91	4.82

Note: Dollar amounts are billions of current dollars.

Source: U.S. Department of the Treasury (1985) and Simenauer (1986).

businesses, the efforts of U.S. multinationals to transfer at reduced prices their high-profit assets to CFCs and away from U.S. taxing jurisdiction, and other business activities of multinationals. Furthermore, it is not obvious how one is to interpret evidence on profit margins, since firms try to maximize profits rather than their margins. Given the limited financial data available, however, the size of CFC profit margins as measured by U.S. accounting principles suggests that use of these principles may substantially overstate CFC profits (relative to the U.S. definition) and, by extension, reduce U.S. multinational tax credits and discourage CFC reinvestment.

Table 8 presents calculations of adjusted effective tax rates for investments made out of retained earnings by CFCs of U.S. multinationals in selected industrial countries in 1982.[15] Column 4 contains estimates of effective tax rates for reinvested CFC earnings without correcting for the U.S. definition of foreign income. These effective tax rates are basically the same as those faced by foreign firms reinvesting in their own countries. Column 5 presents corrected effective tax rates for U.S. CFCs. With the exception of West Germany, the corrected effective tax rates are higher than the uncorrected rates, significantly so in Canada and the United Kingdom where the governments offer very fast depreciation write-offs on new capital as investment incentives. By contrast, West Germany insists on slow capital cost recovery so the U.S. tax system encourages investment there relative to the incentives faced by West German firms.

These effective tax rate calculations are based on the same assumptions

---

[15] Among these countries, the United Kingdom has significantly changed its taxation of corporate profits since 1982.

TABLE 8
Effective Tax Rates and U.S. Affiliate Investment Abroad, 1982

	Start of year property, plant and equipment, U.S. affiliates	Investment, all industries (manufacturing investment)	Investment/capital: all industries (manufacturing) (%)	Foreign ETR, reinvestment (%)	Adjusted ETR for U.S. CFCs (%)
All countries	$155.7	$44.0 ($16.5)	28.3 (10.6)		
Canada	$31.9	$6.9 ($2.4)	21.6 (7.5)	19.2	36.9
West Germany	$12.8	$3.0 ($2.2)	23.4 (17.2)	68.3	66.8
United Kingdom	$28.8	$7.6 ($4.1)	26.4 (14.2)	21.2	52.5
Japan	$2.5	$0.9 ($0.7)	36.0 (28.0)	44.0	46.5
Brazil	$6.8	$1.9 ($1.4)	27.9 (20.6)	61.7	62.6

Note: Data refer to majority-owned nonbank affiliates of nonbank U.S. parents. Investment is plant and equipment expenditures by affiliates. Dollar amount are billions of current (1982) dollars.

Source: U.S. Department of Commerce, Bureau of Economic Analysis (1985).

embodied in Auerbach's (1983b) estimates of effective tax rates on U.S. domestic investment: firms choose accounting policies to minimize taxes, and investors require 4 percent real after-tax returns. For these estimates, inflation expectations are assumed to be static, firms invest in asset combinations similar to aggregate U.S. corporate investment, and these assets depreciate at the same rates as those assumed by Auerbach for the United States. In addition, the average realized U.S. tax rate on foreign income is assumed to be 10 percent, and the average dividend payout ratio on the CFC's *other* investments is assumed to be 50 percent. Though stylized, these assumptions correspond to observed average behavior of U.S. CFCs.[16] Foreign tax parameters are based on data from Price Waterhouse (various), where when necessary values were chosen which correspond most closely to the foreign tax treatment of new manufacturing investment. Given the special tax provisions affecting other important industries, it probably makes the most sense to interpret these effective tax rates as applying primarily to manufacturing firms. As such, they can be compared to effective tax rates of around 25 percent, which Auerbach (1983b) estimates for domestic U.S. manufacturing investment in 1982. The adjusted effective tax rates on foreign investments are uniformly higher.

It is instructive to associate the investment/capital ratios in column 3 of Table 8 with the corresponding effective tax rates. In a first pass there appears to be little correlation: Japan and Brazil exhibit the highest investment ratios without having the lowest effective tax rates. But Japan's adjusted effective tax rate is the second lowest, and the table may illustrate the importance of adjusting foreign effective tax rates to account for the effects of U.S. taxes. Without doing so, Canada and the United Kingdom show by far the lowest effective tax rates, and their 1982 investment ratios suggest that such investment incentives may be absent. In fact, the wedge between domestic effective tax rates and the effective tax rate on foreign investment may partly account for lagging foreign investment behavior.

Naturally, it is a mistake to infer too much from one year's worth of investment and tax data. This is particularly true when different types of investments face different tax rates, and Table 8 presents data only on the tax rates on CFC profits reinvested in manufacturing (though other tax rates should move more or less in tandem). Unfortunately, one has few options in this case. Table 8 presents data for 1982 because it is the only recent year for which the U.S. Commerce Department has detailed survey

---

[16] Of course, these calculations illustrate that marginal investment incentives are sensitive to a firm's average foreign tax rate, and these tax rates differ widely. The reported numbers are based on overall average foreign tax rates, but these may not be the average foreign tax rates of *marginal investors*.

data on U.S. multinationals. The multinational investment and tax picture is likely to look very different with the U.S. passage of the TRA and the excess FTCs it generates. Furthermore, U.S. domestic tax incentives were largely removed by the Act, and it remains to be seen whether U.S. multinationals are thereby encouraged to move more of their operations and investments abroad.

6. CONCLUSION

Taxes have historically played an important role in influencing multinational investment decisions. Although the consequences of the incentives offered by tax havens are plainly visible, the effect of U.S. taxes on the foreign investments of American multinationals may be no less real. Contrary to the claims of earlier authors, the U.S. tax system appears to have had a significant influence on marginal after-tax returns available to investors in foreign assets.

There are several channels for this influence of the U.S. tax system. The U.S. tax code defines income differently than do foreign governments for their own tax purposes, which has generally worked to discourage U.S. multinational investments in countries with strong investment incentives. The potential tax obligation due the U.S. government on repatriation of foreign earnings has influenced multinational financial policy, encouraging firms to pay dividends from high-tax sources and retain earnings (thereby investing) in low-tax countries. The generally heavy taxation of U.S. individual shareholders on dividends encourages U.S. corporations to retain earnings to a greater degree than they would otherwise, and foreign affiliates of U.S. multinationals should be subject to the same incentive. Finally, though not explored here, U.S. taxes may affect the profitability of overseas investments by U.S. multinationals through influencing the rate of accumulation of complementary capital in the United States.

The TRA appears to change many of these incentives. By reducing the U.S. tax rate, the Act all but relieves most U.S. multinationals of U.S. tax obligations on their foreign income. But time will tell what the long-run effects of tax reform will be on multinational investment. Possibly much of the effect will depend on the reaction of foreign governments to U.S. tax changes, a process that is difficult to predict and still appears to be evolving.

REFERENCES

Auerbach, Alan J. 1979. Wealth maximization and the cost of capital. *Quarterly Journal of Economics* 93 (August 1979): 433–46.
———. 1983a. Shareholder tax rates and firm attributes. *Journal of Public Economics* 21 (July 1983): 107–27.

———. 1983b. Corporate taxation in the United States. *Brookings Papers on Economic Activity* 2: 451–505.
Auerbach, Alan J., and James M. Poterba. 1987. Tax loss carryforwards and corporate tax incentives. In *The effects of taxation on capital accumulation* ed. M. Feldstein. Chicago: University of Chicago Press.
Baldwin, Carliss Y. 1986. The capital factor: Competing for capital in a global environment. In *Competition in global industries* ed. Michael E. Porter, Boston: Harvard Business School Press.
Barlow, Mary. 1986. Foreign tax credit by industry, 1982. Internal Revenue Service, S.O.I. Bulletin 5, 9–29.
Boskin, Michael J., and William G. Gale. 1987. New results on the effect of tax policy on the international location of investment. In *The effects of taxation on capital accumulation* ed. M. Feldstein. Chicago: University of Chicago Press.
Bradford, David F. 1981. The incidence and allocation effects of a tax on corporate distributions. *Journal of Public Economics* 15 (April 1981): 1–22.
Brereton, Barbara F. 1987. U.S. multinational companies: Operations in 1985. *Survey of Current Business* 67:6.
Carson, Chris R. 1986. Corporate foreign tax credit, 1982: A geographic focus. Internal Revenue Service, S.O.I. Bulletin 6, 21–48.
Frisch, Daniel J., and David G. Hartman. 1983. Taxation and the location of U.S. investment abroad. NBER Working Paper no. 1241.
Gersovitz, Mark. 1987. The effects of domestic taxes on foreign private investment. In *The theory of taxation for developing countries*. eds. David M. G. Newbery and Nicholas H. Stern. New York: Oxford University Press.
Gordon, Roger H., and Burton G. Malkiel. 1981. Corporation finance. In *How taxes affect economic behavior*. eds. Henry J. Aaron and Joseph A. Pechman. Washington, D.C.: Brookings.
Grubert, Harry, and John Mutti. 1987. The impact of the Tax Reform Act of 1986 on trade and capital flows. In *Treasury Compendium of Tax Policy Research*. Washington, D.C.: U.S. Department of the Treasury.
Hartman, David G. 1981. Domestic tax policy and foreign investment: Some evidence. NBER Working Paper no. 784.
———. 1985. Tax policy and foreign direct investment. *Journal of Public Economics* 26: 107–21.
Horst, Thomas. 1977. American taxation of multinational firms. *American Economic Review* 67: 376–89.
Jun, Joosung. 1987. Taxation, international investment and financing sources. Harvard University, mimeo.
King, Mervyn A. 1977. Public policy and the corporation. London: Chapman and Hall.
Kopits, George F. 1972. Dividend remittance behavior within the multinational firm: A cross-country analysis. *Review of Economics and Statistics* 54: 339–42.
McDaniel, Paul R., and Hugh J. Ault. 1981. *Introduction to United States international taxation*. Deventer, The Netherlands: Kluwer.
Newlon, Timothy Scott. 1987. Tax policy and the multinational firm's financial policy and investment decisions, unpublished Ph.D. dissertation, Princeton University.
Mutti, John. 1981. Tax incentives and reparation decisions of U.S. multinational corporations. *National Tax Journal* 34: 241–48.

Poterba, James M. 1987. Tax policy and corporate saving. *Brookings Papers on Economic Activity* 2.
Poterba, James M., and Lawrence H. Summers. 1985. The economic effects of dividend taxation. In *Recent advances in corporate finances*. eds. Edward I. Altman and Marti G. Subrahmanyam. Homewood, Ill: Irwin.
Price Waterhouse. *Corporate taxes—a worldwide summary*. New York: Price Waterhouse. Various annual editions and individual country guides.
Shoven, John B. 1987. The tax consequences of share repurchases and other non-dividend cash payments to equity owners. *Tax Policy and the Economy* 1: 29–54.
Simenauer, Ronald. 1986. Controlled foreign corporations, 1982: An industry focus. Internal Revenue Service, S.O.I. Bulletin 6, 63–86.
States, Williams. 1986–1987. Controlled foreign corporations, 1982: A geographic focus. Internal Revenue Service, S.O.I. Bulletin 6, 49–80.
U.S. Department of Commerce, Bureau of Economic Analysis 1985. *U.S. direct investment abroad: 1982 benchmark survey data*. Washington, D.C.: Government Printing Office.
U.S. Department of the Treasury, Internal Revenue Service 1979. *U.S. corporations and their controlled foreign corporations, 1968 and 1972*. Washington, D.C.: Government Printing Office.
———. 1980. *U.S. corporations and their controlled foreign corporations, 1974–1978*. Washington, D.C.: Government Printing Office.
———. 1981, *Foreign tax credit claimed on corporation income tax returns, 1974*. Washington, D.C.: Government Printing Office.
———. 1982, *Foreign income and taxes reported on U.S. income tax returns, 1976–1979*. Washington, D.C.: Government Printing Office.
———. 1985, *Compendium of studies of international income and taxes, 1979–1983*. Washington, D.C.: Government Printing Office.

TAX NEUTRALITY AND INTANGIBLE CAPITAL

Don Fullerton
University of Virginia and NBER

Andrew B. Lyon
University of Maryland and NBER

EXECUTIVE SUMMARY

The Tax Reform Act of 1986 (TRA) attempts to "level the playing field" between equipment and other tangible assets by repealing the investment tax credit that was available only for equipment. This change may not increase economic efficiency, however, if there exist substantial amounts of intangible capital. Advertising along with research and development (R & D) are viewed as investments in goodwill and production expertise. As forms of intangible capital, they receive the significant tax advantage of immediate expensing rather than delayed depreciation deductions. This chapter finds that

1. Effective tax rates are mismeasured when this investment is ignored.
2. The United States in 1983 had about $165 billion of advertising capital and $305 billion of R & D capital, which together make up 11 percent of the total capital stock.
3. The inclusion of this intangible capital with a zero effective tax reduces

This paper is for the NBER conference on "Tax Policy and the Economy" held in Washington, D.C. on November 17, 1987. We would like to thank Harry Grubert, Yolanda Henderson, Jon Skinner, and Lawrence Summers for helpful comments. The research reported here is part of the NBER's research program in taxation. Any opinions expressed are those of the authors and not those of the NBER.

by one-third the gain in efficiency from prior law obtained by repealing the investment tax credit for equipment.
4. With more of this untaxed intangible capital, repeal of the investment tax credit can actually reduce overall efficiency.
5. The TRA always increases this measure of production efficiency because it lowers the taxation of other tangible assets at the same time that it repeals the investment tax credit.

Before the TRA the investment tax credit (ITC) was viewed as favoring equipment-intensive industries such as those in manufacturing. The standard view was that nonmanufacturing industries were disadvantaged by receiving a relatively low portion of tax credits for equipment. Measured effective tax rates were often high for nonmanufacturing industries, and a major focus of tax reform was an attempt to "level the playing field" by repealing the ITC. Not surprisingly, perhaps, "the legislation was opposed by the Chamber of Commerce of the U.S.A., the National Association of Manufacturers, ... and a long roster of representatives of corporate America" (Birnbaum and Murray (1987), p. 161).

However, this standard view ignores intangible capital, another set of assets in which firms invest. Intangible capital is "information" or "knowledge" that increases the profits of a firm. Intangible capital includes the knowledge and trust that consumers have for a firm's products—the reputation and brand image. It also includes the knowledge that a firm has of its customers' needs and the know-how essential for providing products to meet these needs. This know-how may be based on the firm's research knowledge, production skills, management expertise, and the goodwill of its employees. Firms invest in intangible capital in many ways, including advertising, research and development (R & D), employee training, and customer relations. But unlike investments in tangible assets, the cost of intangible investments is deducted immediately rather than capitalized and amortized over a depreciation lifetime. We show that intangible investments, rather than equipment, were the most tax-favored assets under prior law. They remain so after tax reform as well. For firms with a relatively intensive use of intangible capital, expenses may be overstated for tax and book purposes. Thus profits may be understated, and effective tax rates are likely to be overstated for such firms.

These firms with an intensive use of intangible capital had much to gain from the corporate tax rate reduction provided in the TRA. Their intangible investments were already written off at the earlier high statutory rate and would generate subsequent income to be taxed at the new low rate. In fact, tax reform was favored by "such powerhouse companies as General Motors, IBM, and Procter and Gamble" (Birnbaum and Murray (1987),

p. 161). Later, we measure intangible capital and find that its ratio to total capital is highest in transportation equipment and ordnance, second in motor vehicles (including General Motors), third in finance and insurance, fourth in chemicals and rubber (including Procter and Gamble), and fifth in machinery (including IBM).

Mismeasurement extends beyond the "average effective tax rate," or ratio of taxes paid to capital income. It also affects the "marginal effective tax rate," which expresses the future tax on a marginal investment as a fraction of the expected future income. Many studies have calculated these rates for tangible assets such as equipment, structures, land, and inventories, but they often omit intangible capital. If the statutory rate is constant, the marginal effective tax rate is zero on intangible capital because an immediate deduction for the outlay is equivalent in present value to exempting from tax all future income generated by the asset.

These marginal effective tax rates are often used to measure the economic cost of tax distortions and misallocations. We calculate the "welfare cost," or the dollar cost of production inefficiency, attributable to tax differences among corporate assets. With only tangible assets such as equipment, structures, inventories, and land in the corporate sector, tax differences under the old law create welfare costs of about $10 billion per year, or 13 percent of federal and state corporate tax revenue. These results accord with existing estimates, where the major distortion is the low tax on equipment due to investment credits. This welfare cost is virtually eliminated by a reform that includes repeal of the ITC.

The existence of intangible capital markedly alters welfare cost calculations because the effective rate of tax on these assets is even less than that on equipment under prior law. We provide alternative measures of the intangible capital stock. With large tax differences between intangible assets and other assets, using our basic measure of intangible capital, we find that the welfare cost measure increases from $10 billion to $13 billion per year. As pointed out by Summers (1987), repeal of the investment credit taxes equipment more like other tangible assets but *less* like intangible assets. The welfare cost still falls, to about $7 billion per year, but it is no longer "virtually eliminated." Our basic estimate of intangible capital is constructed by considering only advertising and R & D expenditures. With additional sources of intangible capital, credit repeal could actually increase welfare costs.

Finally, we note that the TRA also reduced the statutory corporate rate that applies to tangible assets. That is, it does not just raise the tax on equipment (away from intangibles), it also reduces the tax on other tangibles (toward intangibles). With our basic measure of intangible capital, the efficiency cost falls from $13 billion per year under the old law to $4 billion per year under the new law. No amount of increase in the stock of intangible capital in this model reverses the finding that the TRA reduces interasset distortions.

This finding does not mean that the new law is perfectly efficient. There remain tax advantages to investment in advertising, R & D, and other intangible capital. The subsidy to R & D might be justified by the existence of "external spillover benefits": the firm may not receive all of the returns to its discoveries and therefore may not have sufficient incentive to undertake research. Calculations below show the efficiency-improving nature of the subsidy in the presence of such an externality. It is more difficult to justify the advantage to advertising, however. Calculations with a reduction of this benefit show the greatest efficiency gain of all.

The rest of this chapter proceeds as follows. The first section shows how average and marginal effective tax rates are affected by the existence of intangible capital. The second section discusses the nature of intangible capital and the procedures we use to measure it. Tables show the relative use of each type of tangible and intangible capital in each industry. The third section further discusses the tax treatment of tangible and intangible capital; specifics of our tax and efficiency cost calculations are relegated to an appendix. The fourth section reports results of our efficiency cost calculations. The final section summarizes our findings and conclusions.

1. EFFECTIVE TAX RATES AND INTANGIBLE CAPITAL

Much of the discussion about tax differences revolves around measures of effective tax rates that take the ratio of taxes paid to capital income in each industry. This "average" effective tax rate has been used by many to identify high-taxed and low-taxed sectors of the economy. For other applications, such as measuring the effect of taxes on investment incentives, this measure suffers from a number of problems. First, as an aggregate measure, it cannot distinguish the taxation of income earned from the various types of assets in which firms invest. Second, it looks backward at the taxes paid in a given year, rather than forward at the taxes that would be paid on the future income generated by a new investment under consideration in that year. Fullerton (1984) describes many reasons that may cause the two concepts to differ.

For these reasons, many choose to characterize tax differences by the cost of capital or "marginal" effective tax rate. This rate can be calculated for each asset, and it compares the present value of taxes expected to be paid over the life of a given investment with the gross income expected to be generated. It is a "marginal" effective tax rate because it is calculated for an investment that is expected to yield a return just equal to the cost of funds.

Here, however we would like to emphasize that past measures of *both* average and marginal effective tax rates often do not account for intangible capital and thus mischaracterize tax differences across industries. An industry that makes extensive use of intangible capital may pay a tax that is relatively low, even though past reported measures of average or marginal effective tax rates have been characterized as relatively high.

The key feature of intangible capital is that firms can expense it.[1] In accordance with generally accepted accounting practices, advertising and R & D expenses are deducted immediately, for both book and tax purposes. If the firm is growing, the deduction for current investments in advertising and R & D is larger than a deduction for economic depreciation of existing intangible assets. Thus expenses are overstated, profits are understated,[2] and the ratio of taxes to profits is overstated. This is the mismeasurement mentioned above: average effective tax rates may not have been so high in industries receiving the tax advantages of expensing intangible investments.

Because an immediate deduction for the initial expenditure on intangible capital is equivalent to exempting the entire income stream from the investment, the marginal effective tax rate of intangible capital is zero. If industries differ in their relative use of intangible capital, comparisons of marginal effective tax rates that excluded the taxation of intangible capital may be misleading.

An example using actual tax data may help demonstrate the tax advantage of expensing intangible capital and the mismeasurement of tax rates. In 1983, corporations in the chemical and rubber industry had taxable income after deductions of $15.9 million.[3] The tax liability of this industry after the use of tax credits was $3.15 million. The ratio of taxes paid to taxable income is 19.8 percent.

Using data described later in this paper, we calculate that firms in this industry spent $15.5 million in advertising and R & D in 1983. Taxable income before the expensing of these intangible investments is therefore $31.4 million ($15.9 million plus $15.5 million). To measure economic income, however, firms should be allowed a deduction for the depreciation of the existing stock of intangible capital. We calculate that total economic depreciation of advertising and R & D capital in this industry is $13.4

---

[1] For an elaboration of the tax treatment of intangible capital, see Mundstock (1987).

[2] Although the amount of profit is understated, profit *rates* are likely to be overstated if capital in the denominator excludes intangible capital.

[3] All tax and income data are from the Internal Revenue Service, *Statistics of income—1983, corporate income tax returns*. The construction of our data on intangible capital expenditures is described in section 2.

million. Subtracting this amount from the $31.4 million yields taxable income equal to $18.0 million. Actual taxes paid as a fraction of this income is 17.5 percent, about 10 percent less than without this correction. Thus previously reported effective tax rates were overstated.

Finally, if firms in this industry were required to deduct only economic depreciation of advertising and R & D capital, tax payments at a 46 percent statutory tax rate would have been nearly $1.0 million higher, or 22.9 percent of the restated taxable income. As shown in this example, some industries may receive a significant tax advantage from the expensing of these intangible investments.

2. THE MEASUREMENT OF INTANGIBLE CAPITAL

Conceptually, the firm's stock of intangible capital includes its patents, trademarks, copyrights, customer lists, reputation, and any firm-specific knowledge about technology, marketing, or production. These assets may be specific to the firm and difficult to sell in the market, but they are assets nonetheless. They wear out or become obsolete just like other assets, requiring reinvestment to maintain their stock. Although the return to any particular investment may be uncertain, in the aggregate these investments must be expected to generate a viable rate of return since they utilize funds that could have been profitably invested elsewhere.

For many assets, value can be measured using data from market transactions, but intangible assets are rarely bought and sold. For tangible assets in the national accounts, the Commerce Department and others measure capital by the "perpetual inventory" method. Starting with a time series on investment in equipment, for example, and using assumptions about economic depreciation, this procedure simply starts with the earliest available year, adds investment, subtracts depreciation, accounts for inflation, and repeats for successive years up through the most recently available year.

The same procedure can be followed for intangible capital, once the proper investment series and rate of depreciation are established. Time series data are available for advertising and R & D, but not all of these expenditures generate future income. Much advertising information is used by customers immediately, and much research may never pay off. In fact, for a given firm, expenditures on R & D may bear little relation to intangible capital: small R & D in one firm may lead to dramatic scientific discoveries, whereas much R & D in another firm may not. Firms likely invest in R & D until the expense is matched by the *expected* future value of the intangible asset, however, so the aggregation of many firms in the economy or even with one industry may provide a good correspondence between R & D expenditures and subsequent intangible capital.

Some previous research has been directed toward measuring intangible capital. Much of this literature relates to prior claims that industries with high rates of return must have entry barriers and monopoly profits. When measures of intangible capital were added to the denominator of each industry's rate of return, there was much less variation. Clarkson (1977), for example, uses time series on advertising and R & D expenses from a sample of sixty-nine firms representing eleven manufacturing industries. For depreciation, he cites various studies that "indicate that the economic life of advertising capital ranges from less than one year in one industry to more than ten years in some..." (p. 41), whereas "estimates of the average life cycle of a pharmaceutical product, including research and development time, range from twenty to thirty years" (p. 43). He chooses to assume three-year straight-line depreciation for advertising; basic research expenditures are assumed to last for periods of eighteen to twenty-one years, and development expenditures last for thirteen to sixteen years. Sensitivity analyses on alternative assumptions do not substantially affect his major conclusion, namely, that proper measurement reduces the variation of rates of return among industries. Grabowski and Mueller (1978) use a questionnaire study concerning mean R & D project durations and R & D output life-spans. They assign each of the eighty-six firms in their sample to one of nine manufacturing industries and find that "a depreciation rate of 10 percent would be a plausible starting point for all of our industries except pharmaceuticals" (p. 334). They cite other studies showing faster depreciation of advertising, so they use a 30 percent rate of depreciation for that type of capital.

Our own procedure is as follows. First, we want comprehensive measures of advertising and R & D, not just for some firms or just for manufacturing industries. We take advertising data from annual issues of the *Statistics of income corporate income tax returns*, published by the Internal Revenue Service of the Treasury Department. This source provides corporate advertising deductions taken by disaggregated manufacturing and nonmanufacturing industries. From this source, we construct a time series on corporate advertising investment in each industry for the period 1977–1983.[4]

Second, for R & D expenditures, we use annual issues of *Research and*

---

[4] Because of high rates of depreciation assumed for advertising, it is not necessary to collect more years of data. We include constructed estimates for investment in advertising before 1977, as discussed below, but these depreciated investments make up a very small fraction of the 1983 stocks.

development in industry, published by the National Sciences Foundation. We separate the R & D expenditures in each industry into corporate and noncorporate components, which we assume to be allocated in proportion to the tangible capital stock in each sector for each industry. Although the data are provided with sufficient breakdown among manufacturing industries, we are forced to allocate a single relatively small figure of the nonmanufacturing sector among several nonmanufacturing industries using IRS data on the distribution of R & D credits. At this point, we construct a time series on corporate R & D in each industry for the period 1963–1983.

Third, to account for each type of intangible capital at the beginning of the time series, we (a) measure the rate of growth of investment in the asset in each industry during the time period, (b) assume that prior investment grew at the same rate, and (c) construct an infinite series for prior investment.

Finally, we construct a measure of the stock of each intangible asset as of the end of 1983 in a manner similar to the perpetual inventory method used by the Commerce Department for tangible capital. Thus the stock for year-end 1983 includes investment in 1983 with a half year's depreciation and inflation, 1982 investment with one and a half years of depreciation and inflation and similarly for earlier years. We undertake considerable sensitivity analysis on annual rates of depreciation. For advertising, we use rates of one-sixth, one-third, and one-half. For R & D, the rates are 0.10, 0.15, and 0.20. Our central estimates are one-third for advertising and 0.15 for R & D.

Measured stocks of intangible capital are shown in Table 1, where the central depreciation choices imply $165 billion of advertising capital, $305 billion of R & D capital, and $470 billion of total intangible capital. This total could be as low as $330 billion with the high depreciation assumptions or as high as $775 billion with the low depreciation assumptions. Under any assumptions, the largest amount of advertising capital is in wholesale and retail trade, followed by food and tobacco, metals and machinery, chemicals and rubber, and finance and insurance. The most R & D is in our large metals and machinery industry, followed by transportation equipment (including ordnance), chemicals and rubber (including drugs), and motor vehicles.

More important to each industry, however, is the relative use of different capital types. Thus we need measures of tangible capital types used in each industry, and we need to combine several data sources. The Commerce Department's *Survey of current business* provides equipment and structures by industry, but not land and inventories. The Federal Reserve Board's *Balance sheets of the U.S. economy* provides inventories and land, but only in total. Unpublished data of Jorgenson and Sullivan (1981) provide each asset

TABLE 1
Stocks of Intangible Capital from Advertising and R & D in Millions of 1983 Dollars

Industry	Advertising capital, for depreciation rates of			R & D capital, for depreciation rates of			Central case totals
	(1) 0.167	(2) 0.333	(3) 0.500	(4) 0.10	(5) 0.15	(6) 0.20	(7) = (2)+(5)
(1) Agriculture, forestry and fisheries	1,101	496	286	45	32	24	527
(2) Mining	236	101	57	67	48	37	149
(3) Crude petroleum and natural gas	461	268	164	227	162	124	430
(4) Construction	4,088	2,032	1,211	52	37	28	2,069
(5) Food and tobacco	52,306	26,944	16,483	6,374	4,540	3,485	31,484
(6) Textile, apparel and leather	5,638	2,698	1,609	1,213	893	690	3,591
(7) Paper and printing	7,815	4,290	2,664	6,529	4,751	3,674	9,041
(8) Petroleum refining	7,873	3,361	1,872	4,146	2,986	2,320	6,348
(9) Chemicals and rubber	34,560	17,077	10,245	55,859	39,299	30,054	56,376
(10) Lumber, furniture, stone, clay, & glass	4,455	2,098	1,232	4,971	3,524	2,683	5,621
(11) Metals and machinery, including electronics	38,097	18,522	10,985	191,541	135,407	103,725	153,929
(12) Transportation equipment	1,880	841	483	121,158	76,803	56,006	77,644
(13) Motor vehicles	7,731	3,866	2,311	45,745	31,560	23,658	35,426
(14) Transportation, communication, & utilities	11,893	6,457	4,055	2,393	1,709	1,308	8,166
(15) Trade	103,642	51,547	30,792	446	318	244	51,865
(16) Finance and insurance	27,112	13,417	7,964	524	374	286	13,791
(17) Services	21,135	11,431	7,089	3,555	2,538	1,943	13,969
Total	330,023	165,447	99,500	444,843	304,979	230,289	470,426

by industry, but only for 1977. We therefore adjusted the 1977 matrix until it matched appropriate totals for 1983. These data are very similar to the tangible capital data used in earlier efficiency cost calculations by Gravelle (1982), Auerbach (1983), and Fullerton and Henderson (1986).

In Table 2 we show the ratio of each type of capital to total capital in each industry. The most advertising-intensive industry is finance and insurance, followed by food and tobacco. The trade industry falls in this relative ranking because it uses large amounts of other assets, particularly inventories; finance and insurance rises in this ranking because it uses small amounts of other tangible assets. The most R & D-intensive industry by far is transportation equipment, followed by motor vehicles. Metals and machinery had the highest absolute amount of R & D capital, but is third in this ranking of relative intensity. It is followed by chemicals and rubber.

This measure of intangible capital constitutes about 11 percent of the total capital stock. With extreme assumptions about depreciation rates, this figure could almost double. The problem of setting depreciation rates is modest, however, compared to the problem that advertising (as reported to the IRS) and R & D expenditures may only account for a small part of total investment in intangible capital. First, much of what one considers advertising may be deductible as another allowable business expense. For example, a company that hires a consultant to mount an advertising campaign could properly deduct this expense as a consultant fee rather than as advertising. The costs of consumer relations divisions and sales personnel are deductible largely as wages. Second, firms may take less direct methods to create intangible capital. Although advertising is one way to create a reputation, a new firm may sell at lower margins or take greater care in production or customer service as an alternative way to create intangible capital.[5] Here, forgone profits is the mechanism by which the firm invests in future reputation. Firms also invest in the future productivity of their labor force through recruiting and training. Our basic measure of intangible capital is probably an understatement of the total intangible capital stock.

There are no appropriate time series data for the amounts of all such investment, so the perpetual inventory method can never be comprehensive. In related research, we are investigating alternative methods of measuring intangible capital. One method would reverse the logic of above-mentioned attempts to measure variations in the return to properly measured capital: assume instead an equilibrium where all types of capital

---

[5] If consumers have full information about the quality of the product, then extra production costs may not create intangible capital. It may take time, however, for consumers to recognize quality and recommend the product.

TABLE 2
Intangible and Tangible Assets as Percentages of Capital Stock in Each Industry

Industry	Advertising	R & D	Total intangible	Equipment	Structures	Inventories	Land
(1) Agriculture, forestry and fisheries	1	0	1	23	5	4	67
(2) Mining	0	0	0	51	41	5	2
(3) Crude petroleum and natural gas	0	0	0	3	51	1	45
(4) Construction	2	0	2	37	3	31	28
(5) Food and tobacco	18	3	20	28	21	20	11
(6) Textile, apparel and leather	5	2	7	37	20	23	12
(7) Paper and printing	4	4	8	46	22	11	13
(8) Petroleum refining	4	3	7	23	40	12	18
(9) Chemicals and rubber	8	17	25	42	14	12	7
(10) Lumber, furniture, stone, clay, & glass	3	5	8	39	24	17	12
(11) Metals and machinery, including electronics	3	20	23	30	17	23	8
(12) Transportation equipment	1	56	57	10	11	16	5
(13) Motor vehicles	4	30	33	35	12	14	5
(14) Transportation, communication, & utilities	1	0	1	43	50	2	4
(15) Trade	6	0	6	19	13	43	19
(16) Finance and insurance	28	1	28	1	15	0	55
(17) Services	7	1	8	54	30	2	6
Total	4	7	11	31	28	17	14

must earn the same net rate of return. For each industry, we can then divide total net income by the assumed net rate of return to derive the total capital stock, and subtract estimates of tangible capital to get the implied intangible capital stock. Problems include measuring capital income, choosing a rate of return, and accounting for risk differentials.

A second possible method would take the total valuation of capital in the stock market and subtract tangible capital. Problems here include transitory influences and correction for taxes. In fact, the market value of the capital stock divided by its replacement cost is q, a ratio that is expected to depend on taxes and to influence investment. It is typically measured by market value over tangible capital stock. As measured, however, this ratio might exceed 1 if shareholders value intangible capital. Lindenberg and Ross (1981) found that average q was 1.5 over the period 1960–1977 for a large sample of firms. If the entire difference between the firms' market value and the replacement value of their tangible capital stock is attributable to intangible capital, then intangible capital could be as large as one-third of the total capital stock. Further, time series estimates of the effects of taxation on investment using q, such as those in Summers (1981), could be misleading if intangible investments are not just a constant fraction of tangible investments used in the estimation. Even more likely is that intangible capital is not a constant fraction of tangible capital across industries. Thus estimated q would be expected to differ among industries for more than tax reasons.

This other work is not complete, but a simple calculation reveals the possible importance of intangible capital. Feldstein, Dicks-Mireaux, and Poterba (1983) indicate that net capital income divided by tangible capital varies between about 3 and 4 percent. If the properly measured net rate of return were only 2 percent, for example, then the stock of intangibles would be one-third to one-half of the total capital stock. This is four to eight times the estimate of intangible capital from the perpetual inventory method.

We can represent the possibility of greater intangible capital by multiplying the basic estimates of advertising and R & D capital by integers from 1 to 8, or more. We show how efficiency cost estimates depend on the quantity of intangible capital.

3. TAX DISTORTIONS AND EFFICIENCY COSTS

To measure the efficiency cost of tax distortions, we use the cost of capital or marginal effective tax rate in this paper. First, we assume certain conditions about the future environment for marginal investments currently under consideration. In particular, we assume that all investments will earn a risk-free nominal after-tax return of 8.5 percent, that inflation will run at 4 percent, and that firms face a set of tax rules including federal and state statutory corporate tax rates, investment tax credit rates, depreciation allowances, and local property tax rates that may vary by asset. (See King and Fullerton (1984) for derivation of these parameters under prior law.) Second, we assume that firms will undertake all investments for which the present value of all net returns exceeds the outlay for the asset. They stop investing when the present value of net returns just equals the outlay. Third, this equality can be used to solve for the real pretax return on the marginal investment that just allows the firm to earn the assumed 8.5 percent net return (4.5 percent after inflation). The equation is shown in the Appendix. This required pretax return is the "cost of capital" net of depreciation, because it includes tax costs and financing costs (the required net return). Finally, the marginal effective tax rate is the difference between this real pretax return and the 4.5 percent real posttax return, as a fraction of the real pretax return.

Only the cost of capital is used in subsequent calculations, and it does not depend upon actual choices for financing the marginal investment. With arbitrage by the firm among various real and financial assets in this risk-free world, all assets would have to earn the same net return. For example, arbitrage between debt and real capital assures that any asset must earn the after-tax interest rate. All investments thus have the same assumed 4.5 percent real cost of funds, regardless of actual financing.[6] The effective tax rate, calculated only to help interpretations, is the fraction of the cost of capital that would be attributable to business taxes if the investment were financed by equity.

An advantage of this approach is that we do not have to deal with personal tax changes. Although increases in personal exemptions and reductions in personal rates were crucial components of tax reform, they do not relate in this model to the firm's choice among capital assets. Similarly, we abstract from other detailed aspects of tax law that are not directly related to this allocative decision, including passive loss rules, minimum tax, accounting provisions,[7] at-risk rules, bad-debt reserves, foreign tax

---

[6] In a different model, it is possible that financing proportions could affect the cost of capital. Bosworth (1985) and others have pointed out that structures might use relatively more debt finance and take greater advantage of interest deductions. Also, churning might have provided greater tax advantages to real estate, as discussed in Gordon, Hines, and Summers (1987). Other problems are discussed in Summers (1987).

[7] Fullerton, Gillette, and Mackie (1987) consider accounting rule changes and argue that (a) much of the revenue is from existing investment and does not apply to new investment, (b) some of the changes are best modeled as reduced output subsidies rather than reduced

provisions, and loss carryforwards.[8] To simplify further, we do not model the intricate R & D credit.[9] The model captures the important conceptual distinction that advertising and R & D are capital assets substantially favored under both old and new laws. These investments are still expensed, while other assets lose their ITCs or accelerated depreciation allowances.

The effective tax rate includes all business level taxes on the corporation. It would just equal the statutory rate (34 percent under present law) if there were no state taxes or property taxes and if cost recovery were based on economic depreciation at replacement cost. State and local taxes raise the effective rate, whereas the ITC (a maximum 10 percent under prior law) and accelerated depreciation allowances lower it. With no local property tax on intangible capital, the effective rate is zero because an immediate deduction for the initial outlay is equivalent in present value to exempting the entire income stream. For other assets, we summarize complicated depreciation allowances in a single parameter for the exponential rate of tax depreciation. We report for all equipment and for all structures the annual rate of depreciation on historical cost that would provide the same present value of allowances as the actual law.[10]

These tax parameters for present law, as provided by the TRA, are shown in Table 3 for our six assets. The exponential rate of economic depreciation for equipment is 0.13, derived by averaging over estimates in Hulten and Wykoff (1981) for twenty kinds of equipment. Comparison with the 0.38 exponential rate for tax depreciation indicates the degree of acceleration for equipment, but inflation erodes the real value of these allowances since they are based on historical cost. For structures, the average exponential rate of economic depreciation is 0.03, and the rate for

---

investment incentives, and (c) remaining changes have a small effect on marginal effective tax rates.

[8] Any of these aspects may have some effect on our results. For example, Hulten and Robertson (1984) point out that start-up firms may invest relatively heavily in advertising or R & D but may be least able to expense these investments. Early losses mean that deductions must be carried forward and might be lost altogether.

[9] Incentive effects of the incremental R & D credit can be small, or even negative, depending on the circumstances of the firm. See Eisner, Albert, and Sullivan (1984). Details of the effects of tax reform on R & D are provided in Cordes, Watson, and Hauger (1987).

[10] Fullerton and Henderson (1986) provide present-value calculations for depreciation under the old law where many diverse types of equipment receive 150 percent of declining balance, and structures receive 175 percent of declining balance, both switching to straight line. They set a lifetime for each asset, incorporate the half-year convention, and adjust the basis for half the ITC. Similar calculations apply to the new law with double declining balance for equipment of different lives, and straight line for nonresidential structures with a 31.5-year life.

TABLE 3
Tax Parameters and the Cost of Capital under 1986 Law for Each Asset

Asset	(1) Exponential economic depreciation rate	(2) Exponential rate for tax depreciation	(3) Property tax rate	(4) Cost of capital	(5) Real net return	(6) Effective tax rate [(4) − (5)]/(4)
Equipment	0.130	0.380	0.008	0.073	0.045	0.380
Structures	0.030	0.076	0.011	0.081	0.045	0.443
Inventories	0.000	0.000	0.008	0.081	0.045	0.442
Land	0.000	0.000	0.011	0.084	0.045	0.466
Advertising	0.333	∞	0.000	0.045	0.045	0.000
R & D capital	0.150	∞	0.000	0.045	0.045	0.000

Note: The cost of capital is defined here to be gross of tax but net of depreciation. It is based on equation (1) of the Appendix, using a corporate rate of 0.383 including state corporate taxes, a discount rate of 0.085, an inflation rate of 0.04, and therefore a real net return of 0.045 as shown in the table.

tax depreciation on historical cost is 0.076. Inventories and land effectively receive economic depreciation allowances, since they do not depreciate and do not get deductions. Effective tax rates for these two assets would match the 0.383 combined federal and state statutory rate, except that local property taxes push them up to 44 and 47 percent, respectively. The effective rate for structures is 44 percent. The effective tax rate for equipment is 38 percent, which indicates that tax depreciation is a little more generous than economic depreciation at an inflation rate of 4 percent.

These differences are all reflected in the cost of capital in column 4 of Table 3. The cost of capital under TRA for equipment is 7.3 percent, and the cost of capital for other tangible assets is between 8.1 percent and 8.4 percent. Intangible assets have a significantly lower cost of capital of 4.5 percent.

Because the pretax return on tangible assets is higher than that on intangible assets and into tangible assets, total output could be increased by shifting capital out of intangible capital and into tangible assets. For example, replacement of $1 of intangible capital by $1 of structures would increase output by 3.6 cents, the difference in their pretax returns (8.1 minus 4.5). To analyze more than marginal changes in the allocation of capital we need to know the marginal product schedule of each type of capital. We assume that asset demands are Cobb-Douglas: a 1 percent increase in the cost of capital will reduce asset demand by 1 percent.[11] Since

---
[11] The loss in production efficiency depends on the responsiveness of investment demand to

we assume that firms demand capital as long as the marginal product exceeds its cost, this assumption effectively provides all marginal product schedules as well. We use these marginal product schedules to show how much more output would be produced by shifting capital toward the locations with a high cost of capital (and high marginal product) and away from locations with a low cost of capital (and low marginal product). That is, we calculate the additional real value of output that could be produced with a given total stock of capital, if it were simply reallocated to more productive locations and used more efficiently.

These calculations are similar to those of Gravelle (1982) and Auerbach (1983) for different types of equipment and structures under the old law. They represent interasset distortions only and do not include additional misallocations between the corporate sector and noncorporate sector or distortions of saving decisions, risk-bearing, financial choices, housing, and labor markets.[12] Fullerton, Lyon, and Rosen (1984) perform similar calculations, including equipment, structures, inventories, and land. Fullerton and Henderson (1986) include intersectoral distortions and housing, but none of these studies considers intangible assets. In the previous section we calculated large amounts of intangible capital, and in the next section we calculate revised costs of interasset distortions.

4. WELFARE RESULTS UNDER ALTERNATIVE TAX REGIMES

The cost of capital for different assets under the TRA are first compared with prior law and a modification of prior law that merely repeals the ITC (Repeal ITC). Under prior law, firms faced a combined federal and state statutory corporate tax rate of 0.495 and were eligible for an ITC of 10 percent on most equipment and certain structures (as classified in the National Income and Product Accounts). Tax depreciation for equipment is represented by an exponential rate of 0.34, a figure that is less generous than the 0.38 rate under TRA because the basis is reduced by half the ITC. The present value of depreciation allowance for equipment at an 8.5 percent nominal after-tax discount rate under prior law is 2 percent less than under TRA, indicating that in the absence of the half-basis adjustment

---

the change in the pretax return of each type of asset. The greater the responsiveness of demand to changes in this rate of return, the greater is the efficiency cost of tax distortions. Fullerton and Henderson (1986) provide some evidence on the sensitivity of the efficiency cost to this parameter.

[12] These calculations also assume that all corporate assets are separable in production. Feldstein (1985) and others have pointed out that particular substitutability relationships among assets could make nonuniform taxation more efficient.

TABLE 4
The Cost of Capital under Alternative Tax Regimes (percent)

Asset	(1) Prior law	(2) Repeal ITC	(3) TRA
Equipment	5.23	8.70	7.25
Structures	8.47	8.47	8.08
Inventories	9.68	9.68	8.06
Land	10.04	10.04	8.42
Average for all tangible assets	7.52	9.09	7.92
Advertising	4.50	4.50	4.50
R & D capital	4.50	4.50	4.50
Average for all capital	7.19	8.49	7.53

of prior law (a 5 percent reduction in the value of depreciation allowances), depreciation allowance would have been more accelerated under prior law than under TRA. Tax depreciation of structures is represented by an exponential rate of 0.135, providing depreciation allowances that are 30 percent greater in present value than under TRA. Other tax parameters are the same as in Table 3. Repeal of the credit is modeled identically to prior law, except the ITC rate is zero for all assets.

The cost of capital for each type of capital under each of the three tax regimes is shown in Table 4.[13] Because of the ITC, the cost of capital is lower under prior law than under TRA for equipment, while because of the higher statutory tax rate, the cost of capital is higher under prior law for structures, inventories, and land. Because of expensing, however, the cost of capital always equals the real net return for intangible assets. Repeal of the ITC raises the cost of capital for equipment by two-thirds but leaves other assets unaffected.

Average measures of the cost of capital also are shown in Table 4 for all tangible capital and for all capital, including advertising and R & D intangible capital. Under TRA and Repeal ITC, all tangible assets have similar costs of capital, indicating that there is likely to be little loss in productive efficiency due to misallocation of capital across the different types of tangible capital. Major differences in the cost of capital between tangible and intangible capital in all three tax regimes, however, may be a significant source of production inefficiency.

[13] Not shown separately in the table, but included in the overall averages, is the cost of capital under prior law for structures eligible for the ITC. This cost of capital is estimated to be 6.98 percent.

TABLE 5
The Efficiency Cost of Interasset Distortions under Alternative Tax Regimes

	No intangible capital		With advertising and R & D intangible capital	
	Billions of 1983 dollars	Percent of GNP	Billions of 1983 dollars	Percent of GNP
Prior law	9.8	0.29	12.8	0.38
Repeal ITC	0.7	0.02	6.7	0.20
Tax Reform Act	0.4	0.01	4.1	0.12

4.1 The Inclusion of Intangible Capital

Previous studies have calculated the cost of the loss in production efficiency of differential taxation among tangible assets. Because we wish to show how this welfare loss changes with the introduction of intangible capital, we first calculate the welfare loss for the three tax regimes assuming no intangible capital.

Our findings under the assumption of no intangible capital are similar to those of previous research. Under prior law, the annual welfare loss from differential taxation is $9.8 billion per year. This cost is 13 percent of corporate tax revenue in 1983, or 0.3 percent of GNP. With repeal of the ITC, distortions among tangible assets are greatly reduced, and the welfare loss falls to $0.7 billion. The TRA, by reducing the statutory corporate tax rate, provides some further reduction in interasset distortions, and the welfare loss falls to $0.4 billion. In the absence of intangible capital, TRA or repeal of the credit appears quite successful in creating a level playing field.

Next, we repeat these calculations for the three tax regimes using our central estimate of the intangible capital stock attributable to advertising and R & D. Under all three tax regimes, the addition of these untaxed assets increases the interasset distortions and the welfare loss measures. (The addition of any capital with a cost of capital different from the average will increase our measure of the welfare loss.) The cost of interasset distortions under prior law increases to $12.8 billion; under repeal of the ITC it increases to $6.7 billion; and under TRA it increases to $4.1 billion. These welfare losses are compared in Table 5 with the previous estimates under the assumption of no intangible capital.

An important result is that the consideration of intangible capital does not increase the welfare loss by the same amount in each tax regime. Comparing the welfare losses across tax regimes, we find that the absolute welfare gain from repeal of the credit is reduced by one-third when we include intangible capital, from $9.1 billion ($9.8 billion minus $0.7 billion with no intangible capital) to $6.1 billion ($12.8 billion minus $6.7 billion with intangible capital). The ITC can be viewed as less distorting in the presence of intangible capital, because the average cost of capital for all assets is lower.

Under the TRA the inclusion of advertising and R & D intangible capital reduces the absolute welfare improvement over prior law only slightly, from $9.5 billion ($9.8 billion minus $0.4 billion) to $8.7 billion ($12.8 billion minus $4.1 billion). As under repeal of the ITC, intangible capital adds more of a distortion under TRA than under prior law, but the reduction in the statutory corporate tax rate mitigates this effect. The statutory rate reduction lowers the cost of capital for all positively taxed assets, but the cost of capital remains unchanged for intangible capital with a zero effective tax rate. Therefore, TRA still provides significant efficiency gains relative to prior law.

As mentioned in section 2, changes in assumed rates of depreciation for advertising and R & D could nearly double or reduce by one-half our measure of the stock of these assets. More importantly, this study omits many other forms of intangible capital. Because the actual level of intangible capital may be much greater than we have measured here, we also calculate the welfare loss under the three tax regimes for variations in the level of intangible capital between zero and twelve times our measured intangible capital stock. Our results show that inclusion of greater amounts of intangible capital increases the welfare loss from distortionary taxation under each tax regime. Under prior law, if the actual intangible capital stock is four times larger than our measured intangible capital stock, the welfare loss is nearly double the measure in studies that omit intangible capital ($19.2 billion). Figure 1 shows how increases in the level of intangible capital increase the welfare loss measure under each tax regime.

Further, we find that if the actual level of intangible capital is between four and five times our measured level, repeal of the ITC results in a *loss* of welfare. For these magnitudes of intangible capital, the average cost of capital is low enough that repeal raises the cost of equipment away from the average instead of toward the average.

Repeal of the credit in combination with the corporate rate reduction of TRA, however, results in efficiency gains relative to prior law for all levels of intangible capital modeled. The absolute improvement in production efficiency declines from $8.7 billion at our measured level of advertising and R & D intangible capital to $5.6 billion when intangible capital is assumed to be twelve times our measured level.

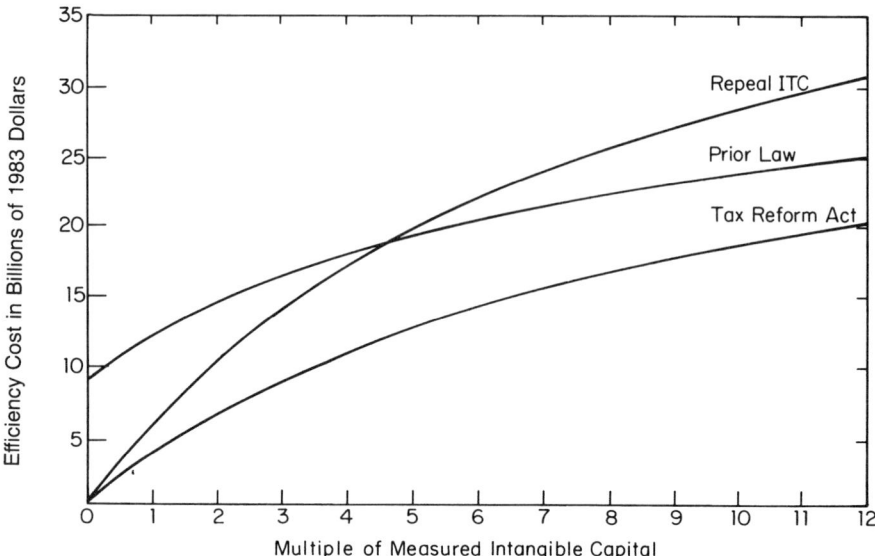

FIGURE 1. *The Efficiency Cost of Interasset Distortions under Alternative Tax Regimes for Varying Levels of Intangible Capital*

4.2 Further Sensitivity Analysis

The favorable tax treatment for R & D is often justified as a proper correction for positive externalities generated by R & D. In this view, firms are unable to appropriate all of the returns from the research they undertake. Competitors or the world at large may benefit from the R & D performed by a firm. Part or all of this effect might be offset by the fact that we ignore the incremental R & D credit. Under TRA, firms can receive a 20 percent credit for qualifying R & D expenditures exceeding a base period amount. Because R & D expenditures increase the base for calculating future credits, however, the marginal incentive of this credit is very difficult to model. We abstract from it here, but this omission is equivalent to the assumption that the marginal incentive of the R & D credit exactly offsets any positive externalities from R & D.

Suppose, however, that these spillover benefits are even greater than the marginal incentive of the R & D credit. To be specific, assume the marginal return to society from R & D is 50 percent greater than the private after-tax return of 4.50 percent (i.e., 6.75 percent). For all other assets we continue to assume no externalities. Under this assumption, the pretax return to R & D including the externality is closer to that of all tangible capital, causing welfare losses to be lower than shown in Table 5 or Figure 1. At our measured level of intangible capital, the welfare loss under TRA and prior law is about $2.0 billion lower than in Table 5, and under repeal of the ITC it is $3.0 billion lower than in Table 5. The absolute welfare gain of TRA relative to prior law is therefore the same as shown in Table 5, while it is slightly greater for repeal of the ITC relative to prior law. At higher assumed levels of intangible capital (but holding the level of R & D fixed), the welfare losses are only slightly lower than those shown in Figure 1.

Next, we consider a modification to the tax treatment of advertising expenditures. One proposal considered during tax reform and again during this year's budget reconciliation is a partial disallowance of the deduction for advertising expenditures. Here, we consider a modification of TRA that provides a deduction for only 80 percent of advertising expenditures. This disallowance is equivalent in present value to capitalizing all advertising expenditures and allowing them to be depreciated at a 34 percent exponential rate, comparable to that for equipment under TRA. To calculate the new cost of capital for advertising, we assume advertising capital has an economic exponential depreciation rate of 33 percent. The partial disallowance of advertising expenditures results in a cost of capital of 9.2 percent, or an effective tax rate of 51 percent. This tax cost is higher than that of other assets because the 80 percent deduction (or equivalently 34 percent rate of depreciation on historical cost) is not enough to cover economic depreciation at 4 percent inflation.

At our measured level of intangible capital (and assuming no externalities for R & D), welfare losses under TRA with a partial deduction for advertising decrease from $4.1 billion to $3.0 billion. At greater levels of intangible capital (while holding constant the level of advertising capital), these welfare gains are smaller.[14]

Finally, some believe that advertising may generate negative externalities, that is, yield a social rate of return below its private rate of return. Some advertising may simply redistribute sales between competing brands but provide no net increase in total sales. Under the assumption that advertising generates negative externalities, welfare losses under all three tax regimes would be greater. A tax on advertising would raise the social rate of return on advertising toward that of other assets and result in welfare gains.

---

[14] In fact, if the total stock of intangible capital is at least eight times greater than our measured stock of advertising and R & D intangible capital, the partial deduction for advertising actually decreases welfare. This result occurs because the cost of capital for advertising is greater than the cost of capital for all other assets. With sufficiently large amounts of untaxed intangible capital, it is more distorting to tax advertising at greater than average rates than to leave it untaxed. At any level of intangible capital, however, a less restrictive partial deduction for advertising would always generate efficiency gains.

5. CONCLUSION

Intangible capital has escaped the attention of many tax researchers and tax policymakers. As a consequence, discussions of a "level playing field" have concentrated on the relative taxation of equipment, structures, and other tangible assets. They have ignored the significant tax advantages of expensing investments in advertising, R & D, and other intangible assets. We have shown that the consideration of intangible capital renders invalid many of the standard views about what constitutes an efficiency increasing reform. For sufficiently large levels of intangible capital, repeal of the ITC can actually increase the cost of distorting firms' choices among assets. Importantly, however, we find that the TRA still reduces the cost of these distortions relative to prior law.

The point of this chapter is not to provide refined estimates of the welfare costs of taxes on income from capital. Indeed, other studies calculate detailed effects of specific tax provisions on distortions among assets, between the corporate and noncorporate sectors, between business capital and housing, among sources of finance, or between present and future consumption. They might use more sophisticated formulas that account for estimated asset demands or particular relationships among assets in production. Other studies do not consider intangible capital, however. This study uses very simple calculations to show that this omission has a major effect on measures of distortions among assets that were a major concern in discussions of tax reform.

These results do not imply that concerns about the level playing fields were misplaced, however. Perhaps they were only too limited by considering only tangible capital. The model in this study starts with the presumption that corporate capital is allocated most efficiently when all types of capital have the same pretax return (or, in the presence of externalities, the same social return). With unequal effective tax rates, efficiency can be increased by any reform that raises the lowest effective rates and uses the revenue to reduce the highest effective rates. Repeal of the ITC may have raised the low effective tax rate for equipment and provided revenue for rate reduction, but it did not deal with the asset having the lowest effective tax rate. Further efficiency gains are possible in this model. If advertising and R & D do create assets that depreciate over time, then expensing provides a zero effective tax rate for that asset. Any cutback from expensing, such as a partial disallowance or delay in deductions, would raise the lowest effective tax rate, remove further distortions, and provide revenue that could be used to reduce or maintain lower rates.

TECHNICAL APPENDIX

In the framework of Hall and Jorgenson (1967), we consider a corporation facing a certain nominal after-tax discount rate r and inflation rate π. The firm makes a \$1 marginal investment in asset j that depreciates exponentially at rate δ_j and earns a net marginal product ρ_j. Income from the asset is taxed at the statutory corporate rate u. The firm receives an immediate ITC at rate k_j and delayed depreciation allowances on the original purchase price. The present value of these allowances per dollar of investment is z_j, where the firm discounts future nominal allowances by the nominal after-tax discount rate. For further discussion of these assumptions, see Bradford and Fullerton (1981).

The profit-maximizing firm continues to make such investments until, in competitive equilibrium, the cost of the asset is just equal to the present discounted value of after-tax returns and tax savings from the asset. This equilibrium condition is used to solve for the net marginal product or pretax return ρ_j, as a function of other parameters:

$$\rho_j = \frac{r - \pi + \delta_j}{1 - u}(1 - k_j - uz_j) - \delta_j. \tag{1}$$

This cost is gross of taxes but net of depreciation. This pretax return can easily vary among assets with different credit rates k_j, depreciation rates δ_j, and/or allowances z_j. With no ITC, however, depreciation could be set so that the firm receives economic allowances at replacement cost for every asset. The firm then discounts by the real net return $s = r - \pi$. In this case, z_j equals $\delta_j/(s + \delta_j)$, and ρ_j reduces to $s/(1 - u)$ for all assets. Alternatively, equation (1) shows that expensing all assets ($k_j = 0$ and $z_j = 1$) provides ρ_j equal to s for all assets. If the total corporate capital stock is fixed, the tax system does not distort its allocation in either of these two special cases. Other tax rules also can provide the same ρ for all assets, as shown in Bradford (1980) and Brown (1981).

In general, taxes do distort the allocation of capital among assets. In this paper, we follow Hendershott and Hu (1980) and Gravelle (1982) in measuring the associated welfare cost by a more recent version of the formula used by Harberger (1966):

$$W = \sum_{j=1}^{N} \left| \int_{K_j^*}^{\bar{K}_j} [\rho_j(K_j) - \bar{\rho}] \, dK_j \right|, \tag{2}$$

where K_j^* is the stock of asset j in the distorted equilibrium, $\bar{K}_j$ is the stock in the undistorted equilibrium, $\rho_j(K_j)$ is the net marginal product given the level K_j, $\bar{\rho}$ is the cost of capital in the undistorted equilibrium, and N is the number of assets. To measure W, therefore, we need to know how the use of K_j depends upon its cost ρ_j. Econometric studies reviewed in Jorgenson (1974) suggest that firms' total use of capital changes by approximately 1 percent for each 1 percent change in its cost. This cost could conceivably be gross or net of depreciation. Gross costs are often used in empirical work that test whether gross output is a Cobb-Douglas function of capital and labor. However, the use of net costs ρ_j in equation (2) guarantees a fixed total stock of capital under all reallocations. No empirical work has measured price elasticities separately for each of the capital assets used in this study, but we assume that the demand for each K_j has unitary elasticity with respect to its price ρ_j.

Expenditure on each type of capital is a constant under our assumptions, so $\rho_j K_j = \rho_j^* K_j^*$ for any K_j. Thus, we can substitute $\rho_j^* K_j^* / K_j$ for $\rho_j(K_j)$ in equation (2). Further algebra then provides

$$W = \sum_{j=1}^{N} \left| \rho_j^* K_j^* \left[\ln\left(\frac{\rho_j^*}{\bar{\rho}}\right) - 1 + \frac{\bar{\rho}}{\rho_j^*} \right] \right|. \tag{3}$$

For the distorted equilibrium under old law, capital costs ρ_j^* are given by equation (1) using parameters for old law derived in King and Fullerton (1984). We obtain the distorted capital allocation K_j^* for 1983 from data in Jorgenson and Sullivan (1981), more recent issues of the *Survey of current business*, the Federal Reserve Board's *Balance sheets for the U.S. economy*, and our constructed stocks of intangible capital. We estimate the long-run distorted allocation for the other tax plans using the same Cobb-Douglas reactions to changes in the cost of capital. Under the TRA, for example, K_j^* is given by capital expenditures $(K_j \rho_j)$ under 1983 law divided by the cost of capital (ρ_j^*) under TRA.

For the undistorted or counterfactual equilibrium, capital costs should be the same for all assets. Our particular choice for $\bar{\rho}$ is the capital-weighted average of ρ_j^* from the distorted equilibrium, such that both equilibria have the same aggregate pretax return, the same aggregate after-tax return, and the same total tax revenue.

Once we specify r, π, and tax parameters for each law, equations (1) and (3) provide the cost of capital for each asset and the efficiency cost of distortions, as reported in the text.

REFERENCES

Auerbach, Alan J. 1983. Corporate taxation in the United States. *Brookings Papers on Economic Activity* 2: 451–505.

Birnbaum, Jeffrey H., and Alan S. Murray. 1987. *Showdown at Gucci Gulch: Lawmakers, lobbyists, and the unlikely triumph of tax reform*. New York: Random House.

Bosworth, Barry P. 1985. Taxes and the investment recovery. *Brookings Papers on Economic Activity*: 1–38.

Bradford, David F. 1980. Tax neutrality and the investment tax credit. In *The economics of taxation*, eds. Henry J. Aaron and Michael J. Boskin. Washington, D.C.: The Brookings Institution.

Bradford, David F., and Don Fullerton. 1981. Pitfalls in the construction and use of effective tax rates. In *Depreciation, inflation, and the taxation of income from capital*, ed. C. R. Hulten. Washington, D.C.: The Urban Institute Press.

Brown, E. Cary. 1981. The 'net' versus the 'gross' investment tax credit. In *Depreciation, inflation, and the taxation of income from capital*, ed. C. R. Hulten. Washington, D.C.: The Urban Institute Press.

Clarkson, Kenneth W. 1977. Intangible capital and rates of return: Effects of research and promotion on profitability. Washington, D.C.: American Enterprise Institute for Public Policy Research.

Cordes, Joseph J., Harry S. Watson, and J. Scott Hauger. 1987. Effects of tax reform on high technology firms. *National Tax Journal* 40: 373–91.

Eisner, Robert, Steven H. Albert, and Martin A. Sullivan. 1984. The new incremental tax credit for R & D: Incentive or disincentive? *National Tax Journal* 37: 171–83.

Feldstein, Martin. 1985. The second best theory of capital taxation. NBER, Working Paper no. 1781.

Feldstein, Martin, Louis Dicks-Mireaux, and James Poterba. 1983. The effective tax rate and the pretax rate of return. *Journal of Public Economics* 21: 129–58.

Fullerton, Don. 1984. Which effective tax rate? *National Tax Journal* 37: 23–41.

Fullerton, Don, Robert Gillette, and James Mackie. 1987. Investment incentives under the Tax Reform Act of 1986. In *Compendium of tax research, 1986*. Washington, D.C.: U.S. Treasury Department.

Fullerton, Don and Yolanda Kodrzycki Henderson. 1986. A disaggregate equilibrium model of the tax distortions among assets, sectors, and industries. NBER, Working Paper no. 1905.

Fullerton, Don, Andrew B. Lyon, and Richard J. Rosen. 1984. Uncertainty, welfare cost and the 'adaptability' of U.S. corporate taxes. *The Scandinavian Journal of Economics* 86: 229–43.

Gordon, Roger H., James R. Hines, and Lawrence H. Summers. 1987. Notes on the tax treatment of structures. In *The effects of taxation on capital accumulation*, ed. Martin Feldstein. Chicago: The University of Chicago Press.

Grabowski, Henry G., and Dennis C. Mueller. 1978. Industrial research and development, intangible capital stocks, and firm profit rates. *The Bell Journal of Economics* 9: 328–43.

Gravelle, Jane G. 1982. Effects of the 1981 depreciation revisions on the taxation of income from business capital. *National Tax Journal* 35: 1–20.

Hall, Robert E., and Dale W. Jorgenson. 1967. Tax policy and investment behavior. *American Economic Review* 57: 391–414.

Harberger, Arnold C. 1966. Efficiency effects of taxes on income from capital. In *Effects of corporation income tax*, ed. M. Krzyzaniak. Detroit: Wayne State University Press.

Hendershott, Patric H., and Sheng-Cheng Hu. 1980. Government-induced biases in the allocation of the stock of fixed capital in the United States. In *Capital, efficiency, and growth*, ed. George von Furstenberg. Cambridge, Mass.: Ballinger.

Hulten, Charles R., and Frank C. Wykoff. 1981. The measurement of economic depreciation. In *Depreciation, inflation, and the taxation of income from capital*, ed. C. R. Hulten. Washington, D.C.: The Urban Institute Press.

Hulten, Charles R., and James W. Robertson. 1984. The taxation of high technology industries. *National Tax Journal* 37: 327–45.

Jorgenson, Dale W. 1974. Investment and production: A review. In *Frontiers of quantitative economics*, vol. II, eds. M. Intriligator and D. Kendrick. Amsterdam: North-Holland.

Jorgenson, Dale W., and Martin A. Sullivan. 1981. Inflation and capital recovery in the United States. In *Depreciation, inflation, and the taxation of income from capital*, ed. C. R. Hulten. Washington, D.C.: The Urban Institute Press.

King, Mervyn A., and Don Fullerton, eds. 1984. *The taxation of income from capital: A comparative study of the U.S., U.K., Sweden, and West Germany*. Chicago: University of Chicago Press.

Lindenberg, Eric B., and Stephen A. Ross. 1981. Tobin's q ratio and industrial organization. *Journal of Business* 54: 1–32.

Mundstock, George. 1987. Taxation of business intangible capital. *University of Pennsylvania Law Review* 135: 1179–1263.

Summers, Lawrence H. 1981. Taxation and corporate investment: A q-theory approach. *Brookings Papers on Economic Activity*: 67–140.

——— 1987. Should tax reform level the playing field? *Proceedings of the National Tax Association-Tax Institute of America* meetings of November 1986, pp. 119–25.

DO WE COLLECT ANY REVENUE FROM TAXING CAPITAL INCOME?

Roger H. Gordon and Joel Slemrod
University of Michigan and NBER

EXECUTIVE SUMMARY

The wide variation in effective tax rates on income from different types of capital received by different investors creates numerous tax arbitrage opportunities that result in a loss in both government revenue and economic efficiency. The objective of this chapter is to estimate the revenue and distributional effects of tax arbitrage, using tax data from 1983, by examining the effects of two tax changes that would each substantially reduce the opportunities for tax arbitrage.

Our principal conclusions are as follows:

1. Taxing real rather than nominal interest income would have raised government revenue in 1983 by $25.5 billion.
2. This increase in revenue would occur mainly at the expense of those in the highest tax brackets.
3. Taxing the cash flow from real capital and exempting from tax any income from financial assets would have raised government revenue by $17.4 billion. Since this tax change eliminates all distortions to savings and investment decisions, our revenue forecast suggests that the tax law in 1983 subsidized savings and investment on average.

We would like to thank Chris Ferrall, Laura Kalambokidis, and Joseph Daniel for careful and able research assistance.

4. This tax change would benefit those in the highest tax brackets, who have large income from financial assets, at the expense of those in lower tax brackets.
5. Either tax change should improve the efficiency of the allocation of existing capital and improve savings incentives.

1. INTRODUCTION

The appropriate tax treatment of capital income has been debated for many years among both academics and government officials. Perhaps as a result of this debate, the actual tax treatment of capital income is extremely complicated and has changed frequently. IRAs, pensions, and equivalent plans are taxed as they would be under a cash-flow tax,[1] and the return to owner-occupied housing and consumer durables is tax exempt. Many other types of capital income are taxed, some quite heavily. The asset whose income is probably taxed most heavily is one that pays interest income, where the entire nominal return on the asset is fully taxable each year.

This chapter argues that the simultaneous presence of these differences in the tax treatment of various types of capital income, and differences in personal tax rates, leads to substantial inefficiencies and inequities in the existing tax system. We argue that if these differences in the tax treatment of various types of capital income were eliminated, the tax system would raise more revenue and be less distorting, even if all capital income were made entirely tax exempt.

The problem with the current tax system is that the combination of differences in the tax treatment of different types of capital and differences in personal tax rates inevitably opens up arbitrage opportunities. In a typical case, an individual or a firm in a high tax bracket borrows heavily to buy a lightly taxed or tax-exempt asset and thereby runs a large tax loss on the transaction. Most likely, the interest payments are ultimately received by an individual in a low tax bracket or a tax-exempt entity such as a pension fund. The possibilities for tax arbitrage are many.[2] For example, high-tax-bracket individuals, say in a 50 percent tax bracket, may borrow money at the going market interest rate, of say 8 percent, from lower-tax-bracket individuals, either directly or more likely through a financial

---

[1] Under a cash-flow tax, investment expenditures would be deductible in the year made, and any future cash flow including revenue from the sale of capital assets would be fully taxable. The government, in effect, acts as a coinvestor, paying some percentage of any expenses and receiving that percentage of the income, and in present value collects no revenue from a marginal investment.

[2] See Steuerle (1985) for an enumeration of various forms of arbitrage.

intermediary, and invest the funds in tax-exempt bonds paying, for example, 6 percent. The interest payments they make on the borrowed funds are tax deductible.[3] The interest payments received by the lower-tax-bracket individuals are taxable, but at a very low tax rate, say 15 percent, so that on net the government loses tax revenue from this transaction. To complete the circle, these lower-tax-bracket individuals could obtain the funds needed to make the loan by having their (low-income) municipality borrow money at the tax-exempt rate and make the funds available to the residents, either through reduced local taxes or through expenditure on goods that local residents would otherwise have purchased directly. Of course, the low-income residents would need to pay the interest on this debt each year. The net result, per dollar of loan, for low-income individuals, high-income individuals, and the government would be as follows:

Transaction	Return to low-income individual	Return to high-income individual	Government tax revenue
Tax-exempt bond	− 0.06	+ 0.06	0
Loan	+ 0.08(1 − 0.15)	− 0.08(1 − 0.5)	.08(0.15 − 0.5)
Total	0.008	0.02	− 0.28

As we see, both low- and high-tax-bracket individuals gain through this tax arbitrage, at the expense of the government.

Several provisions have been enacted trying to restrict specific forms of arbitrage. For example, individuals cannot deduct the interest from loans used to purchase municipal bonds. Also, municipalities are now limited in the degree to which they can issue municipal bonds and invest the proceeds *themselves* in taxable bonds, though they can provide the funds to their residents, who then can invest in taxable bonds, as in the preceding example. However, any of these provisions are difficult to enforce, and in any case many other arbitrage possibilities remain. If this tax arbitrage is important enough, the government's attempt to tax capital income could collect little or no revenue, or even (as we find) result in a loss in tax revenue as well as create a host of distortions affecting capital allocation, risk sharing, and saving-and-investment decisions.[4]

---

[3] The tax law does not allow the deduction of interest on loans where funds are used to buy tax-exempt bonds. This restriction can normally be avoided by using other capital, such as a house, as collateral for the loan.

[4] This point was made strongly in Steuerle (1985). Gordon and Slemrod (1986) focus on arbitrage possibilities available to municipalities.

One objective of this chapter is to provide a preliminary assessment of the importance of tax arbitrage, using data from individual tax returns in 1983 made available to researchers by the Treasury. We focus initially on the tax treatment of interest income, since many types of tax arbitrage involve borrowing to invest in more lightly taxed assets, and attempt to calculate the effect on tax revenue and on the net income of different types of individuals of subjecting to tax real rather than nominal interest income. In the results reported here we find that had this tax change been enacted in 1983, tax revenue would have risen, with the burden of the rise borne heavily by those in higher tax brackets.[5] We also argue that the resulting behavioral responses would have increased revenue further *and* increased efficiency.

We also explore the effects of moving to a modified cash-flow tax in which all forms of capital income from financial assets are made tax exempt, whereas investments in real assets are treated as they would be under a consumption tax.[6] Had these changes been made in 1983, otherwise leaving the tax structure unchanged, government revenue net of interest expense would have increased slightly—we estimate tax revenue would fall very slightly, with a fall in personal taxes just offsetting a rise in corporate taxes, but that the resulting fall in the market interest rate would save the government more than enough in interest payments to offset the net loss in tax revenue. The main beneficiaries from the tax change would be those in the highest income group who have large capital income.

These results do not take into account the effects of the recently enacted tax changes. To some degree, the narrowing of tax rate differentials, the cutback in several tax preference items, and the drop in the inflation rate since 1983 will all reduce the gains from the two tax changes we investigate here. However, the United States is now a large debtor, so any reduction in the interest rate we pay on this debt is now much more important. Data restrictions prevented us from attempting to examine the effects of modifying the current law, so our results that examine the situation in 1983 must be viewed merely as suggestive of what might happen if the changes were made now.

The organization of the chapter is as follows. In section 2 we discuss intuitively what we would expect to happen to the economy if real rather

---

[5] We are aware of the political obstacles to limiting the full deductibility of nominal mortgage interest payments. This chapter estimates the economic returns to overcoming the political obstacles. In Canada, mortgage interest is not deductible. Whether owner-occupied housing is harmed by such a tax change depends on the degree to which the market interest rate falls in response to the tax change.

[6] Specifically, we allowed expensing of new investments and taxed the cash flow arising from these investments.

than nominal interest income were taxed. In section 3 we then use the available data to forecast the size of the change in tax revenue and in the tax payments by different income groups if real rather than nominal interest were taxed or if a modified cash-flow tax were enacted, all assuming no changes in behavior or in market prices. Then in section 4 we discuss how our forecasts would change when behavioral and price changes are taken into account. Finally, we include a brief discussion of the efficiency effects of these two tax changes, an estimate of the revenue losses from likely transition rules were a cash-flow tax enacted, a discussion of how the situation has changed due to the Tax Reform Act of 1986, and a short summary of the chapter.

2. IMPLICATIONS OF CHANGING THE TAXATION OF INTEREST INCOME

It helps to understand the effects of a change in the tax treatment of interest income in the complicated real world if we first think about this tax change in a very simple stylized context. Consider a closed economy in which everyone has the same tax rate and there is no government debt, so all interest payments by one individual represent interest receipts by another individual. If all interest payments are deductible in calculating taxable income, and all interest income is taxable, the interest-related tax base is exactly zero—interest payments exactly offset interest receipts. If all taxpayers face the same tax rate, it follows immediately that tax revenue collected on interest must also be exactly zero. Furthermore, reducing the tax on interest income would not change tax revenue—what is lost in revenue from reducing the tax on interest income is gained in revenue from reducing the deductibility of interest payments. In fact, in response to a tax change the market interest rates would adjust so as to leave the net of tax borrowing and lending rates exactly unchanged. Through this change in the market interest rate, all borrowers and lenders are left unaffected by the tax change, and therefore the bond market continues to clear. This tax change would have no real effects whatsoever.[7]

What if there were government debt as well? In this case, the interest-related tax base becomes positive. Because the government collects revenue on its outstanding debt, it would appear to lose revenue from a reduced tax rate. This is not correct. Because the market interest rate would

---

[7] This argument depends on the presumption that the Internal Revenue Service could defend the zero tax base against attempts to underreport interest income and generate illegitimate interest deductions. The incentive for this type of evasion would likely depend on both the tax rate on interest income and the difference between this rate and the tax rate on other types of capital income.

adjust to leave the net of tax interest rate unchanged, what the government loses in tax revenue from reducing the tax on the interest received by holders of government bonds, it would gain from paying a lower interest rate to the holders of government bonds. As in the absence of government debt, the change in interest taxation has no real effects on the economy or on government revenue.

Forecasting the effects of this tax change becomes more complicated when certain other factors are introduced. Consider a slightly more realistic example in which there are two assets: bonds, where the nominal income is taxable, and physical capital, where only the real income is taxable. (We assume the inflation rate is positive.) In addition, let different investors face different tax rates. In this setting, we would end up initially with those facing the highest tax rates borrowing from the other individuals to buy all the physical capital—the relatively tax-favored status of physical capital is most valuable to those facing the highest tax rates. Those facing lower tax rates end up lending to both the government and higher-tax-rate individuals. If the tax rate on interest income and the deductibility of interest payments were now reduced, the market interest rate would fall as before, although estimating the size of the fall would be more complicated. If the policy change is large enough, bonds would become the tax-favored asset and portfolio holdings would reverse, so those in the highest tax brackets would lend to both the government and those in the lowest tax brackets, and those in the lowest tax brackets would borrow to buy all the physical capital.

To estimate the effect of reducing the taxation of interest on government revenue, we start by calculating the change in revenue arising from a change in the fraction of interest income and payments that are taxable or tax deductible, assuming no other changes in taxable income. In the foregoing example, this would provide a clear gain in tax revenue. As before, we would, in addition, need to take into account the fall in the market interest rate, which again saves the government revenue, though it changes the size of interest income and interest deductions appearing on individual tax returns. Since the interest deductions are taken by those in high tax brackets, and the interest income is received by those in lower tax brackets, the fall in the market interest rate raises tax revenue further by reducing the gains from tax arbitrage. In addition, however, we would need to take into account any rearrangement of individual portfolios, in this case the possible shift in ownership of physical capital from high- to low-tax-rate individuals, and any change in total savings and physical investment. We will discuss these and other complications in section 4.

Recognizing that the United States is open to international flows of capital also has important implications. If, for example, foreigners own

U.S. bonds on net, then cutting the tax rate on interest income (holding the effective withholding tax on interest paid to foreigners constant) raises more revenue than in the previous example, everything else equal, since to that extent interest deductions on domestic tax returns exceed interest income. Any fall in the market interest rate also lowers the amounts paid in interest to foreigners. In 1983, however, according to the data in the *Survey of current business* foreigners paid $47.9 billion in interest payments to U.S. firms while receiving only $28.9 billion in interest in return. Although on net they received $13.1 billion in interest payments from the federal government, they still would gain from any fall in the interest rate. By 1988, however, the net flows should have reversed.

In addition, when the economy is open, a tax change will cause shifts in foreign versus domestic ownership of assets. Since, by assumption, only domestic residents directly benefit from the reduction in the taxation of interest income, foreign residents will find domestic bonds less attractive after the tax change due to any fall in the interest rate. They therefore will shift funds invested in bonds into other securities, both foreign and domestic. Domestic residents, conversely, will shift out of these other securities into bonds. This rearrangement of portfolios raises tax revenue to the extent that bonds remain more heavily taxed than other assets.

Reducing the taxation of interest income is likely to reduce the welfare of taxpayers at the extremes of the income distribution. Those in the highest tax brackets who are net debtors would find it more expensive to borrow, so they are made worse off. But, in addition, those in the lowest tax brackets may suffer because they would receive a lower interest rate on their positive holdings of bonds, but they do not benefit substantially from the lower tax rates. However, a sizable fraction of the funds invested at low or zero tax rates belong to pension plans that are heavily owned by those in higher tax brackets, so these higher-tax-bracket individuals lose on both counts. All residents benefit indirectly, however, from the gain in government revenue that can be used to finance additional expenditures or to lower tax rates. Aggregate individual losses will be less than the net increase in government revenue to the extent that there is an efficiency gain from the tax change and a gain at the expense of foreigners, who now receive a lower return on their holdings of bonds.

Rather than changing proportionately the fraction of interest income and interest deductions entering into the calculation of taxable income, an alternative would be to restrict solely the fraction of interest deductions allowed.[8] Under this alternative, individuals would save considerable

---

[8] The Tax Reform Act of 1986 included a variant of this through its provision to restrict interest deductions, other than mortgage interest payments, to investment income. Individuals can

amounts in taxes simply by using their interest-bearing assets to reduce any debts. Individuals still receiving net interest income would find, as under the current law, that bonds are the most heavily taxed asset. Individuals with net interest deductions, however, would find investments in the retirement of outstanding loans to be tax free, therefore among the most lightly taxed assets. These sharp differences in the relative attractiveness of investments in bonds would create particularly large tax arbitrage opportunities, with taxes falling substantially when net lenders exchange bonds with net borrowers in return for almost any other asset. This arbitrage would therefore take the form of those in debt going short in some other asset and using the proceeds to repay their loans. Such transactions do not occur much now, since taxes discourage them, but presumably financial innovations would quickly occur to facilitate this form of tax arbitrage. As a result, it is difficult to forecast with any confidence the implications of such a tax change.

3. EXPLORATION OF THE DATA

We begin our study of alternative systems of capital income taxation by first calculating the effects of a tax change assuming no changes in reported income. Thus, we ignore price effects, behavioral responses to the tax change, and changes in income from equity resulting from the changes in the corporate tax law. In section 4, we discuss the likely implications of these complications for our results.

In calculating the effects of a tax change, we use data on the 1983 income tax returns of a representative cross section of 29,821 individuals made available by the Treasury. We forecast how tax revenue and the after-tax income of different types of individuals would have been changed had the 1983 tax law included the proposed modifications, in order to understand the historic effects of the tax treatment of interest income, and of capital income generally.

To provide some sense of the distributional implications of these tax changes, we need a measure of how well off people were initially. One straightforward approach is to use the value of adjusted gross income (AGI) reported on the individual's tax return. A crucial problem with this figure, however, is that it measures in part the extent to which individuals have made use of tax arbitrage to reduce their taxable income—a number of seemingly very rich individuals end up with very low AGI through clever use of the tax law. Academics have normally focused on the present value

---

get around this restriction, however, to the extent that they can use their interest-bearing assets to repay existing debt, or they can reclassify existing debt as a mortgage. Only to the extent that these simple remedies are insufficient will the following discussion apply.

of lifetime income as a more reasonable measure of economic welfare; a commonly proposed alternative is comprehensive income. Neither can be calculated with any degree of reliability from the existing data. The measure of well-being we employ is our best estimate of labor income.[9] Labor income has the advantage of being relatively stable over an individual's lifetime, so it is highly correlated with a true measure of the present value of the individual's lifetime income. However, labor income will not be an accurate measure of economic position for those who are retired or for those who have yet to enter the labor force full time. We therefore treat separately any households who report a member over age 65 or who indicate on their tax return that they are being claimed as a dependent on someone else's tax return. For purposes of comparison with other studies of the distributional impact of tax law changes, we also report some of the results broken down by AGI brackets instead of by labor income brackets.

In Tables 1–2, we report our estimates of interest income and payments, other capital income, and various other components that enter into the calculation of individual tax liabilities in 1983, by labor income group. Table 1 reports the aggregate figures across returns in each income group, and Table 2 reports the average value per return. (Tables 1a and 2a report the same figures by AGI brackets.) Given the limited information available from the Treasury, some items had to be estimated. The procedures we employed to make these estimates are described in detail in the appendix. For example, partnership net income, but not the interest deductions of a partnership, was reported in the tax file. To estimate interest deductions, we multiplied reported net income by the ratio of interest deductions to net income observed in the aggregate data in the *1983 statistics of income for partnerships*, doing this separately for partnerships with positive versus negative net income. Also, in constructing the figures for itemized deductions in columns 8 and 9, we defined column 9 as the amount of extra deductions allowed, beyond the standard deduction, due to the availability of all itemized deductions except for interest payments, whereas column 8 measures the additional deduction available due to the deductibility of interest payments. Therefore, the sum of columns 7 and 8 equals the additional deductions taken, beyond the standard deduction, by itemizers.

We also report in column 1 of Tables 3–4 net interest income (income less payments) by labor income group, and in column 2 of Tables 3–4 we report net taxable capital income, defined to equal the sum of net interest income and other capital income, including the capital income component of self-employment income as derived by the procedure described in the

---

[9] There are some complications in measuring the labor income of the self-employed, which are discussed further in the appendix.

TABLE 1
Aggregate Statistics on Income and Tax Payments by Labor Income Group
1983 Individual Income Tax Returns (millions of 1983 dollars)

Labor income group	Returns	Estimated labor income	Schedule B interest income	Other interest income	Other capital income	Adjustment to income	Adjusted gross income	Schedule A interest deductions
<20K	50,105,872	434,457	35,164	−14,140	27,064	−21,203	461,266	14,737
20K–40K	23,816,452	680,622	18,885	−10,093	10,343	−25,764	673,918	46,366
40K–70K	8,114,064	402,447	11,838	−9,024	11,168	−21,925	394,484	37,626
70K–100K	1,028,676	83,481	2,902	−3,436	5,345	−6,475	81,807	8,400
>100K	588,128	102,480	4,889	−8,332	16,855	−6,497	109,400	9,977
>Age 65	11,239,388	106,453	79,859	−6,662	44,542	−3,315	220,876	4,722
Depend.	913,920	783	2,144	7	1,110	−7	4,036	0
Total	95,806,480	1,810,721	155,682	−51,680	116,427	−85,185	1,945,785	121,827

Labor income group	Other excess deductions	Standard deduc. + exemptions	Taxable income	Tax on taxable income	Surtaxes and credits	Investment tax credit	Total tax liability
<20K	8,702	227,077	360,440	41,116	2,238	−704	42,650
20K–40K	16,036	144,914	541,592	85,373	1,337	−954	85,756
40K–70K	19,450	54,124	310,635	64,978	1,275	−908	65,345
70K–100K	6,816	6,831	63,565	17,752	565	−351	17,966
>100K	11,254	4,060	86,825	34,260	535	−1,093	33,703
>Age 65	18,316	65,077	167,147	34,252	1,093	−301	35,044
Depend.	0	3,016	4,608	417	1	−3	415
Total	80,575	505,099	1,534,811	278,147	7,045	−4,314	280,879

1. Returns are classified by labor income, as reported in column 2.
2. Row labeled ">Age 65" includes all returns with at least one age exemption.
3. Row "Depend." includes returns for persons claimed as dependents and having unearned income.

TABLE 1a
Aggregate Statistics on Income and Tax Payments by Adjusted Gross Income
1983 Individual Income Tax Returns (millions of 1983 dollars)

AGI group	Returns	Estimated labor income	Schedule B interest income	Other interest income	Other capital income	Adjustment to income	Adjusted gross income	Schedule A interest deductions
<10K	34,169,012	152,956	23,644	−12,022	6,361	−23,494	147,408	2,817
10–20K	24,369,204	329,295	33,720	−5,845	8,041	−10,254	354,948	9,905
20–30K	16,501,132	388,579	26,540	−6,609	9,907	−13,337	405,034	22,449
30–40K	10,436,080	345,695	20,762	−5,093	10,564	−13,317	358,584	27,162
40–75K	8,699,724	419,120	28,004	−8,731	20,377	−19,247	439,488	40,346
75–100K	803,716	59,538	6,250	−2,941	8,190	−2,731	68,304	5,997
>100K	827,632	115,540	16,761	−10,440	52,986	−2,806	172,022	13,151
Total	95,806,464	1,810,723	155,681	−51,680	116,427	−85,185	1,945,786	121,827

AGI group	Other excess deductions	Standard deduc. + exemptions	Taxable income	Tax on taxable income	Surtaxes and credits	Investment tax credit	Total tax liability
<10 K	2,834	147,446	104,987	6,539	518	−54	7,003
10–20K	5,763	126,017	280,999	32,048	927	−379	32,596
20–30K	8,709	96,772	327,156	47,478	930	−650	47,758
30–40K	11,350	66,658	287,073	48,393	697	−497	48,593
40–75K	24,979	57,360	345,642	73,775	1,744	−871	74,648
75–100K	6,331	5,283	53,402	15,290	508	−350	15,448
>100K	20,609	5,563	135,554	54,625	1,721	−1,513	54,833
Total	80,575	505,099	1,534,812	278,147	7,045	−4,314	280,879

1. Returns are classified by adjusted gross income, as reported in column 7.

TABLE 2
Statistics on Average Income and Tax Payments Per Return by Labor Income Group
1983 Individual Income Tax Returns (millions of 1983 dollars)

Labor income group	Returns	Estimated labor income	Schedule B interest income	Other interest income	Other capital income	Adjustment to income	Adjusted gross income	Schedule A interest deductions
<20K	50,105,872	8,671	702	−282	540	−423	9,206	294
20K–40K	23,816,452	28,578	793	−424	434	−1,082	28,296	1,947
40K–70K	8,114,064	49,599	1,459	−1,112	1,376	−2,702	48,617	4,637
70K–100K	1,028,676	81,153	2,821	−3,340	5,196	−6,294	79,527	8,166
>100K	588,128	174,249	8,314	−14,167	28,659	−11,046	186,014	16,963
>Age 65	11,239,388	9,471	7,105	−593	3,963	−295	19,652	420
Depend.	913,920	857	2,346	7	1,214	−7	4,417	0
Total	95,806,480	18,900	1,625	−539	1,215	−889	20,310	1,272

Labor income group	Other excess deductions	Standard deduc. + exemptions	Taxable income	Tax on taxable income	Surtaxes and credits	Investment tax credit	Total tax liability
<20K	174	4,532	7,194	821	45	−14	851
20K–40K	673	6,085	22,740	3,585	56	−40	3,601
40K–70K	2,397	6,670	38,284	8,008	157	−112	8,053
70K–100K	6,626	6,640	61,793	17,257	549	−341	17,465
>100K	19,135	6,904	147,630	58,253	910	−1,858	57,306
>Age 65	1,630	5,790	14,872	3,048	97	−27	3,118
Depend.	0	3,300	5,042	456	1	−3	454
Total	841	5,272	16,020	2,903	74	−45	2,932

1. Returns are classified by labor income, as reported in column 2.

TABLE 2a
Statistics on Average Income and Tax Payments Per Return by Adjusted Gross Income 1983 Individual Income Tax Returns (millions of 1983 dollars)

AGI Group	Returns	Estimated labor income	Schedule B interest income	Other interest income	Other capital income	Adjustment to income	Adjusted Gross income	Schedule A interest deductions
<10K	34,169,012	4,476	692	−352	186	−688	4,314	82
10–20K	24,369,204	13,513	1,384	−240	330	−421	14,565	406
20–30K	16,501,132	23,549	1,608	−400	600	−808	24,546	1,360
30–40K	10,436,080	33,125	1,989	−488	1,012	−1,276	34,360	2,603
40–75K	8,699,724	48,176	3,219	−1,004	2,342	−2,212	50,517	4,638
75–100K	803,716	74,079	7,776	−3,659	10,190	−3,398	84,985	7,462
>100K	827,632	139,603	20,252	−12,614	64,021	−3,391	207,848	15,890
Total	95,806,464	18,900	1,625	−539	1,215	−889	20,310	1,272

AGI group	Other excess deductions	Standard deduc. + exemptions	Taxable income	Tax on taxable income	Surtaxes and credits	Investment tax credit	Total tax liability
<10K	83	4,315	3,073	191	15	−2	205
10–20K	236	5,171	11,531	1,315	38	−16	1,338
20–30K	528	5,865	19,826	2,877	56	−39	2,894
30–40K	1,088	6,387	27,508	4,637	67	−48	4,656
40–75K	2,871	6,593	39,730	8,480	200	−100	8,580
75–100K	7,877	6,573	66,443	19,024	632	−435	19,221
>100K	24,901	6,721	163,786	66,002	2,080	−1,828	66,253
Total	841	5,272	16,020	2,903	74	−45	2,932

1. Returns are classified by adjusted gross income, as reported in column 7.

TABLE 3
Changes in Aggregate Income and Taxes
(millions of 1983 dollars)

			Policy 1		Policy 2	
Labor income group	Net interest income	Net capital + interest income	Change in taxable income	Change in total tax liability	Change in taxable income	Change in total tax liability
<20K	6,287	33,351	−3,036	−1,038	−30,037	−7,156
20K–40K	−37,574	−27,231	17,048	3,570	26,649	6,150
40K–70K	−34,812	−23,644	14,334	4,392	23,569	7,755
70K–100K	−8,934	−3,589	3,517	1,393	3,539	1,465
>100K	−13,420	3,435	5,326	2,401	−3,254	−1,044
>Age 65	68,475	113,017	−27,361	−5,924	−104,778	−22,086
Depend.	2,151	3,261	−1,278	−113	−4,729	−329
Total	−17,825	98,602	8,549	4,683	−89,042	−15,245

1. Policy 1 involves reducing all interest income and deductions by 40 percent.
2. Policy 2 involves eliminating all interest and capital income and deductions (columns 3,4,5,8, and 14 in Table 1 are zeroed out).

appendix. Table 3 reports the aggregate figures, and Table 4 reports the average of these values per return. As can be seen looking at the last row of Table 3, allowing interest payments to be deducted and making interest income taxable results in a drop in aggregate personal taxable income of $17.8 billion. Only individuals in the lowest labor income group, the elderly and dependents, have higher taxable income due to the existing tax treatment of interest income and interest payments.

In fact, we estimate that individuals on their tax returns report $30.0 billion more in interest payments than they report in interest income.[10] If the economy were closed and all interest income and payments were reported on tax returns, then this figure should equal the sum of net corporate and federal government interest payments. In 1983, according to the data in the *Economic report of the president*, net interest payments by the federal government were $94.3 billion, whereas the *1983 statistics of income for corporations* indicates that corporations (including financial institutions) on net received $19.5 billion in interest income. Therefore, net interest payments by the government and corporations together equaled $74.8 billion. Yet we estimate that individuals on net report making interest

---
[10] Their taxable income falls by only $17.8 billion, however, since those who itemize so as to claim personal interest deductions lose use of the standard deduction.

TABLE 4
Changes in Income and Taxes Per Return
(1983 dollars)

Labor income group	Net interest income	Net capital + interest income	Policy 1		Policy 2	
			Change in taxable income	Change in total tax liability	Change in taxable income	Change in total tax liability
<20K	126	666	−61	−21	−600	−143
20K–40K	−1,579	−1,144	716	150	1,119	258
40K–70K	−4,290	−2,914	1,766	542	2,904	956
70K–100K	−8,685	−3,489	3,419	1,355	3,441	1,424
>100K	−22,816	5,843	9,055	4,082	−5,534	−1,775
>Age 65	6,092	10,055	−2,435	−527	−9,323	−1,965
Depend.	2,339	3,553	−1,398	−123	−5,174	−360
Total	−186	1,029	89	49	−929	−159

1. Policy 1 involves reducing all interest income and deductions by 40 percent.
2. Policy 2 involves eliminating all interest and capital income and deductions (columns 3,4,5,8, and 14 in Table 1 are zeroed out).

payments of $30.0 billion. On net, therefore, interest income of $104.8 billion should be received by a variety of nontaxpaying institutions and individuals, such as pension funds, IRAs, company savings plans, nonprofit organizations, and state and local governments, as well as individuals who do not report interest income or payments because their income is too low, they do not itemize, or they simply evade taxes. These data make clear that a significant amount of tax arbitrage is taking place between taxable and tax exempt entities, perhaps even more than between taxpayers in high and low tax brackets.

In contrast, net capital income of individuals as a group, as reported on their tax returns, is $98.6 billion. As is made clear by Steuerle (1985), this figure is much smaller than the actual real income individuals receive from capital due to a wide variety of provisions in the tax code affecting the definition of taxable income.

3.1 The Impact of Taxing Only Real Interest

We then use these data to forecast the revenue and distributional effects of taxing only real interest payments. As a first step, we ignore any impact of this tax change on the reported capital income figures. We assume that the ratio of the real interest rate to the nominal interest rate is 60 percent, which was approximately true in 1983.[11] We therefore recalculated tax liabilities under 1983 law, including only 60 percent of reported interest income in taxable income and allowing only 60 percent of reported interest payments as a deduction.[12] The results are reported in columns 3–4 in Tables 3–4. Here, we find that aggregate personal income tax revenue goes up by $4.7 billion, with the extra tax payments being made by the nonelderly in the higher tax brackets.

If such a tax change is imposed throughout the tax code, there would also be a change in corporate tax liabilities. According to the *1983 statistics of income for corporations,* net interest payments by nonfinancial corporations as a whole, excluding Subchapter S corporations, were $96.6 billion.[13] Unfortunately, data on individual corporate tax returns are not available for the calculation of how tax liabilities would change, even ignoring behavioral responses, if the interest deduction were scaled back. Doing so is complicated by the importance of loss carryforwards and carrybacks during this period, which imply that an accurate calculation of the change in a company's income due to some tax change must take into account not only the revenue change in 1983 but also the effects on previous and later tax returns arising from carrybacks or carryforwards of 1983 tax losses. Altshuler and Auerbach (1987), in a careful study using internal data at the Treasury, calculated the effective marginal tax rate on interest deductions during the early 1980s to be 31.8 percent. Therefore, if only 60 percent of interest deductions were allowed, the resulting rise in corporate tax payments, ignoring any changes in prices or behavior, would be $0.4(0.318)(96.6) = \$12.3$ billion. Combining this with the estimated increase

---

[11] In 1983, the various nominal interest rates ranged from 8.63 percent for Treasury bills to 13.55 percent for Baa corporate bonds, and the inflation rate in the CPI was 3.8 percent.

[12] This procedure used the tax law simulator developed at the Office of Tax Policy Research at the University of Michigan. In recalculating tax liabilities, numerous minor assumptions had to be made to compensate for inadequate data in the tax file. Details concerning our procedure are available from the authors.

[13] One important assumption we make in trying to model such a tax change is that the tax treatment of banks and insurance companies would be left unaffected. The current tax treatment of these institutions involves a variety of specially designed provisions, with the net result being very little tax payments by these companies. We presume that the amount of taxes paid by financial institutions would not be allowed to fall further as part of a tax change that would appear to raise the tax liabilities of the rest of the corporate sector substantially. In modeling this tax change, we therefore make the simplifying assumption that the tax payments by banks and insurance companies would not change, and we focus only on nonfinancial corporations, including real estate.

of $4.7 billion in personal tax payments yields an initial estimate of a $17.0 billion increase in tax revenue from taxing only real interest income.[14]

3.2 The Impact of Eliminating All Taxation of Capital Income

Our next task is to forecast the effects of shifting to a tax system that does not distort savings and capital investment decisions. This can be done either by exempting capital income from tax entirely or by allowing new investments to be expensed and then taxing at ordinary rates any resulting cash flow from the investments, including the sales price if the assets are sold.[15] We implement this tax by first exempting from taxation all financial income from investments (e.g., dividends and capital gains, as well as interest income). For all other real investments, we replace interest deductions, depreciation deductions, and the investment tax credit with a deduction for expenditures on new capital in that year.[16] The details of this procedure are available in the appendix; it is the same procedure used in separating labor income from capital income. Therefore, in forecasting the effects of this tax change, we zero out net capital income, as reported in column 2 of Tables 3–4 or in the sum of columns 3–5 minus column 7 in Tables 1–2, from taxable income and eliminate the investment tax credit. The resulting change in tax payments is shown in column 6 in Tables 3–4. Here, we find that personal tax payments fall by $15.2 billion. On a per-capita basis, the elderly and the highest income group gain considerably. In contrast, those with labor incomes between $20,000 and $100,000 pay more in taxes, since as a group they had negative taxable capital income.

In implementing this tax, we assume that the same shift to a modified cash-flow tax, requiring expensing of new investment, is made under the corporate tax as well.[17] Our basic strategy was to replace depreciation

---

[14] Attempting a similar calculation for 1982, Steuerle (1985) found that revenue would rise by $29 billion if all interest income and deductions were eliminated from taxation. Steuerle did not provide sufficient information about his procedures to reconcile the differences.

[15] The Treasury's *Blueprints for tax reform*, in describing how a tax that would not distort savings and investment decisions might be implemented, recommended using a combination of these two procedures, giving taxpayers the discretion in most cases concerning the procedure to be used.

[16] In addition, we eliminate the depletion deduction, as would occur under a cash-flow tax.

[17] Under our approach, real assets would be taxed based on their cash flow, but any cash flow from financial assets would be tax exempt. This approach corresponded to the R-base described in the Meade Committee report. Under this type of tax change, there is no important windfall to owners of existing capital, since they continue to face the same tax rate on future income, and there is no change in the taxation of pure profits or any important change in the allocation of risk between investors and the government.

deductions and interest deductions by a deduction equal to the amount of new corporate investment that occurred in 1983 and to eliminate the investment tax credit. A variety of other changes would also be called for in shifting to a cash-flow tax. In particular, expenditures that are amortized should be expensed the same as for depreciable assets. Expenditures on inventories should also be expensed rather than having a deduction made when goods are taken out of inventory. In addition, the depletion deduction should be eliminated. Finally, we eliminate the tax on dividend income and capital gains received by corporations.[18]

On net, we find that under a cash-flow corporate tax, taxable corporate income of nonfinancial corporations would *increase* by $26.8 billion—interest deductions of $96.6 billion would be eliminated, but this change would be mostly offset by allowing expensing rather than depreciation of new investments and by eliminating any tax on financial income. Based on an effective marginal corporate tax rate of 0.318, tax payments by these companies would rise by $8.5 billion. When we also eliminate the investment tax credit and take into account likely changes in foreign tax credits,[19] tax revenue from nonfinancial corporations goes up by $20.8 billion. We further assume that when income from all financial assets is made tax exempt, financial institutions would no longer owe any tax. In 1983, financial institutions paid $7.1 billion in taxes. Therefore, when we take into account the loss of this tax revenue from financial institutions, we forecast that aggregate corporate tax payments would rise by $13.7 billion.

Considering both the corporate and individual taxes, adopting this modified consumption tax leads to a fall in tax revenue of $1.5 billion. This is in contrast to a revenue rise of $17.0 billion if the only change enacted were to tax real rather than nominal interest, a change pushing the tax system much closer to a comprehensive income tax. Note, though, that these calculations assume that the figures reported on the tax returns do not change, whether due to behavioral responses, price changes, or changes in individual income from equity reflecting the corporate tax changes; the calculations also ignore the effect of a drop in the market

---

[18] A detailed description of our procedure is provided in the appendix.

[19] Historically, U.S. operations abroad have paid little or no taxes upon the repatriation of earnings because enough foreign taxes had been paid on these earnings that the foreign tax credit virtually completely offset any taxes due. We make the conservative assumption that this would continue to be true, even after these tax changes are made, implying that the foreign tax credit should increase to offset any extra taxes due on foreign source income. Since we have no direct data on the size of foreign source income, we assume simply that the foreign tax credit offsets the same percentage of the forecasted change in tax revenue that it does of aggregate tax revenue (precredits) prior to the tax change. Taking this correction into account, we find that corporate tax revenue (precredits) would change by only $6.7 billion rather than by $8.5 billion.

interest rate on government interest payments. Addressing these issues is the objective of the next section.

4. IMPLICATIONS OF PRICE AND BEHAVIORAL RESPONSES TO TAX CHANGES

Contrary to the maintained assumption of the previous section, we believe that if either policy were implemented there would be important shifts in portfolios and in rates of return. Furthermore, we have not yet taken into account the losses to individuals arising from the change in corporate tax payments. In this section, we briefly discuss and present some preliminary estimates of how the results in section 3 would change when some of these complications are taken into account.

4.1 Incidence of the Increase in Corporate Tax Payments

In our analysis in section 3 of the distributional impact of these two tax changes, we ignored any impact of changes in corporate tax payments on individuals' pretax income, and the secondary implications of any changes in pretax income on individual tax payments. Since the incidence of the corporate tax is heavily debated, there is no single agreed way to proceed. We adopted the natural starting point of assuming that the losses from these extra corporate taxes are borne by individuals in proportion to their ownership of equity. Since we do not observe asset holdings in the Treasury's file of income tax returns, we also assume that the value of the corporate equity owned by an individual is proportional to his or her dividend income.[20,21]

These changes in equity income are taxable only to the extent that they are received by individuals directly and take the form of dividends or realized capital gains. When we allocate the drop in corporate after-tax income to individuals in proportion to their dividends, we assume that the fraction of this drop in after-tax income that is reflected directly in lower-dividend receipts equals the observed aggregate ratio of dividend income

---

[20] To the extent that the dividend-price ratio is lower on the equity owned by higher-tax-bracket individuals, our procedure attributes too little of the burden of the increased corporate tax payments to these higher-tax-bracket individuals.

[21] Not all dividends are received by individuals and reported on their tax returns. Pension funds, in particular, are large holders of corporate equity. We assume for simplicity that these pension funds are entirely defined-benefit plans, so any changes in their income are borne by corporations, and so by equity owners, rather than by pension recipients. In attributing all the increased corporate taxes to individual equity holders, however, we ignore other nontaxable owners of equity, for example, foreigners and nonprofit institutions.

TABLE 5
Changes in Aggregate Income and Taxes due to Personal and Corporate Tax Changes
(millions of 1983 dollars)

Labor income group	Policy 1			Policy 2		
	Change in total tax liability	Change in pretax income	Change in after-tax income	Change in total tax liability	Change in pretax income	Change in after-tax income
<20K	−1,278	−2,223	−945	−7,156	−2,475	4,681
20K–40K	3,430	−1,046	−4,476	6,150	−1,165	−7,315
40K–70K	4,235	−979	−5,214	7,755	−1,090	−8,845
70K–100K	1,309	−442	−1,751	1,465	−492	−1,957
>100K	2,194	−1,012	−3,206	−1,044	−1,127	−83
>Age 65	−6,832	−6,517	315	−22,086	−7,256	14,830
Depend.	−119	−90	29	−329	−100	229
Total	2,938	−12,309	−15,247	−15,245	−13,705	1,540

1. Policy 1 involves reducing all interest income and deductions by 40 percent.

2. Policy 2 involves eliminating all interest and capital income and deductions (columns 3,4,5,8, and 14 in Table 1 are zeroed out).

of individuals to corporate after-tax profits.[22] The remaining extra corporate tax payments should show up as reduced capital gains to shareholders. We assume arbitrarily that the ratio of realized capital gains to accrued capital gains is 1/4, resulting in an effective accrual-equivalent tax rate on capital gains of 10 percent of the individual's ordinary tax rate.[23]

Tables 5 and 6 take account of our attempt to allocate the changes in corporate tax payments to individuals. Here, we report not only the changes in individual tax payments, which now reflect the changes in dividend income and realized capital gains caused by the higher corporate

[22] According to the *1986 economic report of the president*, 1983 corporate profits after tax, with inventory valuation and capital consumption adjustments, were $136.8 billion, and dividend receipts reported on individual income tax returns totaled $50.4 billion. We assumed that the drop in taxable dividends equaled 36.8 percent (=100×50.4/136.8) of any extra corporate tax payments.

[23] The 1/4 ratio could be obtained, for example, by assuming that half of capital gains escapes taxation by being passed along upon the death of the recipient, and that the effective realization rate is further halved by the discretion shareholders have to postpone realizing capital gains, perhaps to years with lower tax rates, and to hasten realizing capital losses. Because only 40 percent of long-term capital gains were taxable upon realization in 1983, the accrual-equivalent tax rate is (0.25)(0.40), or one-tenth of the ordinary tax rate.

TABLE 6
Changes in Income and Taxes Per Return due to Personal and Corporate Tax Changes
(1983 dollars)

Labor income group	Policy 1			Policy 2		
	Change in total tax liability	Change in pretax income	Change in after-tax income	Change in total tax liability	Change in pretax income	Change in after-tax income
<20K	−25	−44	−19	−143	−49	94
20K–40K	144	−44	−188	258	−49	−307
40K–70K	522	−121	−643	956	−135	−1,091
70K–100K	1,273	−430	−1,703	1,424	−479	−1,903
>100K	3,731	−1,721	−5,452	−1,775	−1,916	−141
>Age 65	−608	−580	28	−1,965	−646	1,319
Depend.	−130	−99	31	−360	−110	250
Total	30	−128	−158	−159	−143	16

1. Policy 1 involves reducing all interest income and deductions by 40 percent.
2. Policy 2 involves eliminating all interest and capital income and deductions (columns 3,4,5,8, and 14 in Table 1 are zeroed out).

tax payments, but also the changes in pretax income of individuals arising from the drop in their dividend income and capital gains, whether realized or unrealized. The net changes in their after-tax income under the two policy experiments are reported in columns 3 and 6, respectively. Under the tax on real rather than nominal interest income, tax payments fall relative to what was reported in Tables 3–4, since dividend and capital gains income has dropped for all income groups. In aggregate, tax revenue is now forecasted to go up by $2.9 billion rather than by $4.7 billion, as reported earlier. Since, pretax income has fallen in aggregate by the $12.3 billion more that would be paid in corporate taxes, however, we now find that all income groups except the elderly and dependents suffer a drop in after-tax income, with the size of the drop increasing with income.

Under the modified cash-flow tax, the fall in dividend and capital gains income has no effect on tax payments since, under this tax, dividend and capital gains are not taxable anyway. But pretax income falls by the $13.7 billion more paid in corporate taxes. In aggregate, individuals now gain only $1.5 billion. But this aggregate gain is divided very unevenly. In particular, the elderly gain $14.8 billion, dependents and the lowest income group gain, but the intermediate income groups lose.

4.2 The Effects of Changes in the Market Interest Rate

Implementing these policies will undoubtedly affect the equilibrium pretax rates of return earned on various assets and result in changes in individual behavior. Any serious attempt to forecast these effects would require an elaborate general equilibrium model, which we do not attempt to construct here.[24] Both types of complications must be considered when estimating the revenue effects of a tax change, but when focusing on the gains or losses to individuals from a tax change, behavioral changes can be ignored, at least when the tax change is small.[25] For example, before the tax change, the individual might borrow to buy more lightly taxed equity until the implicit cost of bearing yet more risk from such a highly leveraged position just offsets the tax savings from further arbitrage. After a small tax change, the individual may modify his or her portfolio slightly, but the gains and losses from doing so still almost exactly offset each other. We therefore focus on the effects of price changes, particularly on the implications of changes in the market interest rate.[26]

What would be a plausible response of the market interest rate if only real interest income were subject to tax? In the new equilibrium, the magnitude of the fall in the interest rate would just balance the decreased demand for loans by investors with above-average tax rates (whose after-tax cost of borrowing rises) and the decreased demand for bonds by foreigners and by investors with below-average tax rates (for both of whom the lower rate of tax does not fully compensate for the fall in the interest rate.) We assume, arbitrarily, that an investor in the 20 percent tax bracket will be left indifferent to the combined effects of the change in the market interest rate and the change in the tax law—those in higher tax brackets will then face higher net borrowing costs, and those in lower tax brackets will face a lower net return on bonds. This implies that if the initial nominal

---

[24] See Slemrod (1983) for a general equilibrium model with endogenous portfolio decisions. In the construction of such a model, it would be important to take into account the effects of these tax changes on international capital flows. In particular, when interest is taxed less heavily, domestic investors would tend to buy more bonds from foreigners in exchange for other assets.

[25] This useful result from economic theory is often referred to as the envelope condition.

[26] In general, all rates of return will change in response to either policy change. However, it would be difficult to forecast the direction of change in other rates of return, let alone come up with a reasonable guess of the size of the change. For example, it is difficult to forecast the effects of either policy change on aggregate savings, since incentives to save go up for those in high tax brackets, but down for those in low tax brackets, so it is unclear whether aggregate investment goes up or down. Similarly, changes in the relative rates of return earned by different types of capital depend on differences in the degree to which different types of capital are affected by these tax changes. We have chosen in this study to focus only on the effects of changes in interest rates.

interest rate is r, the interest rate that must prevail when real interest is taxable, which we denote by r^1, will satisfy $(1-0.2)r = [1-(0.2)(0.6)]r^1$. Hence $r^1/r = 0.909$, implying a fall in the nominal interest rate of 9.1 percent. Similarly, if a modified cash-flow tax were introduced, under this assumption the new market interest rate, r^2, would satisfy $(1-0.2)r = r^2$, implying a 20 percent fall in the market interest rate.

To the degree that the interest rate falls, the government will pay less in interest on its debt. In particular, according to the *1986 economic report of the president*, the federal government paid on net $94.3 billion in interest. If the nominal interest rate were to fall by 9.1 percent, the government would save $8.6 billion in interest payments; if it fell 20 percent, the savings would be $18.9 billion.[27]

In addition, however, interest income and deductions shrink further on individual and corporate tax forms. Under the first tax proposal, this fall in the market interest rate would cause tax revenue to rise just as it did when we lowered taxable interest income and deductions by statute. In particular, the interest deductions of nonfinancial corporations would shrink by 9.1 percent pretax. Since only 60 percent of these payments are deductible, the tax payments of these corporations would rise by $(0.318)[96.6 - (0.6)(0.909)(96.6)] = \$14.0$ billion, instead of by $12.3 billion. Since these corporations save $(0.091)(96.6) = \$8.8$ billion in interest payments, however, the net drop in their after-tax income is only $5.2 billion.[28] However, financial corporations receive on net $116.5 billion in interest income. If the interest rate falls by 9.1 percent while, by assumption, their tax payments remain unchanged, then their after-tax income falls by $10.6 billion. Therefore, the after-tax income of the corporate sector as a whole falls by $15.8 billion.

Under the modified cash-flow tax, this fall in the market interest rate would not affect corporate tax payments since interest payments are not deductible. However, interest payments by nonfinancial corporations would fall by $(0.2)(\$96.6) = \$19.3$ billion. Since their taxes are still forecasted to rise by $20.8 billion, their after-tax income should fall by $1.5 billion. Applying this same procedure to financial corporations would imply that

---

[27] We ignore here the fact that some of the existing government debt is noncallable long-term debt, implying that the fall in the market interest rate will not immediately save the government money on this part of its existing debt. Our intention is to capture the effect of the tax change in a representative future year rather than to measure the impact of the tax change in the year of enactment.

[28] As with government debt, some corporation debt is long term, implying to that extent that a fall in the market interest rate may not affect interest payments. However, since much of corporate long-term debt is either at a floating interest rate or callable, the fall in the interest rate should reduce corporate interest payments on all its existing debt very quickly.

TABLE 7
Changes in Aggregate Income and Taxes Due to Personal Tax, Corporate Tax, and Interest Rate Changes
(millions of 1983 dollars)

Labor income group	Policy 1			Policy 2		
	Change in total tax liability	Change in pretax income	Change in after-tax income	Change in total tax liability	Change in pretax income	Change in after-tax income
<20K	−1,508	−5,208	−3,700	−7,156	−8,353	−1,197
20K–40K	3,870	548	−3,322	6,150	2,655	−3,495
40K–70K	4,788	735	−4,053	7,755	2,976	−4,779
70K–100K	1,462	−83	−1,545	1,465	432	−1,033
>100K	2,431	−630	−3,061	−1,044	26	1,070
>Age 65	−7,991	−18,218	−10,227	−22,086	−30,958	−8,872
Depend.	−135	−380	−245	−329	−710	−381
Total	2,917	−23,237	−26,154	−15,245	−33,932	−18,687

1. Policy 1 involves reducing all interest income and deductions by 40 percent.
2. Policy 2 involves eliminating all interest and capital income and deductions (columns 3,4,5,8, and 14 in Table 1 are zeroed out).

their before-tax profits would fall by 20 percent of their net interest income of $116.5 billion, or by $23.3 billion. Since their tax payments of $7.1 billion are eliminated under this tax change, the after-tax income of financial corporations falls by $16.2 billion, implying that the after-tax income of the corporate sector as a whole falls by $17.7 billion.

Finally, we calculate how individual tax payments and after-tax income change, now taking into account the drop in the market interest rate. To do this, we take into account the drop in interest receipts and payments reported on individual income tax returns, the change in income from equity due to the increase in corporate taxes, and the implications for individuals of the drop in interest income on any nontaxable holdings of bonds in corporate and state and local pension funds, Keogh and IRA accounts, and the drop in interest income on taxable bonds held directly by state and local governments. The assumptions we make in allocating these changes in interest income to individuals are described in the appendix.

The resulting changes in individual tax payments and after-tax income are reported in Tables 7–8. Here, we find that under the first policy, as a result of the fall in dividends and the increase in state and local taxes, to cover the fall in interest earnings on taxable bonds held by state and local governments, personal tax payments rise by only $2.9 billion. However,

TABLE 7a
Changes in Aggregate Income and Taxes Due to Personal Tax, Corporate Tax, and Interest Rate Changes
(millions of 1983 dollars)

Adjusted gross income	Policy 1			Policy 2		
	Change in total tax liability	Change in pretax income	Change in after-tax income	Change in total tax liability	Change in pretax income	Change in after-tax income
<10K	−500	−2,596	−2,096	−625	−4,631	−4,006
10K–20K	−1,239	−4,591	−3,352	−2,123	−8,394	−6,271
20K–30K	264	−2,656	−2,920	360	−4,198	−4,558
30K–40K	1,389	−2,007	−3,396	2,393	−2,496	−4,889
40K–75K	2,641	−3,237	−5,878	3,324	−3,669	−6,993
75K–100K	279	−1,438	−1,717	−1,128	−1,866	−738
>100K	83	−6,713	−6,796	−17,444	−8,678	8,766
Total	2,917	−23,237	−26,154	−15,245	−33,932	−18,687

1. Policy 1 involves reducing all interest income and deductions by 40 percent.
2. Policy 2 involves eliminating all interest and capital income and deductions (columns 3,4,5,8, and 14 in Table 1 are zeroed out).

TABLE 8
Changes in Income and Taxes Per Return Due to Personal Tax, Corporate Tax, and Interest Rate Changes
(1983 dollars)

Labor income group	Policy 1			Policy 2		
	Change in total tax liability	Change in pretax income	Change in after-tax income	Change in total tax liability	Change in pretax income	Change in after-tax income
<20K	−30	−104	−74	−143	−166	−23
20K–40K	162	23	−139	258	111	−147
40K–70K	590	90	−500	956	366	−590
70K–100K	1,421	−81	−1,502	1,424	420	−1,004
>100K	4,133	−1,071	−5,204	−1,775	43	1,818
>Age 65	−711	−1,621	−910	−1,965	−2,755	−790
Depend.	−148	−417	−269	−360	−778	−418
Total	30	−242	−272	−159	−354	−195

1. Policy 1 involves reducing all interest income and deductions by 40 percent.
2. Policy 2 involves eliminating all interest and capital income and deductions (columns 3,4,5,8, and 14 in Table 1 are zeroed out).

TABLE 8a
Changes in Income and Taxes Per Return Due to Personal Tax, Corporate Tax, and Interest Rate Changes
(1983 dollars)

	Policy 1			Policy 2		
Adjusted gross income	Change in total tax liability	Change in pretax income	Change in after-tax income	Change in total tax liability	Change in pretax income	Change in after-tax income
<10K	−15	−76	−61	−18	−136	−118
10K–20K	−51	−188	−137	−88	−344	−256
20K–30K	16	−161	−177	22	−255	−277
30K–40K	133	−192	−325	230	−239	−469
40K–75K	304	−372	−676	383	−422	−805
75K–100K	347	−1,789	−2,136	−1,404	−2,322	918
>100K	100	−8,111	−8,211	−21,077	−10,486	10,591
Total	30	−242	−272	−159	−354	−195

1. Policy 1 involves reducing all interest income and deductions by 40 percent.
2. Policy 2 involves eliminating all interest and capital income and deductions (columns 3,4,5,8, and 14 in Table 1 are zeroed out).

individuals also suffer a fall of $23.2 in pretax income, implying that their after-tax income falls by $26.1 billion. By construction, this loss equals the gains to the government and to foreigners—the government now receives $14.0 billion more in corporate tax revenue, $2.9 billion more in personal tax revenue, and saves $8.6 billion in interest payments on its debt, for a total revenue gain of $25.5 billion; foreigners now pay $0.5 billion less in interest on their net debt to U.S. residents.[29] (To the extent that behavioral changes result in an efficiency gain, ignored in deriving these numbers, the losses to individuals would be less than the revenue gains to the government and foreigners.) We still find that all income groups share in this loss, with the burden increasing quickly across labor income groups.

Under the modified cash-flow tax, personal tax payments still fall by $15.2 billion—the change in interest or dividend income does not affect tax liabilities under this tax, though there is a minor change in state and local tax deductions for itemizers. However, pretax income falls by $33.9 billion, and after-tax income falls by $18.7 billion. As in the previous case, this fall reflects the gains to the government and foreigners. The government now receives $13.7 billion in extra corporate taxes, loses $15.2 billion in personal

[29] In each of the examples, rounding error leads to minor variation in the figures.

taxes, but saves $18.9 billion in interest payments, for a net revenue gain of $17.4 billion; foreigners save $1.2 billion in interest payments to U.S. residents. Our figures suggest that all income groups share in this loss except for the highest income group, which gains substantially from the tax change since it has high capital income that is now exempt from tax. Many writers have forecast large efficiency gains from a move to a cash-flow tax, however, and these figures ignore such efficiency gains.

Tables 7a and 8a provide the same information but are divided among income groups based on initial AGI. These figures are closely consistent with those in Tables 7–8.

4.3 Behavioral Responses

Either of these tax changes should also result in a variety of behavioral responses of both individuals and corporations. When forecasting the revenue effects of these tax changes, one must take these behavioral responses into account.[30]

Under our modified cash-flow tax, however, these behavioral responses will have little or no effect on tax revenue. Under this tax, financial assets are tax exempt, so who owns how much in financial assets has no implications directly for tax revenue. In addition, investments in real assets may change the timing of tax payments, but at least marginal investments should have no impact on the present value of tax revenue under a cash-flow tax. Any capital deepening should raise the wage rate and, therefore, taxable labor income and tax revenue, but only after enough time has passed to allow for significant capital accumulation.

When real rather than nominal interest income is taxed, behavioral responses would likely cause a further rise in tax revenue. To begin with, under this tax change, the portfolio composition of investors should change so as to raise tax revenue. Higher-tax-bracket individuals would reduce their debt to both foreigners and low-tax-bracket investors, and would sell in exchange less heavily taxed assets to these other investors. By domestic investors as a group owning more heavily taxed bonds, shifting some lightly taxed assets to foreigners, tax revenue rises.[31] In addition, rearranging the portfolios of domestic investors, shifting heavily taxed bonds to high-tax-bracket investors and less taxed assets to low-tax-bracket investors, causes tax revenue to rise further.

---

[30] Although we have argued above that, at least to a first approximation, the welfare implications of behavioral responses can be ignored, their revenue implications need to be taken into account.

[31] This type of international portfolio response to a domestic tax change is examined at greater length in Gordon (1986).

The composition of the capital stock should also change so as to raise tax revenue. Capital should shift out of housing and other lightly taxed assets (including tax shelters) purchased by those in high tax brackets, due to the rise in their opportunity cost of funds, and into a broader range of more heavily taxed assets preferred by those in lower tax brackets, causing a further rise in tax revenue.

The effects of this tax change on the aggregate rate of savings and capital accumulation is less clear. Higher-tax-bracket individuals would now earn a higher after-tax rate of return on bonds, so they would have an increased incentive to save; conversely lower-tax-bracket individuals would face a reduced incentive to save. Aggregate effects are unclear. If the interest rate falls by only 9.1 percent, as we have arbitrarily assumed, then investment incentives of corporations and other higher-tax-bracket investors would fall slightly, but this inference would reverse if the fall in the interest rate were slightly larger.

In addition, the effects of given changes in savings and investment on tax revenue may be small, at least in the short run. We find here that a modified cash-flow tax, in which savings and investment decisions are totally tax exempt at the margin, would collect $17.4 billion more revenue than the existing tax system, thus suggesting that savings and investment are now on average slightly subsidized. If we were to modify the existing tax system by taxing real rather than nominal interest income, then under this revised tax system savings and investment may on average be very slightly taxed; we forecast slightly higher tax revenue when this policy is enacted than when the modified cash-flow tax is enacted. However, since the average tax rate on savings and investment seems to be so small, changes in savings and investment rates should have little effect on tax revenue.

5. EFFICIENCY EFFECTS OF CHANGES IN CAPITAL TAXATION

Either of the policy changes we consider will result in behavioral changes that are likely to have a beneficial effect on the efficiency of the economy. By design, the second policy change eliminates all distortions to savings and investment decisions, whereas the first change reduces the tax rate on the most heavily taxed asset toward the effective tax rates on other assets. These efficiency gains would either improve government revenue further or reduce the net loss to individuals. We do not attempt, however, to estimate the size or incidence of these efficiency gains.

Either policy change should cause an improvement in how risk is allocated among individuals. The current tax system causes the portfolios of high-tax individuals to feature relatively risky claims on real capital and causes the portfolios of low-tax individuals to contain mostly relatively riskless interest-bearing securities. The result is that market risk is borne more heavily by upper-income individuals than is efficient. Taxing only real interest will induce a more efficient spreading of risk by lessening the tax distortions to portfolio composition. Abolishing all taxation of capital income will completely eliminate tax-induced distortions in risk-bearing.

Either policy change would also probably improve the sectoral allocation of real capital. Although our shift to a tax on real rather than nominal interest income still leaves in place various distortions to the composition of capital, it lowers the attractiveness of various tax-sheltered activities. The shift to a modified cash-flow tax eliminates any distortions to the allocation of capital.[32]

Assessing the intertemporal efficiency implications of these tax policies requires two steps: first, to understand how they affect the incentive to postpone consumption until the future; second, to understand whether such incentive changes are desirable. We leave the second step, which has been central to the academic debate on the comprehensive versus consumption tax, aside to focus on the first.

Both policy changes reduce the tax rates on various forms of capital income, suggesting that at the initial interest rate there is an increased incentive to save by individuals but a decrease in the incentive to invest due to the rise in the opportunity cost of funds. As a result, the interest rate has to fall to bring investment and savings (plus net capital inflows from abroad) back into equality. Since in equilibrium the after-tax interest rate will fall for those in low tax brackets and rise for those in high tax brackets, effects on savings and direct investments, in owner-occupied housing, for example, will differ across income groups. Whether, in aggregate, investment rises or falls depends on the interest elasticity of savings plus international capital flows relative to that of investment. At this point, the empirical evidence is not adequate to allow any good forecast.

How might savings and investment increase as a result of changes in the tax treatment of capital income that raise government revenue? One part of the answer lies in distinguishing the average return on a taxpayer's portfolio from the marginal return to an additional dollar of savings. That these measures may be different is best illustrated by an example. Consider

---

[32] We have argued that under a cash-flow tax, the present value of tax revenue from a marginal investment is zero. As a result, a cash-flow tax should not distort savings or investment decisions. This result assumes, however, that the individual's tax rate is constant over time. When the individual's tax rate changes over time, there will still be some distortion to savings and investment decisions.

a high-tax-bracket taxpayer in an inflationary environment. The real after-tax return on bonds, and therefore the real cost of borrowing, may very well be negative. Suppose the taxpayer can borrow to buy equity until, at the margin, the higher expected return on equity is just offset by the implicit extra cost of holding an even riskier portfolio. Then, when this individual considers saving more, the available return on equity, taking into account the extra risk-bearing cost, just equals the available after-tax real rate of return on bonds. Given taxes on nominal interest income, this net return can be very low even though the average return on the individual's portfolio, ignoring the costs of risk bearing, can be very high. Through borrowing to buy equity, this taxpayer gains on inframarginal arbitrage and is left indifferent at the margin, whereas the arbitrage results in a loss of tax revenue. In this context, cutting the tax rate on interest income increases the cost of borrowing and causes a reduction in the amount of such arbitrage and a gain in tax revenue from this individual. However, in spite of these higher tax payments, the individual faces an increased marginal incentive to save.

The after-tax return on bonds does not reflect the marginal return to saving if arbitrage gains are limited by a borrowing constraint that is tied to wealth. In this case, saving an additional dollar relaxes the borrowing constraint by some amount. The value to the individual of this relaxation of the borrowing constraint should be included in the marginal return to saving.

6. TRANSITION LOSSES

Our calculations of the revenue effects of shifting to a modified cash-flow tax involve replacing depreciation, amortization, depletion, and inventory deductions that took place under the 1983 law with those that would take place under a cash-flow tax. If a cash-flow tax had first been introduced in 1983, however, presumably businesses would have been allowed to continue to take deductions on existing assets, even as they expense new purchases of assets. Only when the allowed deductions on existing assets are fully exhausted, therefore, would tax revenue equal the figure we report. During the transition period, it would be lower as businesses continue to depreciate and amortize old capital at the same time as they expense new capital.

To calculate the net revenue effects of shifting to a cash-flow tax, we therefore should take into account these likely revenue losses during the transition period as well as the revenue gains that occur later. The size of these transition losses would depend on the transition rules built into any piece of legislation. Measuring their importance relative to the long-run revenue gain also depends on assumptions about discount rates and growth rates that determine the relative importance of the one-time revenue loss and the permanent revenue gain.

In the appendix, we provide a rough calculation of the present value of these transition losses compared with the present value of the long-run revenue gains. In doing so, we assume that depreciation and amortization deductions continue on existing capital under the previous formulae and that depletion deductions cease with the enactment of the new law. We also presume that existing stocks of inventories can eventually be written off even as deductions are taken for new additions to inventories, but that the transition rules will delay these write-offs on average for five years.

Under these assumptions, we find that the long-run revenue gains in present value are more than double the revenue losses that occur due to plausible transition rules, though the exact relation will be quite sensitive to a variety of the assumed parameter values. On average, therefore, new savings and investment are slightly subsidized during the time period even if they were taxed at the margin.[33]

7. THE TAX REFORM ACT OF 1986

All of our results describe the effects of possible changes to the tax law of 1983. Of course, since 1983 major changes in the tax law have been enacted. Several features of the Tax Reform Act of 1986 move the tax law in the direction suggested by this study. The findings of this chapter indicate that the gains from the move in this direction may be substantial, and that further moves in that direction are likely to be beneficial as well.

Among the changes made in the tax law that reduce the revenue loss from tax arbitrage are the following:

1. Flattening the dispersion of individual's marginal tax rates and lowering the statutory corporate tax rate.
2. Fully taxing capital gains.[34]
3. Reducing the dispersion in the effective tax rates on real capital by eliminating the investment tax credit and decelerating depreciation allowances for real estate.

---

[33] Although we forecast that tax revenue increases in present value with this shift to a modified cash-flow tax, even taking plausible transition rules into account, however, tax revenue would drop substantially initially as new investments are expensed and old assets continue to be depreciated.

[34] This change in the capital gains tax also reduces the attractiveness of churning assets to increase depreciation deductions. See Gordon, Hines, and Summers (1986) for further discussion.

4. Directly reducing arbitrage opportunities for state and local governments.

In addition, the drop in the nominal interest rate through the reduction in the inflation rate makes tax arbitrage less valuable and less important.

8. CONCLUSIONS

By 1983 the arbitrage possibilities inherent in our system of differentially taxing different individuals and different forms of capital income had grown so large that abandoning entirely any attempt to tax capital income while leaving the tax law otherwise unchanged would have resulted in a slight rise in government revenue. Many have argued that this change would provide an important improvement in efficiency. Here, we find that the main beneficiaries of such a tax change would be those in the highest income group who have very large capital incomes. Our estimates do not take into account, however, the distributional effects of either the increased government revenue or the efficiency gains.

A more modest change in the system of capital income taxation, subjecting real rather than nominal interest to taxation, would lead to an even larger increase in revenue and should also provide an efficiency gain, all at the expense mainly of those in upper tax brackets. (Again, however, our figures ignore the incidence of the extra government revenue or the efficiency gains.) Although our data do not allow us to test it, we also believe that a move to a comprehensive income tax, where all real capital income and not just real interest income is fully taxed, would have similar beneficial effects.

Arbitrage opportunities disappear whenever all forms of capital income are taxed uniformly,[35] whether they are all tax exempt, as under a cash-flow tax, or all subject to the same tax rate as labor income, as under a comprehensive income tax. Our results suggest that, given the tax system that existed in 1983, *any* move toward more uniform tax rates on real capital income would raise revenue and improve efficiency, whether the uniform tax rate is zero, as under a consumption tax, or equal to each individual's tax rate on labor income, as would occur under a comprehensive income tax.

---

[35] Arbitrage opportunities also disappear if everyone is in the same tax bracket—in this case, the relative before-tax rates of return on different assets adjust to equalize all after-tax rates of return.

Appendix

The data available to us on the Treasury's file of individual tax returns did not include all the information necessary to calculate interest income and payments, to calculate cash flow from corporations, to separately identify labor versus capital income, to calculate the ownership pattern of nontaxed interest-bearing assets, and to calculate the likely transition losses were a cash-flow tax enacted. To circumvent these problems with missing data, we used the following procedures.

Calculation of Interest Income and Payments. The tax file includes interest income reported on form 1040 or Schedule B and itemized interest deductions reported on Schedule A. However, individuals can also report interest deductions or receipts in a variety of other places in their tax returns. In each case, we used information from the published *Statistics of income* data to estimate the likely size of these figures for each tax return. The procedures used varied by tax form.

For example, net partnership income is reported on the tax file data set, but there is no detail provided about the various sources of income or deductions used in calculating net income. However, in the *1983 statistics of income* are reported aggregate figures for interest income, interest deductions, and net income for partnerships in that year. The data are reported separately for partnerships with positive net income and negative net income. To estimate net interest, we first calculated the ratio of aggregate net interest received to aggregate net income separately for partnerships with net profits and losses; we then multiplied the reported net partnership income by the appropriate ratio. Because the data for 1983 report only the sum of interest and dividend income, and not interest separately, we calculated interest income as a fraction of total interest and dividends in 1981 (when they were reported separately), then multiplied the 1983 figure by this ratio to produce an estimate of interest income in that year.

In addition, net income reported for partnerships from rental property and from farming are themselves taken from separate schedules filed by the partnership. Underlying these net income figures are various income and deduction figures, including interest deductions, which are not reported in the *Statistics of income* data. In these cases, we assume that these interest deductions are the same fraction of net income that we estimate for rental property and farms using the procedures described below.

Finally, partnerships report some net income and losses from other partnerships and fiduciaries. We assumed that the ratio of net interest payments to net income was the same for this income as for other partnership income, and we solved algebraically for the appropriate ratios.

The same method was used for estates and trusts, which received income from partnerships and real estate.

The same basic procedure was followed for Subchapter S corporations, using the *1983 statistics of income* data on corporate returns of active small business corporations, and the 1982 data on the breakdown of interest versus dividend income; here, however, we had one ratio for all Subchapter S corporations rather than separate ratios for those with profits versus losses. For Schedule C income, the same procedure was employed, using data reported in the *1981 statistics of income for sole proprietorship returns* for nonfarm sole proprietorships. For Schedule E rental income, we used the data on interest payments and net income in 1983 from partnerships in a subset of the real estate industry including "operators and lessors of buildings" and "lessors, other than buildings." For estates and trusts, we used information from the *Statistics of income* data for 1982 on the fraction of estate and trust income coming from interest income. Finally, for Schedule F income, we used information from the *1980 Statistics of income* for sole proprietorships in farming.

Calculation of Labor Income. The text uses labor income as a classifier for presenting the distributional impact of taxation and as the tax base for policy simulation. Our procedure for calculating labor income with the data base available to us is described below.

We defined labor income to equal the sum of wages and salaries, unemployment compensation, and pension income (since this is a fringe benefit omitted from the wage and salary figures) minus employee business expenses. The principal conceptual problem arises in the case of self-employed individuals, where the reported income from self-employment includes a return to both labor and capital. Income from self-employment could be reported on Schedules C, E, or F. In these cases, we calculated the income from self-employment as it would be under a cash-flow tax. In particular, we estimated the amount of new investment that year and allowed this amount as an expense, but disallowed depreciation and net interest deductions.

This approach provides a tax base that does not distort new investment decisions. However, it provides only a rough measure of labor income. To measure labor income directly, we would like to subtract an estimate of capital income from total income. If the complicated tax treatment of a particular type of capital in 1983 can be summarized by an equivalent tax on economic income at some rate τ, then (by construction) the gross income earned by that capital would equal $[r/(1 - \tau) + \delta]K$, where δ is the economic depreciation rate, r is the real opportunity cost of funds, and K is the real capital stock.[36] In contrast, if the real capital stock is growing at some constant rate g, then new investment expenditures would equal $(g + \delta)K$. Our approach therefore provides a good approximation of labor income to the degree that $g \approx r/(1 - \tau)$. Given the widely varying approaches used in estimating the real opportunity cost of funds, and the widely varying estimates of the effective tax rate on capital, it is difficult to judge the quality of this approximation.[37]

The only data in the tax file helpful for estimating cash flow is net income from each of these schedules. We proceeded by estimating from aggregate data the ratio of the cash flow to the net income for each type of business; we then multiplied each net income figure in the tax files by the appropriate aggregate ratio. In measuring cash flow, we started with net income, then eliminated interest, depletion, and depreciation deductions, and replaced them with a deduction for the estimated value of new investments.

The key problem is estimating new investment expenditures. The best procedure we came up with was to assume that the ratio for corporations of new investment expenditures to depreciation deductions would have the same value for noncorporate firms. The general strategy was to estimate investment expenditures for each group of noncorporate firms by the depreciation deductions taken by this group of firms multiplied by the ratio in the previous sentence. In fact, we constructed two ratios: one for corporations as a whole, and one for corporations in the real estate industry. We used the second ratio to estimate the investment expenditures for noncorporate real estate firms and for partnerships with losses, since most of these losses arose from firms in the real estate industry. The first ratio was used in all other cases.

This procedure should slightly overestimate investment expenditures to the degree that noncorporate firms expense investment expenditures more frequently under section 176, or overestimate their depreciation deductions, as suggested by the figure for misreporting appearing in Table 8.10 in the July 1987 *Survey of current business*. When we used our procedure to forecast total new noncorporate investment from the net income figures reported in the tax returns, our estimate was about 20 percent larger than the investment figure reported by NIPA for noncorporate and farm capital expenditures. Therefore, our procedure should slightly overestimate the

---

[36] See, for example, Auerbach (1983) for a use of this approach in defining the effective income tax rate.

[37] A clear difference arises in the case of land, since there is no new investment in land, but investments in land earn a return.

revenue loss from shifting to taxing cash flow under the personal income tax.

In defining labor income for partnerships, we then constructed ratios of cash flow to net income from the aggregate data, doing this separately for partnerships with profits or losses, and we multiplied the net income figures reported in the individual tax returns by the appropriate ratio to estimate the labor income from these partnerships. One problem encountered was that the *1983 statistics of income for partnerships* reported depreciation deductions only for all partnerships, for all real estate partnerships, and for all farm partnerships without differentiating between partnerships with profits or losses. We therefore used balance sheet data from 1982 for firms with profits and losses,[38] along with this information on total depreciation deductions, to estimate the depreciation deductions separately for firms with profits and losses.[39]

For rental income from Schedule E, we used the same procedure described earlier to calculate the ratio of new investment expenditures minus depreciation and depletion deductions to net income, but we restricted the procedure to data on real estate partnerships. For Subchapter S corporations, the equivalent procedure was used based on the data reported in the *1983 statistics of income for corporations*. For Schedule C, we used the ratios of new investment expenditures minus depreciation to net income found for partnerships. Finally, for farms we used the ratios of new investment expenditures minus depreciation to net income found for farm partnerships.

These estimates of labor and capital income for 1983 may not be representative of their normal values, given the severe recession that was occurring in 1983. Under our procedure for dividing observed net income between labor and capital components, any drop in new investment in capital or in inventories in 1983 relative to their normal values will result in an unusually low estimate of capital income, whereas any drop in sales revenue relative to other expenses will result in an unusually low estimate of labor income. It is difficult to judge whether our procedure provides a

---

[38] Balance sheet data were not available for 1983.

[39] In particular, for partnerships in farming and real estate, we assumed that the depreciation deductions in 1983 for firms with profits versus losses would be proportional to the book capital stocks in 1982 for firms with profits versus losses. For partnerships as a whole, we formed an initial forecast for the depreciation deductions for firms with profits versus losses, then divided the observed total depreciation deduction in 1983 in proportion to these two estimates. For firms with losses, our initial forecast equaled the product of the book capital stock in 1982 for these firms and the ratio of depreciation deductions to book value for real estate firms in 1982. (The real estate industry generated a large fraction of total partnership losses.) For firms with profits, our initial estimate equaled the remaining depreciation deductions taken by all firms in 1982.

misleading estimate of the normal percentage breakdown between labor and capital income.

Calculation of the Cash Flow from Corporations. Under the version of a cash-flow tax we consider, real assets are taxed based on their cash flow, but cash flow from financial assets is made tax exempt. In calculating the resulting cash-flow tax base for corporations, we proceeded as follows.

To begin with, we eliminated net interest payments, and net capital gains, from net taxable income. Here, capital gains are measured by capital gains taxable at ordinary rates plus 28/46 percent of capital gains taxable at the alternative rate of 28 percent.[40] In addition, we eliminated net dividend income from taxable income, where net dividend income is defined to equal domestic dividends minus the dividends received deduction minus the public utility dividend paid deduction.[41] We also eliminated depletion allowances from taxable income, since they are not justified by any cash flow.

Next, we replaced depreciation and amortization deductions by a deduction for investment expenditures. Note, however, that, under a cash-flow tax, when used capital is sold from one firm to another, the purchasing firm would deduct the purchase cost of the acquired capital, but the selling firm would be taxed on the entire proceeds from the sale of the capital. As long as both firms faced the same tax rate, the net tax effects would exactly offset. Therefore the cash-flow tax base can be measured either by deducting expenditures on *new* capital and exempting all capital gains or by deducting all investment expenditures but adding the entire proceeds from the sale of used assets into the tax base. We adopted the first approach.

Our measure of new investment expenditures was based on the figure for nonfarm nonfinancial corporate capital expenditures in 1983 reported in the July 1987 *Survey of current business*. However, we eliminated the inventory investment component of this figure, since we deal with inventories separately. In addition, our industry definition included farms but not Subchapter S corporations, so we estimated new investment within our industry definition by multiplying the reported figure by the ratio of depreciation deductions taken within our set of industries to depreciation deductions reported in nonfarm nonfinancial industries. Finally, the set of capital investments included in the published figure differs slightly from

---

[40] Capital gains from the sale of financial assets but not real assets would be eliminated under our definition of the tax base. However, as we describe later, since we measure investment expenditures by expenditures only on *new* investment, we need to eliminate capital gains from the sale of real assets from the tax base as well.

[41] Under a cash-flow tax, either this income is tax exempt or it is taxable but the firm paying the dividend gets to deduct this payment; we adopted the first approach.

TABLE A1
Changes in Corporate Taxable Income in 1983 under a Cash-Flow Tax
(billions of 1983 dollars)

+ Net interest payments	96.6
+ Depletion allowances	7.4
+ Depreciation deductions	218.0
+ Amortization	3.4
− New investment expenditures	259.0
− Net dividend income	7.7
− Net capital gains	17.3
− Inventory expend. − deduct.	14.6
= Net change in taxable income	26.8
+ Investment tax credit (ITC)	15.2
− Tax on recapture of ITC	1.1
= Net ITC payments	14.1

the set that is depreciated on the tax forms. For example, investments in foreign branches are depreciated but are omitted from the NIPA figure, whereas various mining expenditures are not depreciated but do appear in the NIPA figure. To make this correction, we multiplied the published figure by the ratio of corporate depreciation deductions on the tax forms to the NIPA figure for depreciation, before adjustment, as reported in Table 8.10 in the July 1987 *Survey of current business*. This yielded an estimate of new investment of $259.0, compared with the published figure of $274.9.

Our final step in developing a measure of cash flow dealt with the treatment of inventories. Under a cash-flow tax, expenditures on inventories would be deductible, but under the existing tax some valuation of withdrawals from inventory is deductible. These two differ on average because withdrawals from inventory are priced using older prices, and because of any growth in the size of inventories, due to purchases exceeding withdrawals. The difference between expenditures on inventories and accounting withdrawals in a year equals the change in the inventory balance sheet during that year. We therefore allowed the difference between the balance sheet inventory in 1983 and 1982 as a further deduction.

The resulting changes in taxable income are listed in Table A1. We estimate that net taxable income under a cash-flow tax would be $41.3 billion dollars higher than net taxable income under the 1983 law. In addition, under a cash-flow tax the investment tax credit would be eliminated. Investment tax credits taken in 1983 minus the taxes collected from the recapture of previous tax credit payments equaled $14.1 billion dollars.[42]

Calculation of Implicit Ownership of Nontaxable Interest-Bearing Assets. In the text, we found that the net interest payments of the government and of individuals and corporations as reported in their tax returns totaled $104.8 billion. Since foreigners paid on net $5.9 billion in interest to U.S. residents, U.S. residents must have received in total $110.7 in interest income in one of a variety of forms that do not directly show up as taxable income of individuals or corporations. When analyzing the distributional effects of the two tax changes, taking into account the effects of the resulting drop in the market interest rate, we therefore face the problem of calculating the incidence among different types of individuals of the drop in this nontaxable interest income.

To do this, we first estimate the interest receipts of corporate pensions by extrapolating from 1980 to 1983 the information about the bond holdings of pensions reported in Kotlikoff-Smith (1983), and applying the market interest rate for Aaa bonds in 1983. We forecast that these pension plans received $45.0 billion in interest income in 1983. Of that total, we assume that three-quarters of the income accrues to defined benefit plans and one-quarter to defined contribution plans. (According to Kotlikoff-Smith, participants in defined benefit plans outnumber participants in defined contribution plans by 3 to 1.) For defined benefit plans, we assume that the benefits are indeed defined by the plan, so any change in the earnings received by these plans accrues to corporate shareholders. This change is assigned to individuals in proportion to their dividend receipts and changes their taxable income in the same way as described when we allocated changes in corporate tax payments. The change in interest receipts of defined contribution plans is assumed to be borne by individuals in proportion to their wage and salary income, but does not affect their taxable income.

State and local governments owned $271.8 billion of taxable debt securities in 1983. By assigning market interest rates separately to their holdings of time deposits, government bonds, and mortgages, we estimate their interest income to be $30.0 billion. We assume that a decline in the interest income of state and local governments will be reflected in increased tax levies on individuals. Thus, we increased the state and local tax payments of itemizers proportionately, assuming that the fraction of the tax increase

---

[42] To the degree that firms are unusually constrained by low profits in 1983 from receiving a credit on all qualified investments, this figure will be too low—more unused credits available from 1983 investments will be carried backward or forward and eventually received than have been carried forward into 1983 from past years.

borne by itemizers equals the ratio of the AGI of itemizers to aggregate AGI, which in our sample is 60 percent. The pretax income of nonitemizers is assumed to change in proportion to their federal tax liability, the proportion being chosen to total in aggregate 40 percent of the change in state and local interest income.

The remaining $35.7 billion of net interest income represents a variety of situations, including underreported receipts, receipts of nonfilers, dividends of interest-receiving mutual funds, receipts of nonprofit organizations, and receipts through IRA and Keogh plans. Rather than attempt a detailed assignment of the effects of interest rate changes in each situation, we assumed that the change in interest receipts earned through these sources is borne in proportion to individuals' Schedule B interest receipts and will not be part of taxable income.

Transition Tax Losses under a Cash-Flow Tax versus Long-Run Revenue Gains. We assume that upon enactment of a cash-flow tax, businesses would be allowed to continue to depreciate and amortize existing capital. We therefore attempt to calculate the present value of the tax loss due to these deductions. In addition, we need to calculate the tax loss from the write-off of existing stocks of inventories.

First consider depreciation deductions. Corporate depreciation deductions on existing capital in 1982 were $194.7 billion. We assume for simplicity that nominal investment has been growing smoothly at rate g, a constant percent s of new investment is in structures, the tax depreciation rate on equipment can be approximated by exponential depreciation of 40 percent per year, and tax depreciation of structures can be approximated by exponential depreciation at 10 percent per year.[43] If new investment in 1982 is I, then depreciation deductions that year should satisfy

$$0.1 \int_0^\infty sIe^{-(g+0.1)t} \, dt + 0.4 \int_0^\infty (1-s)Ie^{-(g+0.4)t} \, dt = 194.7.$$

Given estimates of the various parameters, we then solved this equation for I. We set g equal to the nominal growth rate in investment expenditures between 1962 and 1982, which equaled 0.102, and we set s equal to the average fraction of new investment that went into structures during the previous 10 years, which came out to 0.361; together these parameters imply an estimate of I of $283.0 billion, which is quite close to the value of

---

[43] This assumes that the actual law can be well approximated by double declining balance depreciation with lifetimes of five years for equipment and twenty years for structures. Allowed depreciation rates were somewhat slower, but there was a compensating switch to straight-line depreciation.

$259.0 observed in the data. The discounted present value of future depreciation deductions equals[44]

$$0.1 \int_0^\infty e^{-(i+0.1)\tau} \left[e^{-0.05} \int_0^\infty sIe^{-(g+0.1)t} \, dt \right] d\tau$$

$$+ 0.4 \int_0^\infty e^{-(i+0.4)\tau} \left[e^{-0.2} \int_0^\infty (1-s)Ie^{-(g+0.4)t} \, dt \right] d\tau,$$

where i is the nominal discount rate. We set this rate equal to 0.088, using a before-tax nominal longer-term interest rate in 1983 of 0.11 and a tax rate of 0.2. Given this rate, the present value of future depreciation deductions equals $497.6 billion.

In 1982, partnerships and Subchapter S corporations together took depreciation deductions of $38.9 billion, whereas in 1980 proprietorships took $25.8 billion in depreciation. Ignoring changes between 1980 and 1982, we found that total noncorporate depreciation deductions in 1982 were $64.7 billion. Using the same procedure, we forecast that the present value of depreciation deductions on the existing noncorporate capital would be $165.4 billion.

In 1982, corporations claimed $3.3 billion in amortization deductions. If these intangible assets are all depreciated using a straight-line formula over five years, and investment in these assets was equal in the previous five years, then the present value of future amortization deductions on existing intangible capital would be $\Sigma_0^4 (0.8 - 0.2t)3.3/(1 + i)^t$. If $i = 0.88$, this expression equals $6.1 billion. Amortization by noncorporate firms was trivial, so we ignore it.

The stock of corporate inventories at the end of 1982 was $538.1 billion. After a shift to a cash-flow tax, we assume that corporations will be allowed to gradually write off existing inventories at the same time that they are deducting all new purchases of inventories. In particular, we assume that 20 percent of the remaining stock of inventories will be deducted each year, implying that the present value of inventory deductions from existing stocks will be $0.2 \int_0^\infty 538.1 e^{-(0.2+i)t} \, dt$. Given $i = 0.088$, this comes out to $373.7 billion. Similarly, partnerships had an inventory stock of $100.7 billion in 1982. Using the same procedure, we find that the present value of their inventory deductions would be $69.9 billion.

---

[44] The depreciation taken in 1982 equals approximately the integrated amount during the time interval $-.5$ to $.5$. In calculating later depreciation, we therefore start at time $.5$, so aged the capital stock half a year using the terms $e^{-.05}$ and $e^{-.2}$.

Therefore, the transitory tax losses from depreciation, amortization, and inventory deductions would equal $0.318(497.6 + 6.1 + 373.7) + m(165.4 + 69.9)$, where m equals the average marginal tax rate faced by noncorporate firms. Estimating m to be 0.219, we obtain a one-time revenue loss of $329.8 billion.

In contrast, ignoring these transitory losses, we forecast that the revenue gain from this tax change would be $17.4 billion in 1983, and in future years would be larger in nominal terms due to real growth in the economy as well as due to inflation. The discounted present value of these revenue gains would therefore be $\int_0^\infty 17.4 e^{-(i-\pi-\theta)t}\, dt$, where π is the inflation rate and θ is the growth rate of the economy. In 1983, the inflation rate was 0.038 while the average growth rate in real GNP from 1963 to 1983 was 0.028. Together, these figures imply that the present value of revenue gains equals $790.9 billion, which substantially exceeds the one-time revenue loss in the transition to a cash-flow tax.

REFERENCES

Altshuler, Rosanne, and Alan J. Auerbach. 1987. The significance of tax law asymmetries: An empirical investigation. NBER Working Paper no. 2279.

Auerbach, Alan J. 1983. Corporate taxation in the United States. *Brookings Papers on Economic Activity* 2: 451–505.

Gordon, Roger H. 1986. Taxation of investment and savings in a world economy. *American Economic Review*, vol. 76: 1086–102.

Gordon, Roger H., James R. Hines, Jr., and Lawrence H. Summers. 1986. Notes on the tax treatment of structures. NBER Working Paper no. 1896.

Gordon, Roger H., and Joel Slemrod. 1986. An empirical examination of municipal finance decisions. In *Studies in state and local public finance*, ed. Harvey S. Rosen. Chicago: University of Chicago Press.

Kotlikoff, Laurence J., and Daniel Smith. 1983. *Pensions in the American economy*. Chicago: University of Chicago Press.

Meade Committee Report. 1978. *The structure and reform of direct taxation*. London: George Allen & Unwin.

Slemrod, Joel. 1983. A general equilibrium model of taxation with endogenous financial behavior. In *Behavioral simulation methods in tax policy analysis*, ed. Martin S. Feldstein. Chicago: University of Chicago Press.

Steuerle, C. Eugene. 1985. *Taxes, loans, and inflation: How the nation's wealth becomes misallocated*. Washington, D.C.: Brookings Institution.

DID ERTA RAISE THE SHARE OF TAXES PAID BY UPPER-INCOME TAXPAYERS? WILL TRA86 BE A REPEAT?

Lawrence B. Lindsey
Harvard University and NBER

EXECUTIVE SUMMARY

This chapter examines reasons for the rise in the share of taxes paid by upper-income individuals following the passage of the Economic Recovery Tax Act (ERTA) in 1981. It extends this analysis to estimate the potential revenue consequences of behavioral responses by taxpayers to the Tax Reform Act of 1986 (TRA86). Our major findings are as follows:

1. Wage, salary, and professional income constitute an increasingly large share of the income of upper-income taxpayers.
2. Lower tax rates on earnings and capital gains explain most of the redistribution of tax shares following ERTA.
3. Upper-income individuals received a declining share of dividend and interest income in spite of macroeconomic reasons to expect the opposite.
4. Higher tax revenues due to greater wage, salary, and professional income may increase expected tax revenues by as much as $15 billion annually under TRA86.
5. Potential declines in capital gains realizations may lower expected tax revenues by as much as $30 billion annually under TRA86, relative to a nonbehavioral estimation.

6. The combined effect of all responses to TRA86 implies a decline in the share of taxes paid by upper-income taxpayers rather than an increased share expected under nonbehavioral assumptions.

1. INTRODUCTION

The existence of a substantial taxpayer response to the sharp reduction in the top tax rates under the Economic Recovery Tax Act (ERTA) is now generally accepted. In an earlier paper, Lindsey (1987a) estimated that this response was sufficient to generate as much tax revenue with a 50 percent top tax rate as would have been gathered if the earlier 70 percent rate had been maintained. In an investigation using a slightly different methodology, the Congressional Budget Office (1987, p. 501) concluded that:

The data show considerable evidence of a very significant revenue response among taxpayers at the very highest income levels. This finding of a strong revenue response in the top income group holds true for both projection methods and all target years.

On the other hand, there is little evidence of a substantial positive behavioral response to ERTA by lower- and middle-income taxpayers. In fact, the Lindsey and Congressional Budget Office (CBO) studies both noted that the income of lower-income groups was below predicted levels, just as the income of upper-income groups was above predicted levels. A number of explanations of this have been advanced. First, the data show that overall tax rates for many of these groups, including state income and Social Security taxes, showed little decline or actually increased over the period studied.[1] Second, the income tax changes may have had little or no effect on economic growth. The simulation procedures used by Lindsey and CBO took the level of income as constant, implicitly assuming that taxes had no effect on growth. When this is coupled with the upper-income response, a redistribution of income away from lower-income taxpayers results. Third, these groups may not be tax sensitive. This may be due to limited knowledge of tax avoidance possibilities or difficulty in controlling the form of one's compensation and in changing the income from one's portfolio.

For whatever reason, the small response by lower- and moderate-income taxpayers, coupled with the large response by upper-income taxpayers, greatly raised the share of taxes paid by upper-income taxpayers. For

---

[1] Lindsey (1987a) found that the majority of taxpayers had increased marginal tax rates over the period due to increases in Social Security taxes and the effect of bracket creep on federal tax rates.

example, taxpayers earning over $200,000 paid more than 15 percent of total taxes in 1985, but this share would have been only 10 percent in the absence of a behavioral response by taxpayers.

Section 1 considers the magnitude of the revenue response by upper-income taxpayers in the period 1981–1985 as well as the changing nature of these high-income individuals. Often overlooked in the discussion of the behavior of upper-income taxpayers is the fact that the composition of income of these taxpayers has changed in recent years. In particular, the importance of salary and professional income has grown, and the importance of investment income has fallen.

Section 2 considers possible reasons why the behavioral response of upper-income taxpayers, as measured by the CBO and Lindsey studies, was substantially greater than that for lower-income taxpayers. The existence of taxpayer responsiveness to tax rates is well documented in such areas as labor supply, capital gains realizations, and the use of fringe benefits as compensation. We take a detailed look at some of the separate components of income in order to look for explanations of the response of taxpayers to ERTA.

The final section extrapolates the likely impact of TRA86 from these conclusions. That Act resulted in a reduction of the top marginal tax rate from 50 to 33 percent, with an even lower 28 percent rate for very-high-income taxpayers. If the taxpayer response to the latest tax reform parallels that following the 1981 Act, the tax share paid by upper-income individuals will rise further. However, the changes in the 1986 Act were more complex than in 1981. Some rates increased while others decreased. The final section examines the likely revenue consequences of these conflicting rate changes.

2. CHANGES IN REVENUE AND TYPE OF INCOME AT THE TOP

The Economic Recovery Tax Act of 1981 mandated a 23 percent phased reduction in tax rates between 1981 and 1984. The top tax rate was reduced from 70 to 50 percent beginning in 1982. Indexing of tax brackets was then begun in 1985. In addition, individual retirement accounts were extended to all taxpayers, and a partial exclusion of earned income for the lower-earning spouse of two-earner couples was enacted. In the absence of taxpayer response to lower tax rates, these provisions would have cost the Treasury some $110 billion annually by the time they were fully phased in in 1985.

In analyzing the effects of taxpayer behavior on tax revenue, we must contrast the actual cost of the tax rate changes and the cost estimated under an alternative set of economic assumptions. This section begins with a brief description of the methodology involved. It then focuses on the changing composition of income for top-bracket taxpayers.

2.1 *Estimating the Actual Cost of Tax Rate Changes*

The actual revenue cost of these provisions cannot be known for certain; it is hypothetical. The revenue cost depends on how taxpayers would have behaved had ERTA not been enacted, and on the macroeconomic conditions that would have prevailed had the higher amount of revenue, associated with higher marginal tax rates, been collected by the government. To estimate the actual revenue cost, we must construct a predicted level and distribution of income, known as a baseline. This baseline is an estimate of what the level and distribution of income would have been had the tax cut not been passed. The baseline is constructed by pooling information on the income distribution in a year prior to the tax cut with changes in the level and composition of income between that earlier year and the year being studied.

The emphasis of this chapter, and of the Lindsey and CBO papers, is on the microeconomic behavior of individual taxpayers, not the effect of tax cuts on macroeconomic conditions. The macroeconomic conditions that actually prevailed during the period were taken as given. The revenue estimates that result from this approach do not, therefore, take account of the feedback effect of lower tax rates on macroeconomic activity. Only the redistribution of the shares of that activity among different income groups is measured.

To control for as many macroeconomic factors as possible in constructing the baseline, we set the level of income equal to the actual level of income for each component of personal income. That is, the baseline level of components of income such as wages, interest, dividends, and business income were each targeted to match the actual level of that component of income. Therefore, factors such as the rapid rise in interest income and interest rates were factored into the creation of the baseline. The changes in the overall distribution of income brought about by these macroeconomic factors are consequently also incorporated into the baseline. The residual difference between the actual and baseline distributions not caused by tax factors is minimized.

The resulting estimates of the effect of the tax rate cuts on tax revenue are shown in Figure 1. Tax revenue is shown under three different scenarios. The first scenario is that the old tax law is continued. In this scenario, the baseline level and distribution of income are applied to the old tax law and the resulting amount of tax computed. The second scenario predicts the level of taxes given the baseline income distribution under the new tax law. A comparison of these two lines shows the revenue cost of the tax law change assuming no change in taxpayer behavior. This comparison shows that the cost of the tax bill rises from about $5 billion in 1981 to more than $110 billion in 1985.

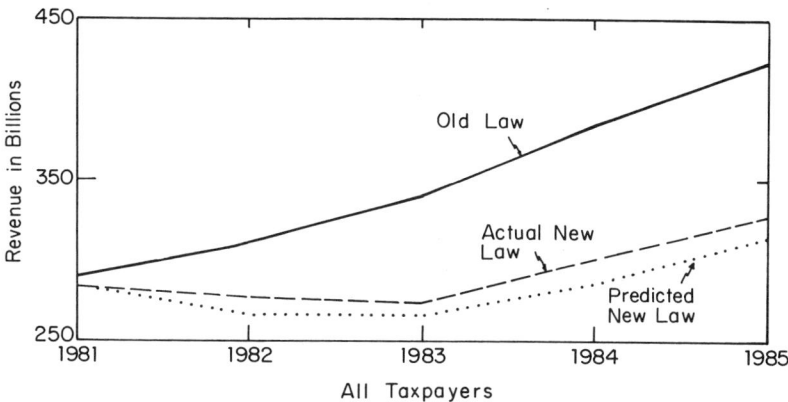

FIGURE 1. *Actual and Predicted Tax Revenue*

The third scenario presents the actual tax revenue collected in each year under ERTA. In Figure 1, this line runs between the old law and new law predictions. The distance between the actual revenue line and the old law line shows the actual revenue loss due to the tax law change. On the other hand, the distance between the actual revenue line and the new law line shows the additional amount of revenue loss that would have occurred had there been no behavioral response by taxpayers.

Figure 1 clearly indicates that the behavioral response made up only a small portion of the total revenue loss due to the tax bill. For example, in 1982 the added revenue amounted to about $11 billion, or only one-quarter of the total prospective loss from the bill. In 1983 the behavioral response was only a bit more than $8 billion, out of a total possible revenue loss of $75 billion. In 1984 the response amounted to about $15 billion out of a possible loss of $100 billion, whereas in 1985 about $13 billion was recaptured out of a possible loss of $110 billion. These numbers suggest that only about 10 to 15 percent of the revenue loss from the ERTA tax cuts was recouped as a result of the behavioral response of taxpayers. The claim by some supply side economists that across-the-board rate reductions would produce added revenue is discredited by this data.

On the other hand, Figure 2 shows a different conclusion regarding the revenue collected from upper-income taxpayers—those earning over $200,000.[2] These data indicate that upper-income taxpayers paid more

---

[2] In each year, baseline taxpayers were ranked by income. The figure presents the taxes paid by the same number of taxpayers in the baseline as had incomes over $200,000 in each year. The result is that taxpayer groups are comparable in each of the years illustrated. Of course,

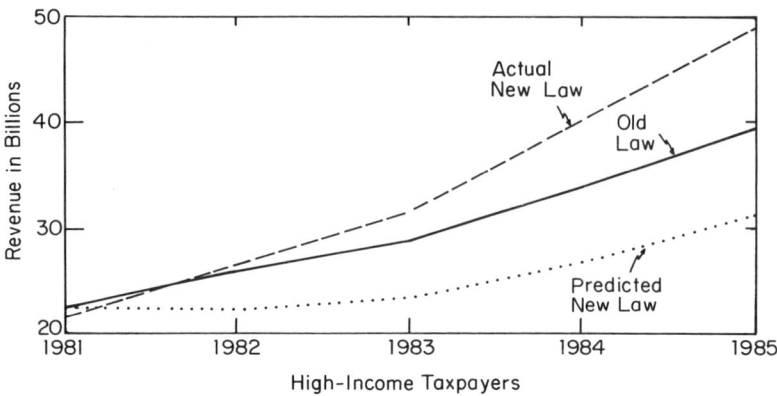

FIGURE 2. *Actual and Predicted Tax Revenue*

taxes under the new law than they would have paid under the old tax law. The difference between the old-law and predicted new-law figures shows that in the absence of a behavioral response, upper-income taxpayers would have received a substantial tax cut under ERTA. This scheduled tax reduction was about $3.5 billion in 1982, $5.5 billion in 1983, $7 billion in 1984, and over $8 billion in 1985.

The actual taxes paid under the new law exceeded the amount predicted by the baseline by substantial amounts. This difference is the amount of revenue attributable to taxpayer response. Upper-bracket taxpayers paid $4.2 billion more than predicted in 1982, $8 billion more in 1983, $13 billion more in 1984, and nearly $18 billion more in 1985. In each year, this taxpayer response exceeded the scheduled amount of the tax cut. As a result, the Treasury netted $0.6 billion more in 1982 from top-bracket taxpayers under the new law than the baseline predicted they would have under the old law. The comparable amounts of extra revenue are $2.7 billion for 1983, $6.3 billion for 1984, and $9.6 billion for 1985.

These data suggest that the across-the-board tax rate reductions of ERTA not only did not produce extra revenue but resulted in a significant decline in revenue. However, reductions in the top rate did increase total tax receipts from that income class. The combined effects of these two facts produced a sharp rise in the tax share paid by upper-income individuals.

---

the number of taxpayers earning over $200,000 rose over the period, as did their incomes. Thus, intertemporal comparisons do not involve the same sizes of taxpayer groups.

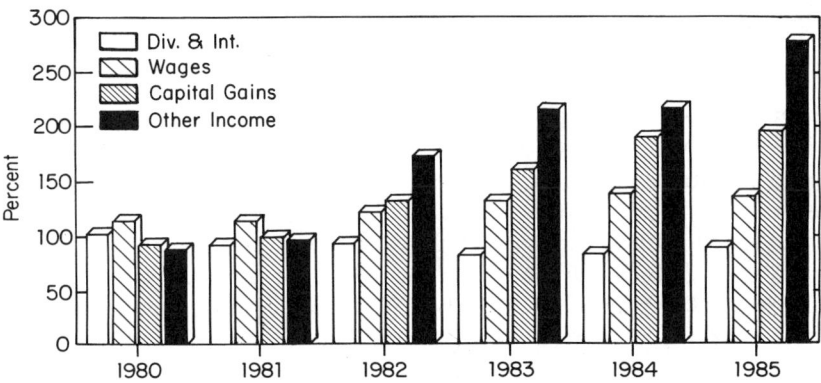

FIGURE 3. *Actual as a Percent of Predicted Income, High-Income Taxpayers (Over $200,000)*

2.2 Changes in the Composition of Top Incomes

This revenue increase from upper-income individuals was the result of an increase in the taxable income they reported. Different components of income for upper-income taxpayers increased more than others in response to the tax rate changes. Figure 3 presents the ratios of the actual level of income to the level predicted by the baseline for four types of income: portfolio (dividends plus interest), wage and salary, capital gains, and "other." The last category is primarily composed of income from businesses, including partnerships, proprietorships, small business corporations, rents, and royalties, and is calculated by subtracting portfolio income, wages and salaries, and capital gains from adjusted gross income (AGI).

The figure indicates that greater reporting of income by upper-income taxpayers was due to greater reporting of business income, capital gains income, and wage income. The level of portfolio income reported by upper-income taxpayers was actually lower than predicted by the baseline.

The rising share of wage and business income and capital gains income in the total income[3] of upper-income taxpayers is also indicated in an historical trend. It is inaccurate to think of top-bracket individuals as deriving the bulk of their income from passive sources such as interest and dividends. In 1983, only 21 percent of the income of the top 0.1 percent of the income distribution came from interest, dividends, and other non-

---

[3] For this analysis, total income represents AGI plus the excluded portion of capital gains, IRA contributions, Keoghs, and the two-earner deduction. It is comparable to the expanded income concept used by CBO.

capital-gains investment income. In contrast, 25 percent of the income of these top taxpayers came from earned sources.

This relatively high earnings share, and relatively low share of investment income, is a recent phenomenon. For sake of comparison, contrast 1983, the first year of economic expansion after the deep recession of 1981–1982, with 1975, the first year of expansion following the oil-shock recession of 1973–1974. After controlling for macroeconomic changes between 1975 and 1983, the top 0.1 percent of income recipients in 1975 received only 20.5 percent of their income from earned sources, compared with 24.7 percent in 1983. The 1975 share of other capital income was 23.5 percent, compared with 21.3 percent in 1983. Capital gains fell from 56 percent of their income in 1975 to 54 percent in 1983. In short, the earned share of compensation for these very-high-income taxpayers rose by more than 4 percentage points, or more than 20 percent, between 1975 and 1983.

This historic trend dates back at least to 1960. Controlling for macroeconomic changes between 1960 and 1983, the top 0.1 percent of 1960 income recipients would have gotten only 14.7 percent of their income from earned sources. Of the rest, 34.1 percent came from capital gains, and 51.2 percent from other sources of capital income. Between 1960 and 1983, the 30-percentage-point decline in the share of ordinary capital income in total income for these very-high-income taxpayers occurred. Roughly one-third of this represented a shift into wage income, and the remaining two-thirds comprised a shift into capital gains income. Figure 4 presents these changes in the income shares of the top 0.1 percent of taxpayers.

This change is even more dramatic when the top 2 percent of taxpayers are considered. Again controlling for macroeconomic changes, the earnings share in total income rose from 30.7 percent in 1960 to 48.3 percent in 1975 and to 55.1 percent in 1983. In contrast, the earnings from non-capital-gains investment income fell from 54.6 percent of income in 1960 to 27.8 percent in 1975 and to 18.6 percent in 1983. The capital gains share rose from 14.7 percent in 1960 to 23.9 percent in 1975 and to 26.3 percent in 1983. For the top 2 percent, the 36-point decline in ordinary capital income went about two-thirds into wages and one-third into capital gains. This is represented graphically by Figure 5.

3. DIFFERENT BEHAVIOR OF VARIOUS INCOME COMPONENTS

The previous section considered the changes in the reporting of income by upper-income taxpayer groups. Not only did the share of income and taxes

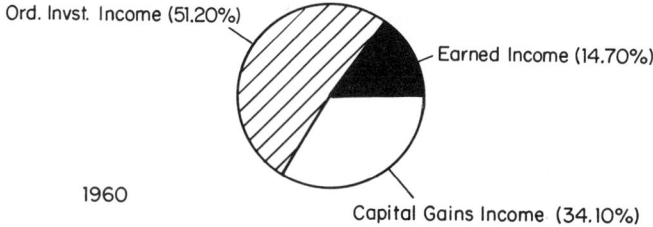
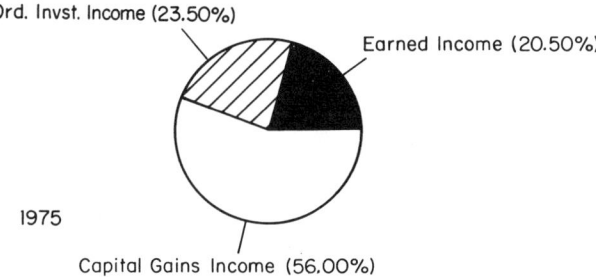
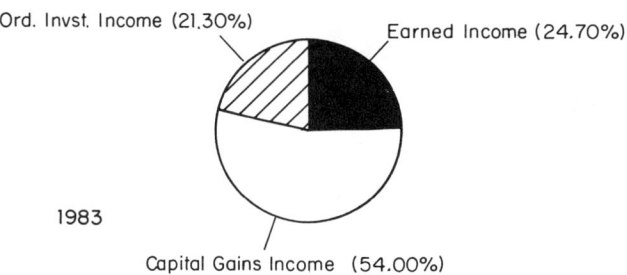

FIGURE 4. *Sources of Income (adjusted for macroeconomic conditions of very-high-income taxpayers—the top 0.1%)*

paid by top-bracket taxpayers rise when the top tax rate was reduced, the composition of income of these upper-income taxpayers also changed. By disaggregating the data into the individual components of income (wages and salaries, capital gains, business income, and interest and dividends), we can gather further information about the cause of these changes.

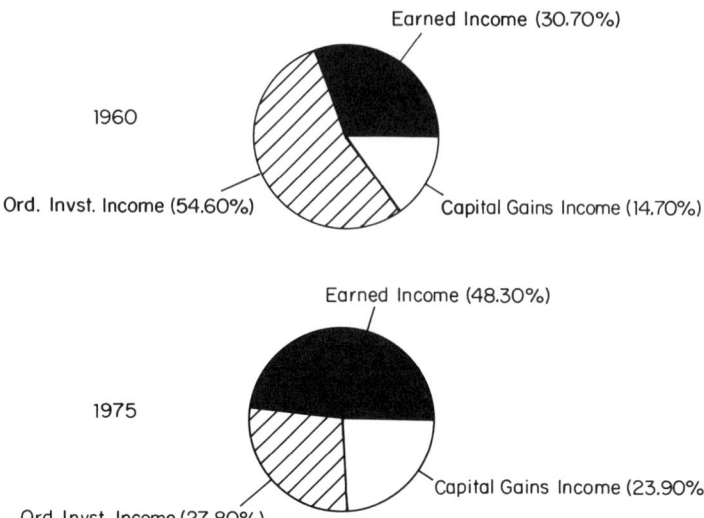

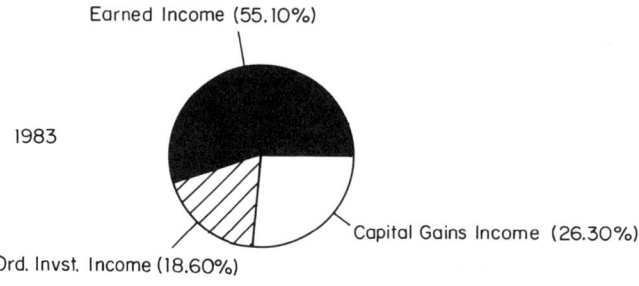

FIGURE 5. *Sources of Income (adjusted for macroeconomic conditions of high-income taxpayers—the top 2%)*

3.1 The Investigation of Behavioral Responses

Note that the preceding analysis, indicating a rise in taxes paid by upper-income taxpayers, ignores what is usually termed "supply side" effects. That is, the effect of tax rate changes on the amount of labor and capital supplied to the economy is omitted from the analysis. This is necessary because the effect of such macroeconomic factors as monetary policy cannot be separated from the supply side effect of tax changes in

ERTA Raise Taxes of the Upper Income 141

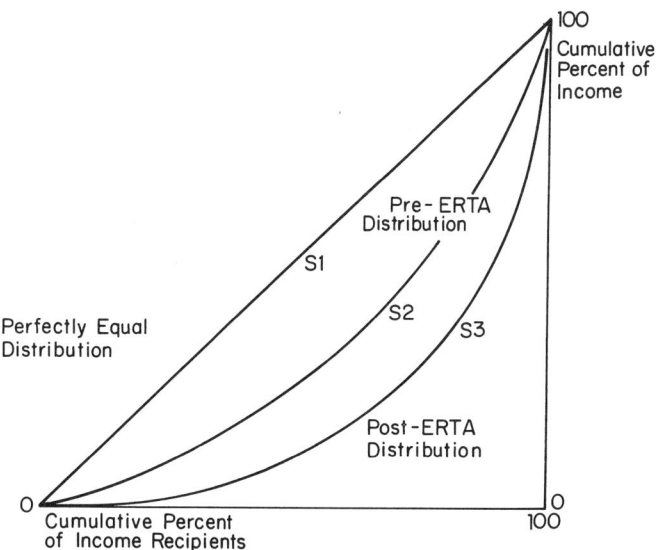

FIGURE 6. *Perfectly equal distribution*

determining the level of nominal income. Therefore, in determining the baseline level of income, we take the actual levels of each component of income as given, which is equivalent to assuming that there was no change in income due to supply side effects.

However, the existence of possible supply side effects can be discerned indirectly. Most of the nontax factors, such as monetary policy, that determine the level of a particular component of income have little or no effect on the *distribution* of that component of income. But the various tax rate changes are likely to have dramatic distributional consequences. These distributional consequences resulted from the differential reduction in tax rates applied to different recipients of each type of income. If the change in the actual distribution of income is systematically related to the change in the distribution of income that can be predicted using results from the literature, then a case exists that a tax-induced change in behavior occurred.

The test of the data for a behavioral response involves a two-step process. Figure 6 illustrates the first step in the test for a tax-induced behavioral change. It shows the calculation of the income distribution measure known as the Gini coefficient. The horizontal axis represents the cumulative percent of the population, and the vertical axis represents the cumulative percent of income. A line of perfect equality would be perfectly straight and connect the endpoints of the horizontal and vertical axes. Less equal distributions of income will be indicated by lines increasingly bowed in from this line of perfect equality. The Gini coefficient measures the inequality of the income distribution by comparing the ratio of the area between the actual distribution and the perfect equality line to the area of the triangle formed by the line of perfect equality and the two axes.

For most components of income, the distribution of income after the tax cut was less equal than the distribution of income before the tax cut. Figure 6 illustrates this with "pre-ERTA" and "post-ERTA" distributional lines. For this study the old-law line reflects the distribution of income in 1979, whereas the ERTA line reflects the distribution of income in 1983. The ERTA line is illustrated as more bowed in than the old-law line because of the less equal distribution of income in the latter year.

To test for the effectiveness of tax explanations for the observed changes in income, we created a simulated distribution of income based on the change in prevailing tax rates and an assumption about the amount of response expected from taxpayers drawn from existing research. In each case we start with the post-ERTA cut distribution of income and use tax rate changes to simulate what the distribution would have been had the pre-ERTA rates prevailed.

This simulated response can fall in any of three regions in Figure 6, indicated by S1, S2, and S3. If the simulation line is in region S1, then the simulation assumptions *overpredict* the actual behavioral response. That is, the actual distributional change turned out to be less than the distributional change predicted by the set of assumptions used. If the simulation line is in region S2, then the simulation assumptions *underpredict* the actual behavioral response. This can be because the chosen parameter is too small, or because some other effect correlated with income is at work. Finally, if the simulation line is in region S3, then the simulation assumptions *wrongly predict* the actual response. That is, the actual change went in the direction opposite to that predicted by the model.

The region in which the simulation line lays provides the qualitative answer regarding the existence of a supply side response. A quantitative answer regarding the predictive power of the simulated response can be tested by comparing the distribution of income in the tax simulation with the pre-ERTA and post-ERTA distributions. To determine the ability of the simulated response to explain the change in the distribution, we divided the continuous distribution shown in Figure 5 into twelve discrete segments. These segments are the bottom 25 percent, the 25th–50th percentiles, the 50th–70th percentiles, the 70th–80th, 80th–85th, 85th–90th, 90th–95th, 95th–98th, 98th–99th, 99th–99.5th, 99.5th–99.9th, and the top 0.1 percent of income recipients.

The share of income received by each group is calculated for the pre-ERTA, post-ERTA, and simulated distributions. As noted above, the simulated distribution fell in area S2 of Figure 6. This means that the simulated distribution explained part of the change from the pre-ERTA distribution to the post-ERTA distribution. To calculate how much of the change was explained, we compared the variance between the pre-ERTA and post-ERTA distributions with the variance between the predicted and post-ERTA distributions. Dividing the latter variance by the former provides the share of the variance between the pre-ERTA and post-ERTA distributions explained by the simulated response. Under this measure, the closer the simulated response is to the post-ERTA distribution from which it originated, the less is the share of the variance that is explained. The closer the simulated response is to the pre-ERTA distribution, the greater is the share of the variance that is explained. This approach measures both the overall ability of the simulation parameters to explain distributional changes and the ability of that approach to explain the changes observed in particular income groups.

3.2 Evidence of Omitted Supply Side and Pecuniary Changes

3.2.1 Wage and Salary Income.
The first test for supply side effects is performed in the area of wage and salary income. The economic literature suggests that the labor supply response of prime-age males is quite low, whereas the response for females tends to be quite high. The differential response is important because the ERTA provided for an extra marginal tax rate reduction for the lower-earning spouse in a two-earner family. This extra marginal rate reduction (equal to 10 percent of the regular rate) was directly targeted to the worker in the family likely to be most responsive to a tax rate change. Although the tax model we used does not specify the sex of the worker, it does provide separate data on the earnings of the higher- and lower-earning spouses.

For simulation purposes, the labor supply elasticity of the higher-earning spouse with respect to the marginal share of compensation retained after tax was set equal to 0.1. The elasticity for the lower-earning spouse was assumed to be 1.0. The pre-ERTA and post-ERTA tax rates for each earner were computed. The post-ERTA earnings were reduced for each worker in accordance with the assumed elasticity and the change in the tax rate. The result was a simulated level and distribution of wage and salary income for each taxpayer unit. The distribution of this simulated result was then plotted and compared with the pre-ERTA distribution.

The elasticities chosen for the simulation are on the high side of the range of estimates of male and female labor supply elasticities in the literature. In spite of this, the simulated distribution of wage income is in region S2 on

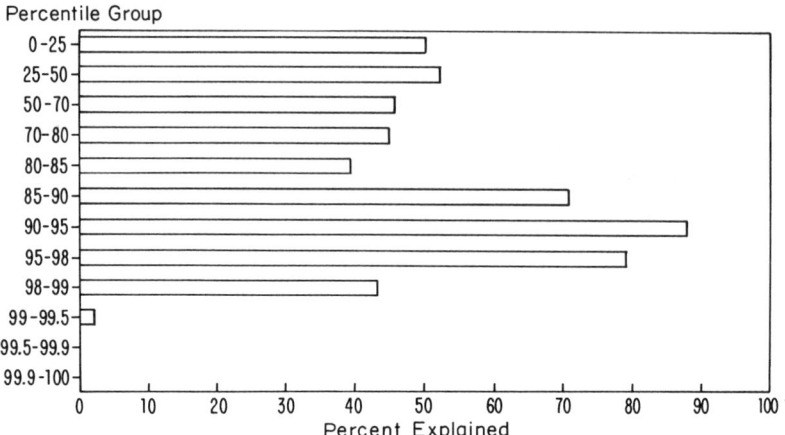

FIGURE 7. *Labor supply response of wages (percent of variance explained)*

Figure 6, implying that the assumed elasticities underpredicted the change in the distribution of wage and salary income.

Figure 7 illustrates the ability of the simulated response to explain the difference between the pre-ERTA and post-ERTA earned income shares for different income classes. The figure shows that the simulated response explained about half of the change in the income distribution for the bottom 99 percent of the taxpayer population. It was particularly effective at explaining the income change for the upper middle class—those between the 85th and 98th percentiles. These taxpayer groups had wage income between $40,000 and $80,000 in 1983. On the other hand, the simulated labor supply response was unable to explain the enormous increase in the wage and salary income reported by the upper 1 percent of wage and salary recipients.

This provides an indication that at least some supply side change was at work. The change in wages and salaries in this simulation amounts to $38 billion out of total wages and salaries of $1645 billion, or a bit less than 2.5 percent. Of this change, $23 billion, or 61 percent of the change, was due to the behavioral response of secondary earners[4], whereas the response of

---

[4] Corroborating evidence of an increase in female labor supply includes a dramatic decline of the difference between female and male unemployment rates beginning in 1982 and a rise in the ratio of female-to-male earnings at the same time. In 1982, for the first time since 1949, the adult female unemployment rate was below the adult male unemployment rate. In the five-year period during which this provision was in place, the adult female unemployment rate averaged 0.2 percent lower than the adult male unemployment rate. By contrast, in the five-year period immediately preceding 1982, the female unemployment rate exceeded the male

primary earners and single earners amounted to only $13 billion. This response is relatively small at the top of the income distribution because the importance of secondary earners incomes in total wages and salaries in that income range is quite small.

If this extra labor supply is attributable to the supply side effects of tax rate reductions, then ceteris paribus an additional $8 billion annually was added to federal income tax collections. This occurs because the simulations described in section 1 took the economic conditions of the period as given. Had this extra labor supply not been forthcoming, the real level of wage income and the resulting level of tax revenue would have been lower.

However, this supply side response leaves about half of the change in the distribution of wages and salaries unexplained. One possible explanation for this unexplained residual is a switch from fringe benefits to wages as the preferred form of compensation. Given that fringe benefits are untaxed, a drop in the tax rate would indicate the greater likelihood for such a substitution.

Empirical evidence for a very high responsiveness of fringe share to tax rates is not present. However, evidence for modest responsiveness does exist. For example, work by Turner (1988) suggests that taxation of fringes under the pre-ERTA personal income tax would cause the fringe share of total compensation to fall by one-third. Because the changes under ERTA were far less dramatic than the full taxation of fringe benefits, a substantially smaller change in the fringe share of compensation would be expected. Turner's work suggests an elasticity of fringes with respect to federal tax rates of about 0.18. Such an elasticity would imply that wage income was $30 billion, or 1.8 percent, higher as a result of the switch from fringes to taxable wages.

Combining this elasticity assumption for fringes with the labor supply elasticities already reported produces a far better explanation of the change in the distribution of wage and salary income. Figure 8 illustrates the share of the variance between the 1979 and 1983 distributions explained by the simulated response. As the figure indicates, over 90 percent of the distributional change in the upper middle class is now explained. Between 50 and 80 percent of the change was explained for the bottom 80 percent of the income distribution. (The result shown for the 80th–85th percentile is low because 1979 and 1983 income shares for this group were quite similar.)

Furthermore, there is some evidence that this fringe benefit explanation

---

unemployment rate by an average of 1.2 percentage points. In the ten-year period preceding 1982, the female unemployment rate exceeded the male unemployment rate by an average of 1.3 percent. The earnings of full-time year-round female workers rose to an average 63 percent of the earnings of full-time year-round male workers in the first year that ERTA was in effect, after having been just 60 percent for each of the preceding eight years. The average of this ratio since ERTA took effect has been 64 percent.

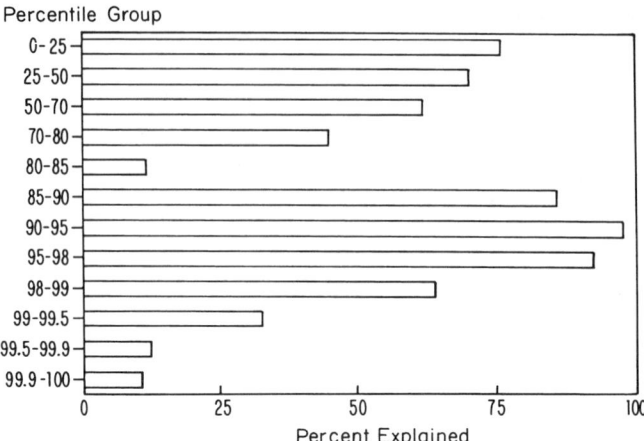

FIGURE 8. *Labor supply and fringe response of wages (percent of variance explained)*

had some effect at the top of the income distribution. Roughly one-third of the variance for the bottom half of the top percentile is explained by the fringe benefit effect. The combined explanatory power of labor supply and fringe benefit effects is about 10 percent for the very top earners, compared to nil explanatory power for the labor supply effect by itself. The fringe elasticity of 0.18 was derived from data on middle-income workers and applied to all groups. Had a variable elasticity simulation been performed, with a higher elasticity for upper-income taxpayers, a greater explanatory power would most likely have resulted.

The revenue effect of the reduction in fringe benefits induced by ERTA's rate reductions would amount to an additional $6 billion of federal income taxes annually. It is important to consider whether this extra revenue is permanent or simply an acceleration in the payment of taxes. In large measure the answer depends on the type of fringe compensation given up. Fringe benefits in the form of pension contributions produce future taxes when the taxpayer receives the pension benefits. On the other hand, office "perks" and insurance-type fringe benefits provide untaxed future benefits. In this latter case, the extra taxes received are not at the expense of future tax payments.

Turner's data show that pension benefits and insurance benefits make up roughly equal shares of total fringes. His results suggest that pension benefits are probably less sensitive to taxes than are insurance benefits, implying that less than half the reduction in fringes was due to a reduction in pension benefits.

Furthermore, the amount of forgone taxes on future pension benefits is likely to be far less than the taxes gained in the present by smaller pension contributions. To avoid the issue of present value, we can assume that the pension contributions grow in value at a rate equal to the rate of discount of future tax liability. The only difference in tax revenues will be due to the differential taxation of wage and pension income. In the aggregate, the marginal tax rate on wage income is 22 percent under the new tax law but only 19 percent on pension benefits. In fact, since pension contributions accrue primarily to upper-income workers, this greatly understates the extra taxes from wages. Furthermore, wages are subject to social insurance contributions, but pensions are not. This would add an additional 14 percent to the total federal taxes received and raise the federal tax burden on wages to 36 percent. In sum therefore, the extra revenue forgone from lower future pension benefits is less than half the extra revenue received in the present from lower pension contributions. Because less than half of the switch from fringes to wages is in the form of pensions, it is safe to assume that less than one-quarter of the revenue gained in the present from the switch in form of compensation is at the expense of future revenue.

The extra revenue received from the switch from fringe benefits to wages cannot be considered a supply side response because no additional factor supplies are forthcoming. Instead, a pecuniary change has occurred in the form of compensation that a worker receives.

Although no extra economic growth is attributable to the change, this fringe benefit effect raises wages and salaries relative to what they otherwise would have been. The level of wage and salary income in the baseline income distribution described in section 1 was overstated. As a consequence, the behavioral response to the tax rate reduction was understated. To measure the true behavioral response to the tax changes, we must add the labor supply and fringe benefit effects to the effects measured in section 1.

. The supply side and pecuniary changes in wage and salary compensation provide two possible explanations of the enormous behavioral response of upper-income taxpayers relative to other taxpayers. If these responses were neglected in forming the baseline income distribution, then the actual response of middle- and upper-middle-income taxpayers is much larger than previously estimated. This would make the total responses of upper-income and moderate-income taxpayers more comparable. As Figure 7 showed, the labor supply and fringe benefit simulation had relatively little explanatory power at the very top of the income distribution, but it was a signficant factor at other levels, thus indicating that the ignored response was at these lower levels.

3.2.2 Business Income. As in the case of wage and salary income, the possibility of an omitted supply side response exists in the case of business income. As the data presented in the first section indicated, business income—income from proprietorships, partnerships, small business corporations, farms, rents, and royalties—rose far more rapidly than predicted for upper-income taxpayers. Part of this response might be a supply side response of these individuals working harder. However, applying labor supply elasticities from the literature to the changes in after-tax compensation due to ERTA produces a labor supply response that is far smaller than the observed rise in business income. The likelihood of a supply side response being the dominant factor in the change in business income is therefore likely to be remote.

However, individuals who own their own businesses have a substantial ability to convert taxable business income into untaxed business expenses. Work by Clotfelter, for example, indicates that the travel and entertainment expenses of small firms is highly sensitive to the after-tax cost of the compensation. These businesses also have a greater capacity to convert current income into insurance and pension benefits than does the population at large.

The test for tax effects on business income is performed in the same manner as the tests on wage and salary income. Empirical estimates of the effects of taxes on proprietorship and partnership decisons do not exist. Therefore, an arbitrary selection of 0.56 was made. This value assumes that business income is derived from primary earners with a labor supply elasticity of 0.1 and a fringe elasticity of 0.18. It further assumes that small businesses are twice as responsive as large firms to the tax effects on their owners. Simulations done using this elasticity place it in region S2 of Figure 4, indicating an underprediction of the actual effect by the model.

Figure 9 shows that over half the variance between the pre-ERTA and post-ERTA distributions is eliminated by the simulated response to the tax rate changes. The results in Figure 9 show that the tax changes were particularly effective in explaining the variance in the share of earnings received by middle-income professionals and proprietary businesses. However, in the case of income at the top of the business income distribution, only about half of the variance was explained. This, coupled with a similar result for top-bracket wages, suggests that additional factors are at work.

As in the case of wages, some of the extra revenue resulting from the response of taxpayers to the change in tax rates is transitory. As discussed previously, pension contributions that are currently untaxed will eventu-

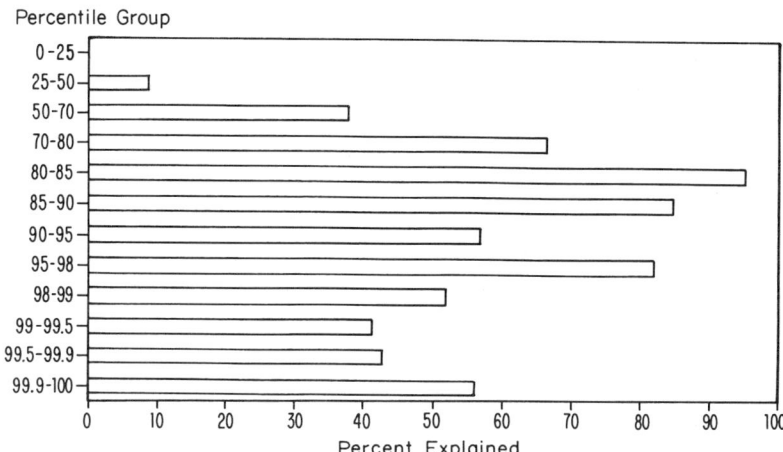

FIGURE 9. *Response of Business Income (percent of variance explained)*

ally produce pension income that will be subject to tax. The more complex types of deferred benefit packages are subject to the same analysis. Furthermore, a case can be made that the tax bracket of these taxpayers is less likely to drop when the benefits are received because they tend to be near the top of the income distribution. This would suggest that a greater degree of the revenue gain from extra business income is less likely to be transitory for these taxpayers than it is for the population as a whole.

On the other hand, taxpayers receiving business income are more able to change their compensation between taxable income and consumption-type perks such as travel and entertainment. The transformation of perks into taxable income may change the consumption mix of the individual, but this change will not alter the amount of tax liabilities generated from other sources or at a later date. This type of behavioral change will produce a revenue gain that is more likely to be permanent and not offset by tax effects.

3.2.3 Capital Gains. The evidence that capital gains realizations are sensitive to tax rate changes has been demonstrated by many researchers (Auten and Clotfelter (1983), Feldstein and Yitzhaki (1977), Lindsey (1987b), Minarik (1981), and U. S. Department of the Treasury (1986)), although the magnitude of the response is far from certain. In addition, macroeconomic factors contributed to the level of capital gains realizations as well as tax changes.

The baseline income distribution that underlies this study assumes that, absent any tax changes, capital gains realizations rise at the same rate as "tradable" household wealth. Tradable household wealth is composed of corporate equities, real estate, and the value of unincorporated businesses as estimated in the Federal Reserve Board's *Flow of funds*.

One can distinguish between the effects of macroeconomic factors, such as the rise in household wealth, and the effect of tax changes. An overall rise in wealth would be likely to cause an increase in the level of capital gains, but not a redistribution of the share of capital gains received by different taxpayers. On the other hand, a tax rate reduction is likely to cause both a rise in the overall level of realizations and a change in the distribution of those realizations, reflecting the different changes in incentives for different taxpayers under ERTA. If the change in the distribution of capital gains resembles the distributional change predicted by behavioral simulations of the response of capital gains realizations to tax changes, then the tax changes are the likely cause of the rise in capital gains.

The test of the hypothesis that tax-induced changes were at work resembles the tests performed to check for tax effects in the distribution of wages. The 1983 level and distribution of capital gains realizations was adjusted to take account of the changes in marginal tax rates between 1979 and 1983. An elasticity of capital gains realizations with respect to an after-tax share of 5.2 was selected to simulate the tax effect using the result from Lindsey (1987b). This elasticity is equivalent to an elasticity of 0.8 with respect to the tax rate.

The simulation placed the distribution line in region S2 of Figure 6, indicating that the assumption underpredicted the actual change. However, the simulated distribution was quite close to the pre-ERTA distribution, indicating a high degree of explanatory power by the simulation. Figure 10 shows the amount of variance between the 1979 and 1983 distributions, which was explained by the tax effect. On average, the simulation explained over 80 percent of the variance between the 1979 and the 1983 distributions.

It should be stressed that any behavioral response to changes in capital gains tax rates is not supply side in the usual meaning of the term. The observed response of extra realizations is not evidence that existing supplies of capital are brought forth as a result of the tax change. It might be argued that the existing stock of capital is more likely to be efficiently allocated with the lower capital gains tax rate, since taxpayers are less likely to be locked in to their existing portfolios because of tax considerations. It might also be argued that lowering the total tax rate on capital income will increase the rate of savings on the margin above what it otherwise would have been. However, the benefits of such changes are only likely to evolve

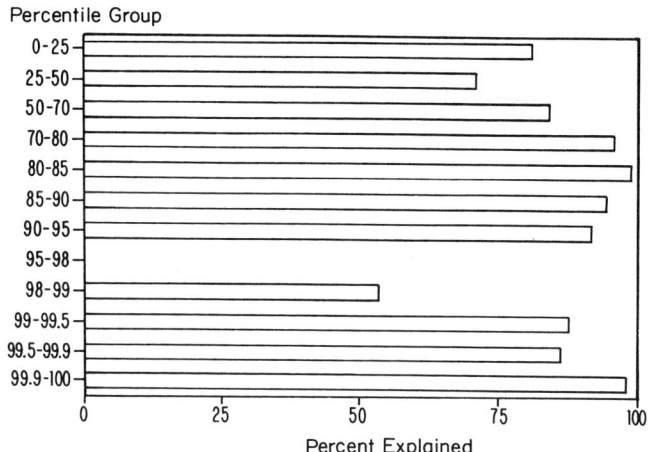

FIGURE 10. *Response of Capital Gains (percent of variance explained)*

over a long time and are probably too small to be observed in the existing data.

The revenue gain from such a change in capital gains realizations might best be termed pecuniary rather than supply-side because the behavioral response represents a rearrangement of the existing supply of capital rather than an increase in the overall quantity. This rearrangement of portfolios raises the further question of whether this revenue gain is permanent or temporary.

3.3 The Surprising Case of Ordinary Investment Income

The period between 1979 and 1983 was one of rapidly rising interest and dividend income for taxpayers as a whole. Interest and dividend income rose by $97 billion between 1979 and 1983, or by 90 percent. This was nearly three times as fast as the growth in AGI over the same period. Furthermore, interest and dividend income is highly concentrated among upper-income brackets. For example, the top 1 percent of interest and dividend recipients receive about a quarter of total income from these sources.

The combined effect of the sharp rise in interest and dividends and the concentration of that income among high-income taxpayers would be a large redistribution of total personal income toward top-bracket taxpayers. Further enhancing this expectation are indications that the share of wealth in the country, which produces interest and dividend income, held by the top of the income distribution may have increased. In addition, the tax rate reduction and increase in after-tax share for top-bracket taxpayers was at least as dramatic in the case of interest and dividend income as it was in the case of wage and professional income. All of these factors would lead to the expectation that the increased share of income received by upper-income taxpayers between 1979 and 1983 would be due in part to the overall rise in capital income.

This turns out not to be the case. Greater interest and dividend income was not a factor in the increase in the share of total income received by the top 1 percent of the income distribution. The total income of this group was nearly $23 billion higher than it would have been had its share of income remained unchanged. Of this figure, $22 billion can be explained by the rising share of capital gains income and a further $8 billion by the rising share of earned income. The net change in the share of interest and dividend income was a negative component in contributing to the higher share of total income received by the top 1 percent. This result is one of the most unexpected findings in the tax data.

The reason for this is a sharp reduction in the share of interest and dividend income received by the top recipients of this income. Unlike the other types of income considered, the share of income from interest and dividends received by upper-income taxpayers was lower in 1983 than in 1979. The top 1 percent of recipients of this type of income received 27.1 percent of interest and dividend income in 1979 and 23.2 percent in 1983.

This decline in the share of interest and dividend income received at the very top did not move to the bottom of the distribution, however, but stayed in the top half of the income distribution. The lower half of interest and dividend recipients received the same share of interest and dividend income in the two years: 2.2 percent. On the other hand, taxpayers in the 50th to 90th percentiles of interest and dividend income recipients saw their share rise from 30 to 33 percent. Taxpayers in these percentile classes typically received between $300 and $5000 in interest and dividends in 1979 and between $600 and $9000 in interest and dividends in 1983.

Tax law changes are unlikely to account for this change. If saving is positively related to the after-tax share of portfolio income kept by the taxpayer, then a redistribution of this income to top-bracket taxpayers would be indicated. The pattern of response would be similar to that seen in the cases of wages, capital gains, and business income.

In this case, an institutional factor can be identified to explain this data. Money market mutual funds became widely available between 1979 and 1983. Furthermore, the deregulation of the banking system afforded savers with moderate-sized portfolios saving instruments that yielded market interest rates previously available only to the very wealthy. Taxpayers with small portfolios probably had fewer increases in the options available to them than did taxpayers with portfolios of $10,000 or more. Thus, the share change did not extend down to the bottom half of the distribution of income and dividend recipients.

The revenue consequences of this institutional change are likely to be negative. The opening of these money market accounts either raised the total cost of borrowing above what it otherwise would have been or reduced the spreads of financial intermediaries. It probably had the added effect of lowering the return to lenders other than those who availed themselves of these new financial instruments. The tax status of these groups can be compared. The taxpayers with the new money market accounts were in an above average personal tax bracket, say 30 percent, but well below the top rate. On the other hand, final borrowers and financial intermediaries are taxed at the marginal corporate rate of 46 percent. Lenders who previously had access to market rates were probably also at or near the top marginal personal rate of 50 percent. Thus, the beneficiaries of these accounts had lower marginal tax rates than those whose income may have declined due to the new accounts.

4. TAXPAYER BEHAVIOR AND THE 1986 TAX REFORM

The previous section described a number of possible behavioral phenomena that followed the tax rate reductions of the 1981 Tax Act. TRA86 continued the rate-cutting tradition of the earlier act. The maximum tax rate on ordinary income was reduced from 50 to 33 percent, with a further reduction to 28 percent for very-high-income taxpayers. Unlike the 1981 Act, TRA86 aggressively expanded the income tax base. The expansion of the base offset in large measure the potential revenue loss from the reduction in tax rates.

This section examines the potential effects of the base broadening and rate reduction in the 1986 Act. The possible supply side ramifications of rate reductions are considered as well as the revenue effects of pecuniary changes in taxpayer behavior. The revenue estimates presented here are intended to convey only the potential magnitude of supply side assumptions; they do not represent a forecast of what is likely to happen.

As in the case of the analysis presented earlier, the major potential behavioral response involves top-bracket taxpayers. These taxpayers will have the largest reduction in their tax rates and the greatest increase in the after-tax share of income. The earlier analysis also indicated that the degree of responsiveness to tax rate changes may also be greater for upper-income taxpayers than for the taxpaying population as a whole. For all of these reasons, the magnitude of revenue response at the top of the income distribution is the key to whether or not TRA86 is revenue neutral as claimed, raises taxes, or reduces taxes. The magnitude of the behavioral response will also determine whether the share of taxes paid by upper-income taxpayers will rise, as it did after the 1981 Tax Act, or fall.

4.1 Revenue Estimates With No Taxpayer Behavior

The first step in simulating the effect of the 1986 Act is the creation of a baseline income distribution for a year in which the new law will be in effect; 1988 was selected. The baseline for a future year involves a procedure not required for simulating a past event: forecasting future macroeconomic levels. The use of any economic forecast necessarily creates added uncertainty regarding the accuracy of the revenue estimates, because actual economic conditions may differ from those forecast. For these simulations, the economic forecast contained in the 1988 budget of the United States was used.

The 1988 baseline income distribution was extrapolated from the 1983 Individual Tax Model File Public Use Sample using the NBER TAXSIM model. The resulting distribution presumes that taxpayers behave as they behaved in 1983, the year from which the original data are obtained. Each taxpayer is allotted a higher income level, reflecting economic growth over the period, and a different composition of income, reflecting the forecast change in economic conditions between 1983 and 1988. Any possible behavioral response by the taxpayers to the new tax rates implied by the change in income and the new tax law are ignored in the first set of simulations.

Table 1 presents the results of these simulations. Taxpayers are classified by income class based on the definition of adjusted gross income in a fully phased-in version of TRA86. The total tax paid by taxpayers in that income group is reported for three different tax laws: the old or prereform tax law, the TRA86 tax law for the year 1988, and a fully phased-in version of TRA86. The latter two laws differ in that some of the new base-broadening provisions of the TRA are only partially implemented in 1988.

The table shows that absent any behavioral response, the new tax law will raise taxes on all income groups earning over $50,000, and lower taxes on all income groups earning less than $50,000. Given the 1988 tax rules, this will mean that total taxes will be about $2.6 billion higher under the new tax bill than under the old tax bill. Taxpayers earning over $200,000 will pay $4.6 billion more, and taxpayers earning between $100,000 and $200,000 will pay $3.1 billion more. Each figure represents an 8 percent increase in taxes. In contrast, taxes for taxpayers earning under $10,000 will be cut nearly in half, and those for taxpayers earning between $10,000 and $20,000 will decline by about 10 percent. In total, the share of taxes paid by taxpayers earning over $50,000 will rise from 54.0 percent under the old law to 56.7 percent under the new law.

TABLE 1
Tax Revenue Assuming No Behavioral Response

Income class	Old tax law	TRA86 1988 rules	TRA86 fully phased in
Under 10	3.2	1.7	1.8
10–20	28.2	25.5	25.9
20–30	44.4	43.3	44.0
30–40	51.7	50.0	50.8
40–50	47.8	46.2	47.3
50–75	78.8	80.9	82.9
75–100	32.1	34.2	35.3
100–200	38.8	42.3	44.3
Over 200	61.7	68.4	71.3
Total	386.6	392.5	403.7

All numbers are for calendar 1988.

Income classes are in thousands.

Revenue figures are in billions.

The table also shows that the phase-out provisions of the new tax law involved $10.9 billion of revenue in 1988. Although all groups would see their taxes rise if the phase-out provisions were eliminated, most of the extra revenue would come from upper-income taxpayers. Nearly one-quarter of the revenue consequences of the phase-out provisions involve taxpayers with incomes over $200,000, whereas more than 70 percent of the phase-out revenue involves taxpayers with incomes over $50,000. Therefore, as the tax provisions are phased out, the share of tax payments by upper-income taxpayers will continue to rise. If these provisions were fully subject to tax in 1988, 57.1 percent of taxes would be paid by taxpayers earning more than $50,000.

These results indicate that absent any behavioral response by taxpayers, the new individual income tax provisions will increase personal income tax revenue. Furthermore, they show that the 1986 Act increased the share of taxes paid by upper-income taxpayers, even though the tax rate on these taxpayers dropped dramatically. This is evidence that the base broadening more than compensated for the lower tax rate.

4.2 The Potential Taxpayer Response

Previously, we identified a number of possible supply side and pecuniary responses that taxpayers might undertake. On the supply side, increased real wage income would result from increased labor supply. The same would occur in the case of professional income. In addition, pecuniary reallocations of compensation into taxable wages along with out-of-tax-exempt compensation would be likely to result from the tax rate reduction. On the other hand, the 1986 Act produced the largest increase in capital gains tax rates on record. This would cause fewer capital gains to be realized and cause tax revenue to decline relative to the no-behavior revenue figures.

These potential responses were simulated separately for each of the types of income involved: wages, professional income, and capital gains. The elasticities used were the same as those used in the previous section. For wages, a labor supply elasticity with respect to after-tax share of 0.1 was used for single individuals and for the higher earner in married couples. An elasticity of 1.0 with respect to after-tax share was used for the wages of the lower-earning spouse if both spouses worked. Turner's fringe benefit elasticity of 0.18 was added to each of these figures. For professional and proprietary income, an elasticity of 0.56 with respect to the after-tax share was used. Finally, a capital gains elasticity of 4.5 with respect to the after-tax share was used in the simulation of taxpayer response to the increase in the capital gains tax rate. A final simulation was also run, which incorporated the effects of all of these responses. The total effect might differ from the sum of the individual effects due to the interaction of different types of income in determining a taxpayer's taxable income and tax rate.

As stated previously, these elasticities should not be considered precise estimates or predictions. They were selected in order to estimate an order of magnitude for any potential taxpayer response. As such, these estimates tend to err on the high side. Readers who feel that the behavioral parameter is twice as high as it should be will find that a revenue effect half as large as estimated is in line with their prior expectations.

It is also important to note that these simulations presume that any supply side response would be reflected in a higher level of nominal income. In fact, this is unlikely to be the case. Given a constant monetary policy, a rise in labor supply will increase nominal income by less than it will increase real income. These simulations therefore overstate the rise in nominal tax revenue that would result from the simulated supply side response. They represent the change in revenue that would be expected at a given level of prices and rate of inflation.

Table 2 presents the revenue results from each of the simulations of these behavioral responses. In each case, the behavioral simulation was performed at 1988 income levels, assuming that TRA86 was fully phased in. The revenue effect is given for each income class based on the new law's fully phased-in definition of adjusted gross income.

The table shows that the simulated behavioral response of wages would produce an additional $13.8 billion of revenue, or about 3.5 percent more

TABLE 2
Potential Revenue Impact of Behavioral Responses

Income class	Revenue effect due to response of			
	Wages and salaries	Business income	Capital gains	All responses
Under 10	−0.1	−0.0	−0.1	−0.2
10–20	−1.4	−0.0	−0.2	−1.6
20–30	+0.1	+0.0	−0.5	−0.4
30–40	+2.0	+0.1	−0.6	+1.5
40–50	+0.8	+0.1	−0.8	+0.1
50–75	+2.7	+0.2	−2.7	+0.2
75–100	+2.6	+0.2	−2.3	+0.5
100–200	+3.0	+0.5	−5.3	−1.8
Over 200	+4.4	+0.5	−18.4	−13.5
Total	+13.8	+1.6	−30.8	−15.5

All figures for 1988.

Income classes are in thousands.

Revenue effects are in billions.

than expected. Of this additional revenue, 53 percent would be derived from taxpayers with incomes over $100,000 and 91 percent from taxpayers earning more than $50,000. This extra tax revenue results from a $57 billion, or 2.4 percent, rise in total wage and salary income. A 17 percent rise in wage income for taxpayers earning more than $200,000 is indicated. More than one-quarter of the total rise in wage and salary income will accrue to taxpayers in this income class, and nearly three-quarters will accrue to taxpayers earning more than $50,000. The share of wages and salaries received by taxpayers earning more than $50,000 will rise from 35.3 to 36.2 percent. These changes in the distribution of wage and salary income are of roughly the same order of magnitude as the changes that followed the 1981 Tax Act.

Table 2 indicates that professional and proprietary income would rise enough to generate $1.6 billion in extra revenue in 1988, given the simulation parameters described above. This extra revenue would result from a $6 billion increase in business and professional income, a 6 percent increase.

In sum, the simulated potential increase in revenue from greater labor supply and lower fringe benefits amounts to $15.5 billion. To individuals not familiar with the magnitudes involved in the federal budget, this may seem like a large number. However, it amounts to slightly less than 4 percent of personal income tax revenue and roughly 1.5 percent of total federal revenue. It represents the extra revenue produced from a typical year's economic growth of 2.5 to 3.0 percent. In short, potential supply side responses should not be relied on to balance the federal budget or to be sufficient to finance further marginal tax rate reductions.

In addition, although the wage, salary, and professional income responses will produce more tax revenue than predicted by the behavior-free model, the reverse is true for capital gains behavior. The 1986 Act mandated the largest increase in capital gains tax rates on record. Absent a behavioral response, this tax rate increase would boost tax revenues by roughly $15 billion in 1988. This $15 billion increase is factored into the revenue estimates presented in Table 1. There is general agreement that at least some reduction in capital gains realizations will result from this tax rate increase, however (Turner (1988)). Thus, the behavior-free revenue estimates in Table 1 exaggerate the amount of tax revenue that will be collected.

To estimate the magnitude of the possible revenue effect, an elasticity of 4.5 with respect to the after-tax share was used. The third column in Table 2 presents the revenue consequences of such an assumption. Total revenue declines $30.8 billion due to the reduced realization of capital gains. This represents 7.7 percent of total personal income tax revenue and twice the simulated response of wage, salary, and professional income.

The table also shows that the great majority of this revenue decline would occur among upper-income taxpayers. Fully 60 percent of the decline would occur among taxpayers earning over $200,000, and 93 percent of the revenue decline would occur among taxpayers making over $50,000. This would have a dramatic effect on the share of taxes paid by different income groups. Taxpayers earning more than $100,000 would see the share of taxes they pay drop from 29 percent under the behavior-free simulation to 25 percent. The share of taxes paid by taxpayers earning under $40,000 would rise from 30 to 33 percent. In short, the potential behavioral response to the capital gains tax changes would have important distributional consequences as well as a substantial effect on total government tax collections.

The final column presents the combined effect of the three behavioral responses. The data presented here show that the tendency of TRA86 to increase the share of taxes paid by upper-income taxpayers in the behavior-free model is reversed when potential taxpayer behavior is taken into account. Taxpayers earning more than $200,000 pay 16 percent of total taxes under the old tax law. This rises to nearly 18 percent under the no-behavior simulation of a fully phased-in TRA86. However, the tax share for this group of taxpayers falls to 15 percent when all behaviors are simulated together.

In sum, potential taxpayer behavior in response to the changes in the tax law may completely reverse the tendency of TRA86 to increase the tax share at the top. This is exactly opposite to what happened after the tax rate reductions of ERTA. In that case, the behavior-free tax rate effects indicated a reduction in the share of taxes paid by upper-income taxpayers. When the actual results were reported, the reverse occurred, and the tax share paid by upper-income taxpayers rose. Absent the behavioral response to the capital gains tax rate increase, TRA86 would extend the trend of greater tax shares at the top. However, the potential response to the capital gains tax increase is so great that the 1980s may end with the tax share paid by upper-income taxpayers back at the level at which it began the decade.

REFERENCES

Auten, G., and C. Clotfelter. 1982. Permanent vs. transitory effects and the realization of capital gains. *Quarterly Journal of Economics*.

Boskin, Michael J. 1973. The economics of the labor supply. In *Income maintenance and labor supply*, eds. Glen G. Cain and Harold W. Watts. Chicago: Rand McNally.

Burtless, Gary, and Jerry A. Hausman. 1978. The effect of taxation on labor supply: Evaluating the Gary negative income tax experiment. *Journal of Political Economy* 86: 1103–30.

Clotfelter, Charles T. 1979. Equity, efficiency, and the tax treatment of in-kind compensation. *National Tax Journal* 32: 51–60.

———. 1983. Tax-induced distortions and the business-pleasure borderline. *The American Economic Review* 73: 1053–65.

Congressional Budget Office. 1981. A review of the accuracy of treasury revenue forecasts 1963–1978. Washington, D.C.: U.S. Government Printing Office.

———. 1983. Forecasting individual income tax revenues: A technical analysis. Washington, D.C.: U.S. Government Printing Office.

———. 1986. Effects of the 1981 tax cut on the distribution of income and taxes paid, mimeo.

———. 1987. CBO replies to Lindsey. *Tax Notes* May: 496–501.

Economic report of the president. 1987. Washington, D.C.: Government Printing Office.

Feenberg, Daniel, and Harvey S. Rosen. 1982. Alternative tax treatment of the family: Simulation methodology and results. In *Simulation methods in tax policy analysis*, ed. Martin Feldstein. Chicago: The University of Chicago Press.

Feldstein, Martin. 1978. The rate of return, taxation, and personal savings. *The Economic Journal* 88: 482–87.

Feldstein, Martin, and Joel Slemrod. 1978. The lock-in effect of the capital gains tax: Some time series analysis. *Tax Notes* 8, no. 6: 134–35.

Feldstein, Martin, Joel Slemrod, and Shlomo Yitzhaki. 1980. The effects of taxation on the selling of corporate stock and the realization of capital gains: Reply. *The Quarterly Journal of Economics* 94: 777–91.

Feldstein, M., and S. Yitzhaki. 1977. The effect of the capital gains tax on the selling and switching of common stock. *Journal of Public Economics* (February).

Gwartney, James, and James Long. 1984. *Income tax avoidance and an empirical estimation of the Laffer curve*. Florida State University, mimeo.

Gwartney, James, and Richard Stroup. 1982. Tax cuts: Who shoulders the burden? *Economic Revenue of the Federal Reserve Bank of Atlanta* March: 19–27.

Hausman, Jerry A. 1981. Exact consumer's surplus and deadweight loss. *The American Economic Review* 71: 662–76.

———. 1981. Labor Supply. In *How taxes affect economic behavior*. Washington, D.C.: The Brookings Institution.

Joint Committee on Taxation. 1981a. *General explanation of the Economic Recovery Tax Act of 1981*. Washington, D.C.: U.S. Government Printing Office.

———. 1981b. *General explanation of the Tax Reform Act of 1986*. Washington, D.C.: U.S. Government Printing Office.

Lindsey, Lawrence B. 1987a. Individual taxpayer response to tax cuts: 1982–1984 with implications for the revenue maximizing tax rate. *Journal of Public Economics* 33 (1987): 173–206.

———. 1987b. Capital gains: Rates, realizations, and revenues. In *Taxes and capital formation*, ed. Martin Feldstein. Chicago: University of Chicago Press.

———. 1987c. Criticizing the CBO analysis of ERTA's effect on the distribution of income and taxes. *Tax Notes* May: 491–96.

———. 1987d. Capital gains taxes under the Tax Reform Act of 1986: Revenue estimates under various assumptions. *National Tax Journal*.

Long, James E. 1982. Income tax and self employment. *National Tax Journal* 43: 43.

Minarik, Joseph J. 1981. Capital gains. In *How taxes affect economic behavior*, eds. Henry J. Aaron and Joseph A. Pechman. Washington, D.C.: The Brookings Institution.

———. 1984. The effects of taxation on the selling of corporate stock and the realization of capital gains: Comments. *The Quarterly Journal of Economics* 99: 93–110.

Pechman, Joseph, and Benjamin A. Okner. 1974. *Who bears the tax burden?* Washington, D.C.: The Brookings Institution.

Statistics of income. 1960. Washington, D.C.: U.S. Government Printing Office.

———. 1975. Washington, D.C.: U.S. Government Printing Office.

———. 1979. Washington, D.C.: U.S. Government Printing Office.

———. 1980. Washington, D.C.: U.S. Government Printing Office.

———. 1981. Washington, D.C.: U.S. Government Printing Office.

———. 1982. Washington, D.C.: U.S. Government Printing Office.

———. 1983. Washington, D.C.: U.S. Government Printing Office.

———. 1984. Washington, D.C.: U.S. Government Printing Office.

———. 1985. Washington, D.C.: U.S. Government Printing Office.

Turner, Robert W. The effect of taxes on the fringe share of compensation. Colgate University, Dept. of Economics, Discussion Paper 88-05. 1988 mimeo.

U.S. Department of Treasury. 1985. *Capital gains tax reductions of 1978*. Washington, D.C.: U.S. Government Printing Office.

Wyscarver, Roy A. 1982. *The Treasury individual income tax simulation model*. Washington, D.C.: Office of Tax Analysis.

PENSION BACKLOADING, WAGE TAXES, AND WORK DISINCENTIVES

Laurence J. Kotlikoff
Boston University and NBER

David A. Wise
Harvard University and NBER

EXECUTIVE SUMMARY

The federal government is actively involved in encouraging the formation and growth of private pensions and in regulating their behavior. The primary form of encouragement is the government's tax subsidization of pensions. A primary attribute of pension plan provisions is an implicit tax on employment after certain ages. The primary form of pension regulation is through ERISA, the Employee Retirement Income Security Act. The government's involvement in encouraging and regulating private pensions appears to reflect its desire that workers have a secure source of old-age income that will lessen their reliance on Social Security. In recent years the government has reacted to demographic changes, their effects on Social Security funding, and the increase in early retirement by also using its pension and Social Security tax and regulatory policies to encourage workers to delay their retirement decision.

This chapter examines the structure of pension plans with two questions in mind. First, have government pension backloading regulations aimed at ensuring future pension benefits been effective? Second, has the structure of old-age pension accrual at the end of the workspan, an implicit tax,

We thank John Bound for providing some very useful data and William M. Lieber of the Joint Committee on Taxation for many helpful discussions concerning recent pension legislation.

greatly limited the effectiveness of government policy in reversing the trend to early retirement? The answers to these questions are important for assessing the benefits of the government's tax subsidization of pensions as they are currently structured.

Our principal findings are as follows:

1. ERISA regulations notwithstanding, a significant proportion of defined benefit plans exhibit severe backloading. Indeed, backloading is an inherent property of defined benefit pension plans.
2. A large fraction of defined benefit plans embed very substantial old-age work disincentives through an implicit tax on wage earnings.
3. These pension retirement incentives are often much greater than Social Security's retirement incentives.
4. Evidence from one large Fortune 500 firm indicates that pension retirement incentives can greatly increase the extent of early retirement.

1. INTRODUCTION

The federal government is actively involved in encouraging the formation and growth of private pensions and in regulating their behavior. The primary form of encouragement is the government's tax subsidization of pensions. Workers are taxed on their pension benefits not when they accrue but when they are received, at which time their tax brackets may be much lower. In addition, pension saving accumulates tax-free interest. The primary form of pension regulation is through ERISA, the 1974 Employee Retirement Income Security Act. The government's involvement in encouraging and regulating private pensions appears to reflect its desire that workers have a secure source of old-age income that will lessen their reliance on Social Security. In recent years the government has reacted to demographic changes, projected Social Security financial problems, and the increase in early retirement by adjusting somewhat its policies to encourage workers to delay their retirement decision. But, as yet, the government does not appear to have recognized the extent to which the provisions of private pension plans encourage early retirement.

This chapter examines the structure of pension plans with two questions in mind. First, have government pension backloading regulations aimed at securing workers their future pension benefits been effective? Second, has the structure of old-age pension accrual at the end of the workspan greatly limited the effectiveness of government policy in reversing the trend to early retirement? The answers to these questions are important for assessing the effects of the government's tax subsidization of pensions, as they are currently structured.

1.1 Government Concern with Pension Backloading and the Labor Supply of the Aged

Over the past two decades the government has been concerned with the backloading (delaying) of the accrual of vested pension benefits. Limiting the backloading of pension benefit accrual is an important objective of ERISA as well as subsequent legislation. The government's main concern with pension backloading, reflected in ERISA's vesting and minimum benefit accrual requirements, appears to be to ensure that older workers are not terminated, either intentionally or unintentionally, just in advance of accruing significant pension benefits. Senator Bentsen expressed this concern in introducing ERISA to Congress: "There are instances where workers have not received pension benefits that they have earned through years of long hard labor. Their dreams of financial security after retirement have been shattered." Although the legislation appears intended to limit the extent of backloading in defined benefit pension plans, it seems not to recognize that backloading is inherent in the benefit formulae of most defined benefit plans; it cannot be legislated away.

Another reason for concern about excessive pension backloading and, more generally, the pattern of pension benefit accrual involves retirement incentives. If most pension benefits accrue before a particular age, say the age of early retirement, beyond which additional accrual is negligible or possibly negative, workers will have an incentive to remain with the firm up to early retirement and then leave the firm. In effect, pension provisions often impose a tax on earnings after a particular age; wage earnings are offset by loss in pension wealth. This implicit tax could thus be a major explanation of the trend toward early retirement, a trend that the government is seeking to reverse through planned increases in the age at which Social Security benefits are received.

Although the backers of the ERISA legislation were apparently prompted by the potential avoidance of pension liabilities through layoff, backloading of pension accrual has much more general implications for worker mobility. Job change, by itself, reduces pension benefits. Even if it involves no change in future wage earnings and even if the provisions of the pension plans on the old and new jobs are the same, workers who change jobs will typically have much lower pension benefits at retirement age than those who remain with the same employer. Thus, pension provisions may inhibit worker mobility and, therefore, adjustment to changing economic circumstances.

The 1980s have witnessed a marked shift in government policy toward promoting the labor supply of the elderly. The government has virtually eliminated mandatory retirement and scheduled a gradual increase in

Social Security's retirement age. It has limited somewhat Social Security's earnings test that reduces Social Security benefits for "retired" workers earning more than an "exempt amount"; it has eliminated the earnings test after age 70 and is increasing the actuarial incentive to delay the receipt of Social Security benefits beyond age 65. The government has also required that pension plans provide continued pension benefit accrual for workers who remain with the firm beyond the pension plan's normal retirement age.

1.2 Demographic Change Meets the Trend Toward Early Retirement

The change in government policy toward the labor supply of the elderly is responsive to the major demographic swing currently underway, with its important implications for retirement finances in the next century. The elderly (those over 64), who now constitute about one-fifth of all adults, will constitute about two-fifths of all adults by 2040. Given Social Security's pay-as-you-go method of finance, the projected increase in the ratio of beneficiaries to contributors means either significant cuts in future benefits or significant future increases in Social Security's payroll tax rate. Although the 1983 Social Security legislation provides a plan for dealing with the baby boomer's demographic bulge, there is real concern that the plan will not be fully implemented; and if it is fully implemented, there is concern that it will not be sufficient.

Reversing the trend toward early retirement represents an important alternative for addressing the demographic transition. Additional labor supply of the elderly would relieve Social Security's finances as well as offset a potential shortage in the supply of labor relative to that of other productive factors. Despite recent changes in government policy, the early retirement trend remains quite strong. Table 1 presents the labor force participation rates of men between ages 40 to 64 since 1967. In 1967 the labor force participation rate of men aged 55 to 59 was 90.1 percent; it was 81.9 percent in 1980 and 79.0 percent in 1986. For males 60 to 64 the 1986 labor force participation rate was 54.9 percent, down from 61.0 percent in 1980 and 77.6 percent in 1967. The participation rate of men over 65 fell from 35 percent in 1960 to below 20 percent in 1980 (figures not shown in the table).

1.3 Are Pension Plans the Major Old-Age Work Deterrent?

Economists have pointed to Social Security as well as general increases in living standards as the key explanations for increased early retirement, but little attention has been given to the retirement incentives associated with

TABLE 1
Labor Force Participation Rates of Men

	Age				
Year	40–44	45–49	50–54	55–59	60–64
1967	97.0	96.2	94.2	90.1	77.6
1968	97.0	95.9	93.9	90.0	77.3
1969	96.7	95.7	93.5	89.6	75.8
1970	96.5	95.4	93.1	89.5	75.0
1971	96.3	94.9	92.8	88.8	74.1
1972	96.2	94.6	91.9	87.4	72.5
1973	95.8	94.3	91.7	86.2	69.1
1974	95.5	94.0	90.4	85.7	67.9
1975	95.2	94.1	90.1	84.4	65.7
1976	95.0	93.3	89.9	83.6	63.7
1977	95.3	93.2	89.2	83.2	62.9
1978	95.1	93.0	89.7	82.9	62.0
1979	95.3	93.4	89.6	82.2	61.8
1980	95.1	93.3	89.3	81.9	61.0
1981	94.9	93.4	89.6	81.3	58.7
1982	94.7	92.8	89.7	81.9	57.2
1983	94.8	93.3	89.1	80.7	57.0
1984	95.1	93.3	88.9	80.2	56.1
1985	94.7	93.3	88.6	79.6	55.6
1986	94.3	92.9	88.9	79.0	54.9

Source: Employment and earnings, various years.

private pension plan provisions. Our analysis of a recent Bureau of Labor Statistics cross-section survey of pension plans indicates a large proportion with substantially backloaded pension plans; these plans typically have very sizable accrual as the age of either early or normal retirement approaches, and they often have more lower, or even negative, pension accrual, thereafter. Such accrual profiles engender very large implicit taxes on labor supply beyond the age at which the significant pension accrual occurs. These old-age pension work disincentives often exceed those arising from the effect of Social Security provisions on Social Security accrual and from the effect of the Social Security earnings test. In addition to fostering early retirement, such accrual profiles raise the concern, voiced by Senator Bensten, that workers may be terminated, or change jobs for other reasons, immediately prior to accruing the great majority of their pension benefits.

1.4 Organization of the Paper

Before presenting the new evidence on pension backloading practices, we briefly discuss in the next section a possible economic rationale for pension backloading as well as the potential economic problems arising from the government's regulation of the pattern of pension accrual and, more generally, its anti-age-discrimination policy.

Section 3 introduces the concept of pension accrual and demonstrates how in many instances it imposes an implicit tax on wage earnings; sometimes it increases total compensation, and sometimes it reduces it. Illustrative graphs indicate that defined benefit pension plans are typically severely backloaded. Section 4 discusses ERISA's antibackloading rules and suggests why they are ineffective in limiting backloading. Section 5 presents findings on the accrual of pension benefits based on the 1979 Bureau of Labor Statistics Level of Benefits Survey (BLS-LOB). This survey of 1,469 establishments with 3,386,121 pension participants provides extremely detailed information concerning vesting, early and normal retirement benefits, supplemental early retirement benefits, and Social Security offset formulae, each of which is a crucial input to the calculation of pension accruals.

Section 6 examines the retirement response of workers in a large Fortune 500 company to the pattern of pension accrual. The pension accrual profile for this firm exhibits very substantial backloading with disproportionate benefit accrual at the age of early retirement and only modest accrual thereafter. This pension accrual profile appears to substantially increase the early retirement of the firm's employees. We estimate that the firm's accrual profile increases from 14 to 44 percent the probability that a worker at age 55 will leave employment prior to age 60. The last section briefly summarizes our findings and raises some questions relevant to pension policy.

2. AN ECONOMIC RATIONALE FOR PENSION BACKLOADING

In recent years the traditional spot-market view of the labor market, in which compensation equals productivity at each point in time, has given way to a contract view. According to the contract view, workers and firms enter into long-term relationships, which may be explicit or implicit, in which there is a relationship over time between compensation and productivity but not necessarily an equality between the two at any given point in time.

The economic rationale for long-term labor contracts as opposed to short-term spot-market arrangements is that firms can structure compensation over the workspan to improve worker incentives. For example, by paying workers for less than they produce when young and for more than they produce when old, the firm provides the worker with an enhanced incentive to remain with the firm. It may also provide an incentive to work harder; the cost of shirking becomes not only the loss of one's current salary but also the lost opportunity to earn more than one produces in the future. This carrot-stick age-related structure of compensation is potentially beneficial not only to employers but to workers as well. By reducing worker turnover and increasing effort, the firm can afford to pay workers a higher present value of compensation. Such higher present-value payments to workers reflect not the benevolence of employers but the outcome of a competitive contract market in which firms compete with each other in hiring workers.

Although the long-term contract view of labor arrangements implies that the firm will compensate the worker in excess of his or her productivity after an initial period in which the reverse is true, the length of time during which compensation exceeds productivity cannot be unlimited. The firm's competitive interest is in reimbursing the worker when old for earning less than he or she produced when young, not paying the worker more than is necessary to balance the account. Hence, the firm's interest is in fixing the length of time in which compensation exceeds productivity. As pointed out by Lazear (1981,1982), mandatory retirement provides a convenient mechanism for limiting this time period.

Compensation can be paid as wage earnings or as pension accrual. Therefore, one mechanism for paying deferred compensation at certain ages and for reducing compensation at subsequent ages is to provide significant positive pension accrual prior to a critical age and small or even negative pension accrual thereafter.

In eliminating mandatory retirement the government may have reduced one important mechanism by which employers were able to limit the amount of deferred compensation. If Congress were also to proscribe abrupt changes in the age-profile of pension or any other form of compensation, firms might find it even more difficult to structure deferred compensation efficiently.

In addition to potential assistance in providing work incentives, the age profile of pension accrual may represent a graceful mechanism to lower the wages of older workers if, as seems likely (Kotlikoff (1987)), they become less productive with age. As described below, pension accrual after early and/or normal retirement ages is often quite small, if not negative.

3. PENSION BENEFIT ACCRUAL FORMULAE AND IMPLICIT TAX ON WAGE EARNINGS

Vested pension benefit accrual at age a, $I(a)$, equals the difference between pension wealth at age $a+1$, $Pw(a+1)$, and pension wealth at age a, $Pw(a)$, accumulated to age $a+1$ at the nominal interest rate r: that is,

$$I(a) = Pw(a + 1) - Pw(a)(1 + r). \tag{1}$$

Pension accrual is thus the increment to pension wealth in excess of the return on the previously accumulated pension bank account. Pension wealth at age a is defined as the expected value of vested pension benefits discounted to age a. The term "expected" refers to the use of mortality probabilities to assess the chances that the worker will be alive at future ages when benefits are available. Intuitively, $Pw(a)$ can be thought of as the worker's pension bank account. If $I(a) = 0$, the worker continuing employment with the plan sponsor at age a has exactly the same pension wealth at age $a + 1$ as an identically situated worker who terminates employment at age a. The worker receives no compensation in the form of increased future pension benefits.

Figure 1 presents the age profile of accrued pension benefits divided by wages for a hypothetical plan under different assumptions about real wage growth and nominal interest rates. The top profile, for example, is based on a 3 percent rate of real wage growth and a 9 percent nominal interest rate. The inflation rate assumed in each profile is 6 percent. The plan provides 100 percent vesting at ten years of service and calculates normal retirement benefits as 1 percent of average earnings over the last five years of service times the number of years of service. The plan's early and normal retirement ages are 55 and 65, respectively. Workers can retire early and receive early retirement benefits that equal normal retirement benefits reduced by 3 percent for each year that retirement precedes the normal retirement age.

There are two significant discontinuities in the profiles. One occurs at age 40 when the worker becomes vested; clearly in going from age 39 to age 40 the worker's vested pension wealth changes abruptly from zero to a positive number explaining the jump in the profile. The second discontinuity occurs at the age of early retirement. It arises because the 3 percent per year early retirement reduction factor is much more generous than an actuarial reduction. By retiring a year earlier, the worker gains a year's benefit with only a modest, 3 percent, payment for that delay. To understand more clearly why there is a discontinuous fall in pension

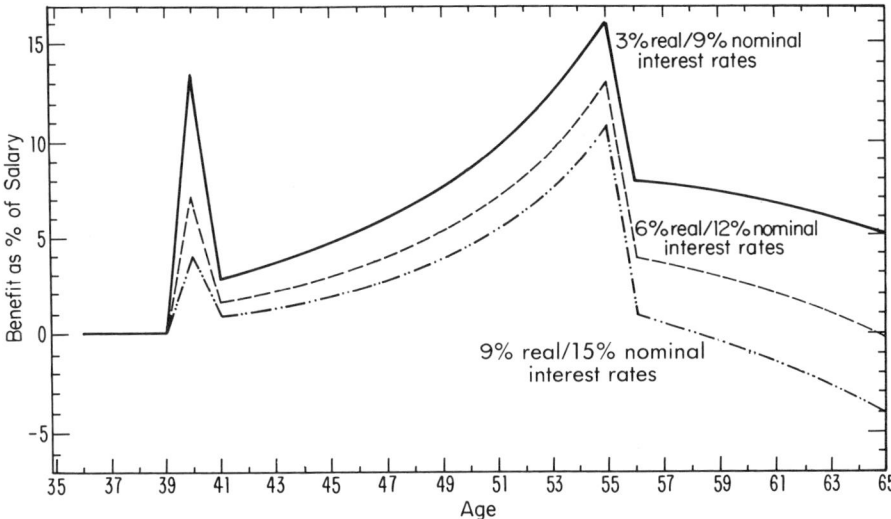

FIGURE 1. *Pension increments as a percentage of salary, by age, for a wage stream with 6 percent inflation discounted at real interest rates of 3 percent, 6 percent, and 9 percent.*

accrual at early retirement, consider the case in which the early retirement reduction factor is zero. In this case by working an additional year after age 55, the worker loses that year's benefit entirely. Although it is true that the worker's future benefit will likely be larger because of an additional year of service and possibly an increase in the earnings base, the loss of this year's benefit may significantly offset or even outweigh, in present value, this benefit increase, implying a small or negative pension accrual during the period after early retirement.

The diagram indicates roughly a halving in the accrual ratio between ages 55 and 56. Beyond age 55 the accrual ratio declines gradually. If one assumes a sufficiently high interest rate, the accrual after age 55 is negative. According to the three curves, total compensation is roughly 8 percent lower, ceteris paribus, at age 65 than at age 55. The diagram also indicates that much of the accrual of vested pension benefits occurs in the ages immediately preceding age 55. Figure 2 shows the effect of the lower-than-actuarial reduction for early retirement on the hypothetical plan's accrual profile. It compares the top profile of Figure 1 with the profile that would occur if the reduction factor were actuarial or, what is equivalent, if workers were forced to wait until the normal retirement age to collect benefits. Notice that the discontinuity at age 65 disappears. Also note that the

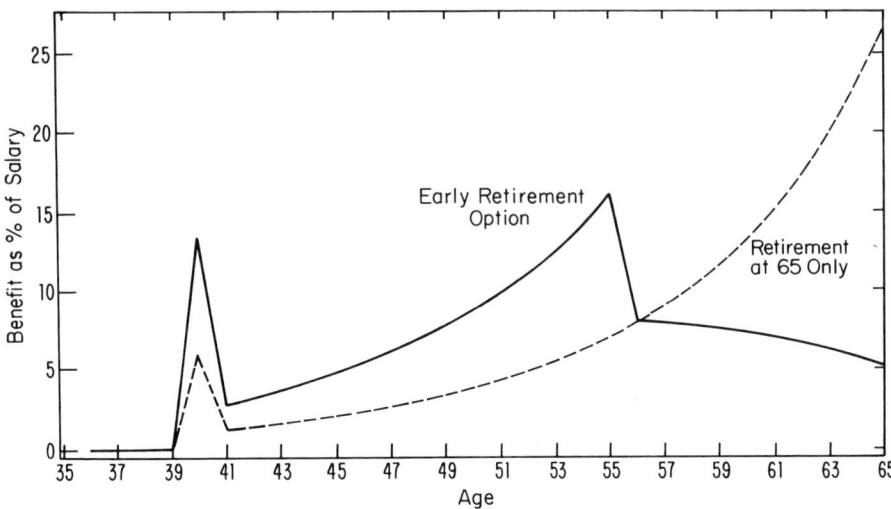

FIGURE 2. *Pension increments as a percentage of salary, by age, for plans with an early retirement option versus retirement at 65. 6 percent wage inflation, 3 percent real interest rate.*

backloading in the "Retirement at 65 Only" profile is even greater than that in the profile with the early retirement option. This is inherent in the defined benefit formula, with the benefit at age a typically given by $B(a) = kW(a)T(a)$, where $W(a)$ is the wage at age a, $T(a)$ is years of service at age a, and k is a multiplier often between 0.01 and 0.02. If $k = 0.02$, the worker's benefit, in nominal dollars, is 2 percent of his final wage for each year of service; after working thirty years, the pension would equal 60 percent of the final wage.

3.1 The Accrual Profile for a Large Fortune 500 Firm

The profiles presented in the first two diagrams, although indicative of a considerable degree of backloading, are based on a hypothetical plan with rather simple features. But if one thing is true of private pension plans, it is that there is enormous variation among them. Figure 3 presents the pension accrual profile of male managers hired at age 20 in the Fortune 500 firm whose retirement behavior is discussed in Section 6. The diagram also includes the estimated age-wage profile in absolute 1985 dollars for the managers as well as the age-accrual profile of Social Security benefits.

In addition to having ten-year "cliff" vesting, a two-step earnings-related normal retirement benefit formula, this plan has a Social Security offset, a supplemental early retirement benefit, and special early retirement benefit

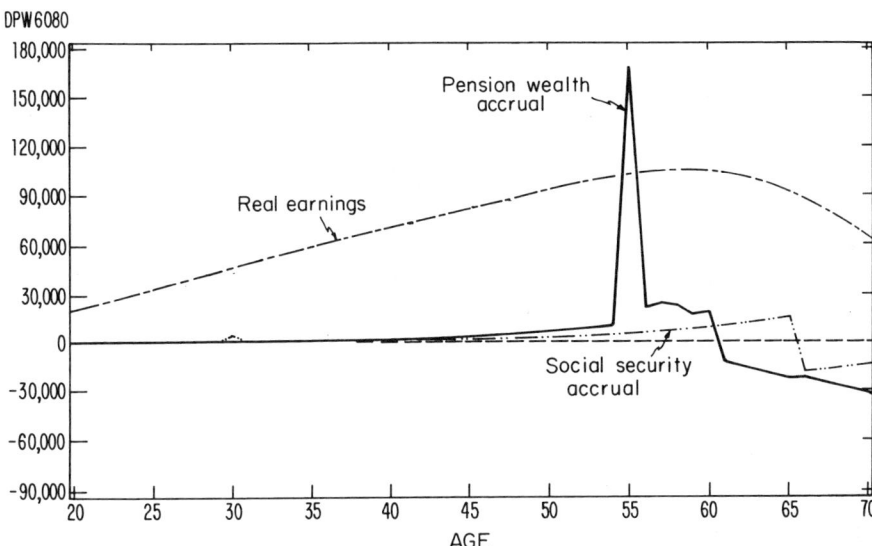

FIGURE 3. *Pension wealth accrual, SS accrual, and wage earnings for male managers born in 1960 and hired in 1980, in real 1985 dollars.*

reduction factors. The supplemental early retirement benefit and the less-than-actuarially fair reduction factors are available only to workers who remain with the firm through age 55, the early retirement age. Workers who leave at age 54 or earlier can start collecting their vested benefits at age 55, but these benefits are actuarially reduced. In addition, such pre–early retirement terminators receive benefits that are immediately reduced by the Social Security offset. In contrast, for workers retiring at age 55 or later, the Social Security offset does not occur until age 65; hence, the supplemental early retirement benefit corresponds to the Social Security offset for each year between the age of retirement and age 65.

Thus there are two important reasons for the accrual spike at early retirement in Figure 3. The first is the nonactuarial early retirement reduction factors and the fact that they are available only to those remaining with the firm until age 55; the second is the delay in the Social Security offset, which is also only provided to workers remaining through early retirement.

Now that we understand the source of the large accrual spike in Figure 3, let us consider its size and implications. First the spike at age 55 is very large—over one-and-one-half times a year's earnings. Second, between age 55 and 60, accrual, though small in comparison with the spike at 55, is still quite important. However, after age 60 accrual is negative, becoming significantly negative by age 65. Clearly, this is an extremely backloaded pension plan that provides workers with a strong incentive to remain with the firm through early retirement and a strong incentive to leave the firm thereafter. For workers who quit or otherwise lose their jobs at, for example, age 54, there is a very substantial loss in benefits compared with remaining on the job through age 55. In its effect accrual profiles of this kind recreate the situation of some plans prior to ERISA in which workers *could* be terminated immediately before they accrued the bulk of their potential pension benefits. There is clear evidence that this does not happen in this firm, however.

4. HOW FIRMS MAY CIRCUMVENT ERISA'S ANTIBACKLOADING RULES

ERISA stipulates that defined benefit pension accrual must satisfy one of three provisions. The first is a 3 percent rule that says that workers' accrued benefits must exceed their years of service times 3 percent of the normal retirement benefit they would have if they had begun service at the earliest possible age of participation and had remained with the firm until normal retirement. That is, for each year of employment pension, accrual must be at least 3 percent of the amount the workers will have if they stay until normal retirement. The second provision is a 133 percent rule that says that future projected annual pension accrual cannot exceed 133 percent of current annual pension accrual. The third provision stipulates that the terminating worker's benefit be not less than his or her projected normal retirement benefit times the ratio of actual completed service to the service the worker would have if he or she remained with the firm through early retirement. That is, if the worker leaves after twenty years and normal retirement would be after forty years, the benefit must be 50 percent of what the worker would have if he or she worked twenty more years.

Each of these three provisions specifies that the projection of future normal retirement benefits and future pension accrual be determined by assuming that a worker's future wage equals the current wage. But if there is wage inflation, future wages may be much greater than current wages, and the real value of current accrual may be quite low. Thus even a modest rate of wage inflation could permit a quite backloaded plan that, nonetheless, meets one of the three antibackloading provisions. The choice of other assumptions in the accrual calculation, such as the interest rate, also give firms additional latitude in deferring pension accrual.

However, the main method of backloading that does not appear to be ruled out by the three ERISA rules involves early retirement provisions. The accrual rules pertain to normal retirement benefits rather than early retirement benefits. Extra benefits arising from supplemental early retirement benefits or from less-than-actuarial reductions of early retirement benefits do not appear to be considered in the three antibackloading rules. Thus a firm could structure its plan to have small normal retirement benefit but to have substantial early retirement benefit, for example. It could easily conform its accrual of the small normal retirement benefit to one of the three ERISA rules, yet remain free to specify quite large early retirement benefits that only accrue if the worker stays with the firm through a critical age. Recall the example of the large firm considered here; this firm provides extra early retirement benefits in the form of (1) a waiver until the age of normal retirement in their offset of benefits due to Social Security and (2) less-than-actuarial early retirement reduction rates.

5. PENSION ACCRUAL IN THE BLS-LOB DATA

In this section we examine accrual ratios for earnings-based defined benefit plans from the BLS-LOB survey. Earnings-based plans account for approximately 80 percent of BLS-designated usable plans from the survey and about 65 percent of plans weighted by pension coverage. Each of the earnings-based plans we examine stipulates cliff vesting at ten years, but the plans have different normal and early retirement ages. Other earnings-based plans with different vesting ages have accrual profiles similar to those that we shall describe, but for convenience of exposition we have not included them in our analysis here. Of the 1,183 earnings-based plans we examine, 508 are integrated with Social Security under an offset formula. The accrual profiles were calculated under the assumption of a 6 percent nominal wage growth up to age 65, after which nominal wage growth is assumed to be zero. We also assume a 9 percent interest rate. Our calculations are based on the industry-occupation-age-earnings profiles reported in Kotlikoff and Wise (1987).

5.1 The Decline in Pension Wealth Accrual at Early and Normal Retirement Ages

Age profiles of the average ratio of pension accrual to the wage for the percent of earnings plans with ten-year cliff vesting are shown in Table 2 by early and normal retirement ages. Three of these average profiles, corresponding to plans with the respective early and normal retirement ages—55–55, 55–65, 65–65—are graphed in Figure 4. The 55–55 and the 65–65 profiles show a considerable degree of backloading, the first with dispro-

TABLE 2
Weighted Average Accrual Rates for Percent of Earnings Plans With Ten-Year Cliff Vesting, by Early and Normal Retirement Age[a]

Early ret.	55	55	55	60	60	62	62	65
Normal ret.	55	60	65	60	65	62	65	65
No. of plans	152	115	513	78	53	19	8	50
Age								
40	.244	.111	.071	.034	.047	.038	.054	.036
41	.045	.022	.013	.007	.010	.016	.009	.010
42	.051	.026	.016	.008	.011	.017	.010	.011
43	.058	.029	.018	.010	.013	.120	.011	.012
44	.066	.033	.020	.011	.015	.029	.013	.014
45	.075	.036	.023	.013	.017	.036	.013	.016
46	.085	.043	.026	.016	.019	.042	.015	.018
47	.097	.050	.031	.028	.022	.047	.017	.021
48	.110	.057	.035	.039	.025	.054	.019	.024
49	.124	.064	.040	.056	.029	.060	.021	.027
50	.141	.077	.046	.065	.034	.068	.023	.031
51	.159	.072	.052	.084	.040	.077	.026	.033
52	.180	.087	.062	.091	.050	.090	.028	.043
53	.204	.099	.072	.105	.060	.101	.032	.050
54	.231	.113	.083	.117	.068	.114	.035	.055
55	.261	.130	.097	.149	.082	.128	.039	.065
56	−.003	.100	.068	.170	.094	.144	.036	.068
57	−.012	.111	.072	.192	.107	.162	.039	.076
58	−.020	.118	.076	.224	.127	.184	.044	.089
59	−.028	.129	.077	.241	.146	.208	.048	.105
60	−.038	.143	.079	.269	.167	.241	.054	.118
61	−.048	−.090	.068	−.061	.113	.220	.059	.128
62	−.058	−.091	.064	−.091	.115	.248	.066	.145
63	−.067	−.091	.056	−.114	.114	−.130	.017	.163
64	−.076	−.092	.053	−.121	.114	−.136	.012	.186
65	−.085	−.094	.044	−.121	.112	−.144	.006	.211
66	−.292	−.169	−.152	−.138	−.088	−.266	−.081	−.194
67	−.294	−.174	−.162	−.155	−.115	−.263	−.080	−.204
68	−.295	−.179	−.171	−.171	−.142	−.260	−.079	−.213
69	−.296	−.182	−.179	−.184	−.162	−.258	−.078	−.221
70	−.297	−.184	−.186	−.196	−.182	−.255	−.077	−.234

[a] Plans with early or normal retirement supplements are excluded.

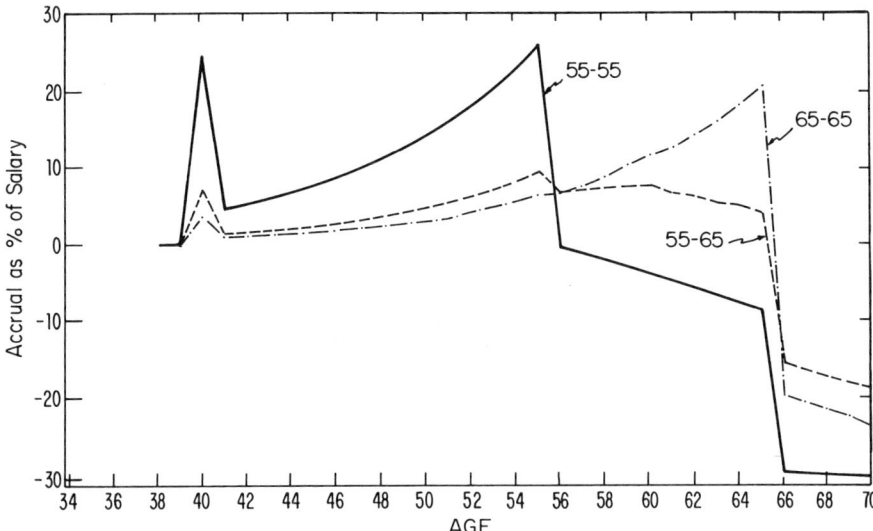

FIGURE 4. *Weighted average accrual rates for percentage of earnings plans with ten-year cliff vesting, for selected early and normal retirement ages.*

portionate accrual as age approaches 55, and the second as age approaches 65. In addition, each graph shows substantial declines in the rate of pension wealth accrual at several critical ages. The first is the age of normal retirement, which equals the age of early retirement for plans with no early retirement option. Second, there is a sharp decline in the rate of accrual at the age of early retirement, but this decline is substantially lower than the decline at the normal retirement age. Third, there is a very substantial decline between ages 65 and 66 in the average accrual rate no matter what the ages of early and normal retirement. This age 65 decline would, however, be smaller under current law, which mandates continued participation in the plan's benefit formula after the plan's normal retirement age. This 1986 legislation was not incorporated in these accrual analyses because the law postdates our information on the pension plans. The new law may have temporarily altered the postnormal retirement accrual pattern. But, if the patterns depicted here were chosen for a specific reason, and there is little evidence that they were or that they were not, plans could add additional features that will restore the pre-1986 decline in pension accrual after normal retirement.

The declines in average accrual rates at the critical ages indicated in Table

TABLE 3

Early and normal retirement age

Age	(1) 55 55	(2) 55 60	(3) 55 65	(4) 60 60	(5) 60 65	(6) 62 62	(7) 62 65	(8) 65 65
40	.244	.111	.071	.034	.047	.038	.054	.036
55	.261	.130	.097					
56	−.003	.100	.068					
60		.143		.269	.167			
61		−.090		−.061	.113			
62						.248	.066	
63						−.130	.017	
65	−.085	−.094	.044	−.121	.112	−.144	.006	.211
66	−.292	−.169	−.152	−.138	−.088	−.266	−.081	−.194
70	−.297	−.184	−.186	−.196	−.182	−.255	−.077	−.234
65–66	20	8	19	2	20	12	8	40

2 are highlighted in Table 3. The ages of early and normal retirement are identical in columns 1, 4, 6, and 8 of the table with respective retirement ages of 55, 60, 62, and 65. At these ages the accrual rate as a percentage of wages declines from 0.26 to 0, 0.27 to 0.06, 0.25 to −0.13, and 0.21 to −0.19, respectively. Thus, total annual compensation (wage plus pension accrual) from working declines at these ages by 21 percent, 26 percent, 30 percent, and 33 percent, respectively. Surely the incentive beyond these ages to continue work with the current employer is substantially reduced.

In instances where early and normal retirement ages do not coincide, there is also a substantial decline in the average ratio of pension accrual to the wage at the age of normal retirement. For example, among plans with early retirement at 55 and normal retirement at 60, the average decline is from 0.14 to −0.09. There is also a decline at the age of early retirement for these plans, although it is considerably less than the decline at the age of normal retirement. For example, of plans with early retirement at 55 and normal retirement at 65, the average decline at 55 is from 0.10 to 0.07, whereas at 65 the average decline is from 0.04 to -0.15.

The figure and the table also show a large variation in average pension accrual at 40, the age of cliff vesting. It is highest, on average, for plans with early and normal retirement at 55 and lowest, on average, for plans with early and normal retirement at 65. As mentioned, because the early retirement reduction is typically less than actuarially fair, pension wealth— the present value of the future stream of benefit payments—is generally greatest if benefits are taken at the age of early retirement. Thus the accrued

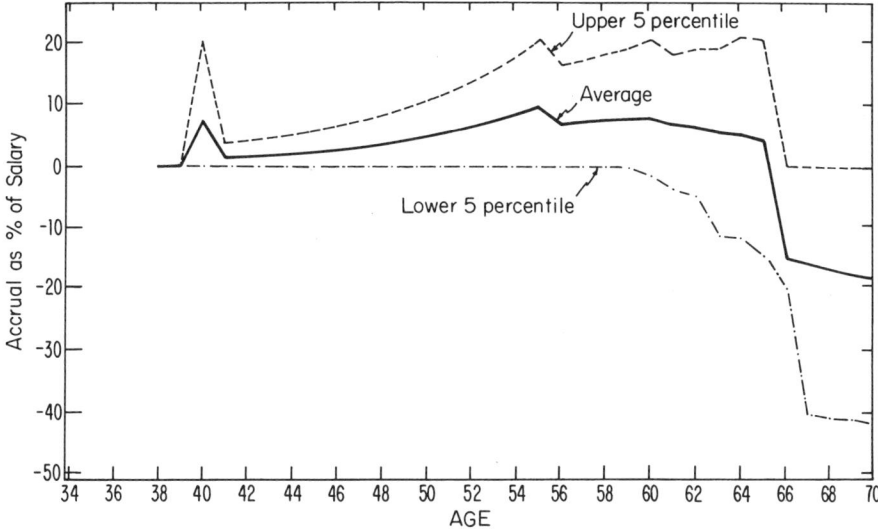

FIGURE 5. *Weighted average accrual rates and upper and lower 5 percentile levels for percentage of earnings plans with ten-year cliff vesting. Early retirement at 55, and normal retirement at 65.*

wealth at the age of vesting is usually calculated by discounting benefits from the age of early retirement, assuming that the worker could begin to collect benefits at that age. Figure 4, for example, shows an average vesting spike of almost 25 percent of earnings for 55-55 plans, 7 percent of earnings for 55-65 plans, and about 4 percent of earnings for 65-65 plans.

5.2 Variation Among Plans

Even among plans with the same early and normal retirement ages there is wide variation in accrual rates at each age, particularly after the age of early retirement. Consider the accrual ratio at age 55. The average ratio for this subsample is 0.097, the maximum is 0.405, and the minimum is 0. The ratio at the lowest fifth percentile is 0, at the highest fifth percentile it is 0.208. There is a similarly large dispersion in annual accrual ratios at each of the ages 40 through 70. Weighted average accrual rates together with upper and lower 5 percentile levels are graphed in Figure 5. The average accrual rates between ages 55 and 65 are positive; for many plans, however, the rates prior to age 65 are very negative. *Thus it is very important not to base judgments about the labor force participation incentive effects of pensions simply on the basis of average accrual rates.*

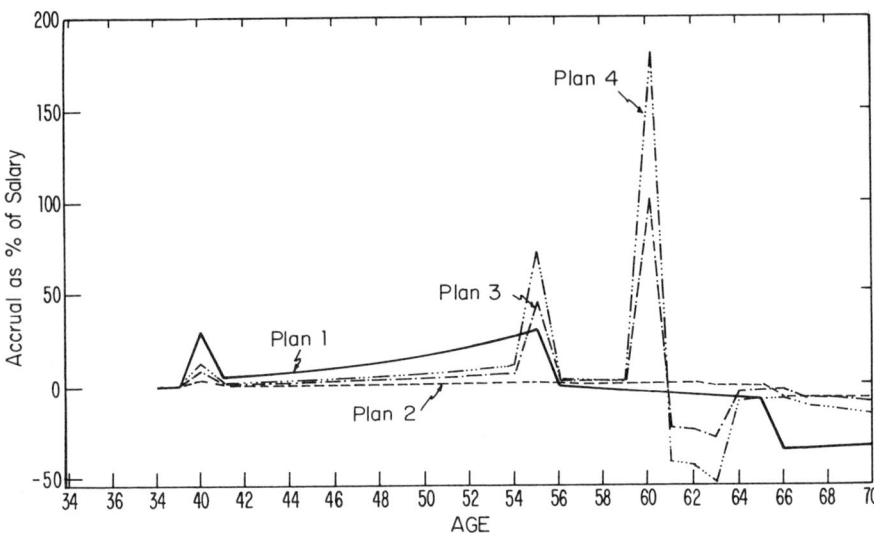

FIGURE 6. *Accrual profiles for four large plans.*

Additional evidence of the variability of pension accrual profiles and the possibility of severely backloaded plans is obtained by comparing profiles of particular plans. Figure 6 plots the accrual profiles of four of the sample's largest plans. Plan 1 exhibits a 29 percent vesting spike, a reduction of 30 percentage points in the accrual ratio at age 55 and a further major reduction at age 65 from −0.063 to −0.351. In contrast, the vesting spike is only 4 percent for plan 2 in the figure. This plan also exhibits no major reduction in the accrual ratio after early retirement and only a minor reduction at normal retirement. Plan 3's vesting spike is much less than that of plan 1, but the drop in accrual at age 55 is very much larger than that in plan 1. This plan also exhibits extremely sharp changes in accrual ratios at ages 60 and 63. Plan 4 exhibits even greater discontinuities in the accrual profile and more backloading than Plan 3. It shows little accrual before age 55, accrual at 55 equivalent to about 75 percent of the wage, little accrual at ages 56 through 59, accrual at 60 almost twice as large as wage earnings, then *negative* accrual at ages 61 through 63 equivalent to about 50 percent of the wage. Clearly, the plans' incentive effects on labor force participation also vary widely.

5.3 Accrual Ratios by Industry and Occupation

Holding fixed the early and normal retirement ages, we see little difference in average accrual profiles across industries or occupations. But since these retirement ages differ, on average, particularly across industries, a typical worker faces a much greater incentive in some industries to leave the labor force early. For example, a large proportion of workers covered by pensions in transportation would experience a 27 percent reduction in effective compensation by continuing to work between 55 and 56. At 55, pension accrual would be equivalent to about 27 percent of wage rates for many workers in this industry, but if the worker continued in the labor force until age 66 the annual loss in pension wealth would be equivalent to 30 percent of wage earnings at 66. A large proportion of workers in manufacturing have plans with early retirement at 55 and normal retirement at 65. In this case, the accrual at 55 averages about 9 percent of the wage at 55 and only declines to about 7 percent of the wage by 65. But then the accrual rate becomes negative, and if the worker were to continued in the labor force between 65 and 66 the decline in pension accrual would amount to an effective reduction in compensation of about 21 percent.

5.4 The Possible Impact of the 1986 Age Discrimination Act on Pension Accrual

Table 4 isolates the potential impact of the 1986 legislation requiring continued participation in the pension formula after the plan's normal retirement age. The table presents the accrual ratios for percentage of earnings plans with early retirement at 55 and selected normal retirement ages calculated by first assuming that all of the plans had a provision to credit fully postnormal retirement service and second by assuming that all the plans had no such credit provision. The table indicates that the effect of crediting service after normal retirement depends importantly on the age of normal retirement. For plans with a normal retirement age of 55, negative accrual ratios are larger in absolute value under no crediting prior to age 66 and smaller in absolute value thereafter. A similar pattern, although less pronounced, is observed after age 62 for plans with normal retirement at that age. The least effect is found for the most common plans, those with normal retirement at 65 (and early retirement at 55). If pension plans do not alter some other features to reproduce the pre-1986 retirement incentives, the 1986 legislation will have a nontrivial affect on retirement incentives for some plans at some ages. But even if plans are not restructured, fully crediting postnormal retirement service has only a minor impact on accrual after age 66 for most pension plans.

5.5 Early and Normal Retirement Supplements and the Potential for Backloading

Approximately 11.4 percent of plans have early retirement supplements, and 7.5 percent have normal ones. The typical normal retirement supple-

TABLE 4
Weighted Average Accrual Rates for Percent of Earnings Plans With Ten-Year Cliff Vesting and Early Retirement at 55, by Normal Retirement Age, **Assuming** *Full Credit and No Credit Postretirement Provisions*

Normal ret.	55 FC[a]	55 NC	62 FC	62 NC	65 FC	65 NC
No. of plans	152	152	187	187	513	513
Age						
40	.244	.244	.106	.106	.071	.071
41	.045	.045	.023	.023	.013	.013
42	.051	.051	.027	.027	.016	.016
43	.058	.058	.032	.031	.018	.018
44	.066	.066	.035	.035	.020	.020
45	.075	.075	.045	.045	.023	.023
46	.085	.085	.046	.046	.026	.026
47	.097	.097	.055	.055	.031	.031
48	.110	.110	.064	.064	.035	.035
49	.124	.124	.076	.076	.040	.040
50	.141	.141	.090	.090	.046	.046
51	.159	.159	.104	.104	.052	.052
52	.180	.180	.120	.120	.062	.062
53	.204	.204	.140	.140	.072	.072
54	.231	.231	.160	.160	.083	.083
55	.261	.261	.185	.185	.097	.097
56	−.002	−.244	.102	.102	.068	.068
57	−.011	−.229	.105	.105	.072	.072
58	−.019	−.215	.118	.118	.076	.076
59	−.027	−.202	.117	.117	.077	.077
60	−.037	−.139	.114	.114	.079	.079
61	−.049	−.178	.099	.099	.068	.068
62	−.059	−.167	.098	.098	.064	.064
63	−.068	−.157	−.060	−.284	.056	.056
64	−.077	−.148	−.069	−.267	.053	.063
65	−.086	−.139	−.079	−.252	.044	.044
66	−.133	−.130	−.150	−.237	−.132	−.225
67	−.177	−.128	−.192	−.233	−.153	−.222
68	−.219	−.127	−.231	−.232	−.172	−.219
69	−.261	−.124	−.260	−.227	−.190	−.216
70	−.301	−.123	−.285	−.223	−.205	−.212

[a] Assumed postnormal retirement provision: FC = full credit; NC = no credit.

ment provides an addition to otherwise calculated benefits if the individual postpones retirement until the normal retirement age. The typical early retirement supplement provides an addition to benefits if retirement occurs after the age of early retirement. Retirement supplements, which are not available to workers who leave before reaching specified ages, thus provide a potentially powerful mechanism for pension backloading.

The average accrual rates for percentage of earnings and flat plans with supplements, with ten-year cliff vesting, and with early and normal retirement at 55 and 65, respectively, are shown in Table 5 by type of supplement. There are just two plans in the category with only normal retirement supplements, but, nonetheless, the effect of the supplements can be seen in the first column of the table. The accrual rate jumps from about 8 percent of the wage at age 64 to 60 percent of the wage at age 65. Thus the supplement generates substantial backloading and provides a relatively strong incentive to remain with the firm until age 65, but thereafter there is a sharp drop in the accrual rate to -18 percent.

Accrual rates for plans with early retirement supplements are shown in the second column of the table. In this case there is a sharp increase in the average accrual rate from 12 percent of the wage at age 54 to 44 percent at age 55, with a sharp drop thereafter. Again, the provision increases backloading and provides a substantial incentive to remain with the firm until the age of early retirement, with a very substantial disincentive to remaining thereafter. Accrual rates for plans with both types of supplements are shown in the last column of the table. In this case there is a rather large spike at the age of early retirement, equal to 62 percent of the wage in that year, with a smaller, but still noticeable, spike at about the age of normal retirement.

Accrual rates for percent of earnings and flat plans with either type of supplement are shown in Table 6 for selected early and normal retirement ages. The spikes in the accrual rates are highlighted with dashed lines. Consider, for example, plans with early retirement at age 55. The spike created by the early retirement supplement is from 0.22 at age 54 to 0.39 at age 55 for plans with normal retirement at 55, from 0.12 at age 54 to 0.50 at age 55 for plans with normal retirement at 60, and from 0.11 at age 54 to 0.48 at age 55 for plans with normal retirement at 65. Of the 56 plans with normal retirement at age 60, the pension accrual rate at that age is, on average, equivalent to 100 percent of the wage rate.

Similar discontinuities in the accrual ratios are evident for plans with other early and normal retirement ages. For example, of plans with early and normal retirement at age 60, the accrual rate at that age is equivalent to 64 percent of the annual wage for persons aged 60. Thus these special supplements create very significant one-time additions to pension wealth

TABLE 5
Weighted Average Accrual Rates for Percent of Earnings and Flat Plans With Ten-Year Cliff Vesting, Early and Normal Retirement at 55–65, and Early or Normal Retirement Supplement, by Type of Supplement

	Normal supplement (2 plans)	Early supplement (10 plans)	Both supplements (10 plans)
Age			
40	.065	.111	.035
41	.012	.197	.009
42	.013	.023	.011
43	.015	.026	.013
44	.017	.031	.018
45	.019	.035	.023
46	.022	.040	.030
47	.025	.047	.037
48	.028	.053	.044
49	.032	.060	.052
50	.036	.069	.060
51	.040	.079	.070
52	.045	.094	.081
53	.051	.106	.095
54	.057	.121	.108
55	.065	.442	.621
56	.047	−.0007	−.051
57	.051	−.008	−.049
58	.054	−.014	−.043
59	.058	−.022	−.046
60	.061	−.011	−.051
61	.066	−.049	−.068
62	.070	−.058	−.072
63	.074	−.073	−.080
64	.078	−.022	.009
65	.601	−.031	.008
66	−.181	−.247	−.092
67	−.180	−.213	−.167
68	−.179	−.207	−.164
69	−.179	−.204	−.163
70	−.178	−.201	−.160

TABLE 6
Weighted Average Accrual Rates for Percent of Earnings and Flat Plans With Ten-Year Cliff Vesting and Early or Normal Retirement Supplements, by Early and Normal Retirement ages[a]

Early ret.	55	55	55	60	60	62
normal ret.	55	60	65	60	65	62
No. of plans	19	56	22	37	2	19
Age						
40	.199	.136	.082	.078	.068	.056
41	.039	.024	.015	.014	.012	.010
42	.045	.027	.018	.016	.013	.011
43	.052	.030	.021	.018	.015	.013
44	.059	.034	.025	.020	.017	.151
45	.068	.038	.030	.022	.019	.180
46	.077	.043	.036	.023	.022	.020
47	.088	.049	.041	.027	.025	.023
48	.100	.055	.048	.030	.028	.026
49	.114	.062	.056	.035	.032	.030
50	.129	.070	.064	.039	.036	.035
51	.148	.080	.074	.044	.040	.029
52	.167	.090	.087	.050	.046	.033
53	.191	.103	.099	.057	.053	.039
54	.220	.117	.113	.066	.061	.044
55	.389	.498	.484	.075	.069	.060
56	−.019	.071	.016	.086	.080	.064
57	−.078	.071	.019	.099	.092	.161
58	−.048	.071	−.021	.114	.107	.097
59	−.057	.069	−.026	.132	.123	.110
60	−.067	1.079	−.008	.643	.233	.127
61	−.085	−.292	−.049	−.208	.048	.146
62	−.093	−.301	−.056	−.212	.045	.183
63	−.108	−.353	−.067	−.227	.039	−.078
64	−.079	−.079	−.006	−.102	.072	−.086
65	−.086	−.043	.018	−.099	.194	−.094
66	−.124	−.088	−.182	−.100	−.048	−.169
67	−.141	−.116	−.195	−.088	−.064	−.111
68	−.150	−.124	−.191	−.092	−.072	−.112
69	−.151	−.132	−.188	−.097	−.112	−.113
70	−.151	−.141	−.186	−.102	−.120	−.114

[a] There are no plans in the 62–65 or in the 65–65 early–normal retirement groups.

and, therefore, provide very important incentives to remain with the firm until the age that the special supplement is awarded. The special supplements also further dramatize the wide variation in the incentive effects implicit in the provisions of private pension plans.

6. PENSION ACCRUAL AND RETIREMENT IN A LARGE FIRM

This section considers the relationship between pension accrual and retirement in the Fortune 500 firm whose plan is described in section 3. The data are the employment and earnings histories between 1969 and 1984 of all workers employed by the firm in any years between 1980 and 1984. There are five sex-occupation groups: male and female office workers, male and female salesworkers, and male managers. The provisions of the firm pension plan are such that different workers face very different pension accrual profiles and, thus, pension compensation. As a consequence, different workers face very different incentives for continued work versus retirement.

To illustrate these provisions, pension accruals and predicted wages (see Kotlikoff and Wise (1987)) for managers with different birth and hire years are shown in Tables 7 and 8, respectively. Those born in 1940 reach age 55 in 1995, and for each of these groups there is a discontinuous increase in pension wealth in that year. It is $29,639 for those with fifteen years of service in that year and $82,953 for those with twenty-five years of service. Comparable jumps occur in 1985 for those born in 1930. Accruals are often negative for persons over 60. The differences in accruals because of different amounts of service indicated in the table reflect the fact that the benefit formula and early retirement reduction factors are service dependent.

Pension accruals provide a large incentive for some groups to stay in the firm for another year and a strong incentive for others to leave. For example, staying with the firm in 1985 brings pension accrual of $72,527 for 55-year-old managers with twenty-five years of service (born in 1930 and hired in 1960), but a *loss* of $14,936 for 65-year-olds with thirty-five years of experience (born in 1920 and hired in 1950). Thus there is enormous variation across older workers in the effective compensation for continued service. One might expect, therefore, that some groups would be much more likely than others to retire in a given year.

The pension accrual profiles for other employee groups look very much like those for male managers. Accrual is minimal during the first years of service. There is a substantial discontinuous increase in pension wealth at age 55; and accrual typically becomes negative after thirty years of service—sometimes before that. Social Security accrual becomes negative after 65. The major differences among the groups stem from different age-earnings profiles. An illustration of the similarity and difference is provided by comparing Figure 3, which depicts accrual profiles for male managers, with Figure 7, which depicts profiles for salesmen.

6.1 The Retirement Response to the Pattern of Pension Accrual

Table 9 presents annual departure rates, the proportion of workers who leave the firm before the end of the year, cross-tabulated by age and years of service. Several aspects of the data stand out. There is substantial turnover in the first nine years of employment, especially during the first five years. On average, about 15 percent of those employed five years or less leave in a given year. The table shows rates only for employees 40 and older. The departure rates are somewhat higher for younger workers, 16 or 17 percent for those employed five years or less, and 10 to 12 percent for those employed 6 to 9 years. There is a sharp decline in departure rates at ten years of service, when employees are about to become vested in the pension plan. Before the early retirement age (55), the typical decline is from 8 or 9 percent to 4 or 5 percent. After 55, when vesting carries with it eligibility for early retirement, it is much sharper, often from 10 percent or more to 3 percent or less.

The availability of early retirement benefits at 55 apparently has a substantial effect on retirement. Before 55, departure rates are typically around 2 percent over a broad spectrum of age-service combinations. At 55, they jump to 10 percent or more. Note that the departure rates stay at that level until age 60, when there is another jump in the rate of departure. The jump at 60 corresponds to the age at which pension accrual becomes negative for many employees.

To understand the potential importance of the early retirement benefits, suppose that if it were not for this inducement, the departure rates would remain at 3 percent until age 60, instead of the 10 or 12 percent rates that are observed. (Notice that the departure rates for employees aged 55 to 61 who are in their tenth year of service—not yet vested and hence not eligible for early retirement benefits—are also 2 or 3 percent on average.) Departure at 3 percent per year would mean that 14 percent of those employed at 55 would have left before age 60. At a departure rate of 11 percent per year, 44 percent would leave between 55 and 59. Such a difference, even if only for a small proportion of all firms, can have a substantial effect on aggregate labor force participation rates.

The jump in departure rates at 60, especially noticeable for persons with twenty-five or more years of service, was just mentioned. There is another

TABLE 7
Accrual in Pension Wealth by Year of Birth and Year of Hire for Managers

Year Born	1960	1950		1940			1930
Year Hired	1980	1980	1975	1980	1975	1970	1980
1980	0	0	0	0	0	508	0
1981	0	0	0	0	0	380	0
1982	0	0	0	0	0	770	0
1983	0	0	0	0	0	582	0
1984	0	0	1,278	0	2,470	1,494	0
1985	0	0	251	0	475	767	0
1986	0	0	663	0	1,335	2,090	0
1987	0	0	353	0	651	994	0
1988	0	0	663	0	1,289	1,978	0
1989	1,008	2,158	767	4,037	1,479	2,323	22,194
1990	194	388	890	688	1,709	2,676	831
1991	341	690	1,051	1,297	2,174	3,168	1,060
1992	418	845	1,260	1,601	2,675	3,820	609
1993	504	1,016	1,485	2,021	3,202	4,515	−89
1994	606	1,220	1,756	2,603	3,851	5,351	−908
1995	716	1,441	2,043	29,639	40,727	82,953	−2,067
1996	843	1,695	2,555	7,130	9,538	9,898	5,217
1997	987	1,986	2,992	7,349	9,672	11,334	4,579
1998	1,153	2,422	3,499	7,437	9,641	10,665	3,902
1999	1,342	2,969	4,085	7,377	9,426	7,844	3,186
2000	1,558	3,492	3,900	7,140	6,196	8,643	2,423
2001	1,807	4,095	4,481	4,432	2,198	−6,178	0
2002	2,093	4,790	5,149	3,750	1,206	−7,237	0
2003	2,517	5,587	5,904	2,870	−15	−8,380	0
2004	3,037	6,502	6,763	1,791	4,378	−9,658	0
2005	2,918	95,433	117,775	−2,553	−8,981	−11,004	0
2006	3,361	11,955	14,674	−1,993	−4,042	−6,843	0
2007	3,872	13,705	16,840	−2,784	−4,988	−7,994	0
2008	4,461	13,022	15,944	−3,601	−5,955	−9,155	0
2009	5,139	9,809	11,879	−4,436	−6,930	−10,299	0
2010	5,910	10,923	13,211	−5,265	−7,875	−11,375	0
2011	6,792	−6,583	−8,668	0	0	0	0
2012	7,801	−7,785	−10,184	0	0	0	0
2013	8,940	−9,069	−11,809	0	0	0	0
2014	10,223	−10,418	−13,531	0	0	0	0
2015	168,439	−11,848	−15,345	0	0	0	0
2016	21,859	−8,684	−12,662	0	0	0	0
2017	25,137	−9,994	−14,317	0	0	0	0
2018	23,904	−11,319	−15,995	0	0	0	0
2019	17,968	−12,627	−17,524	0	0	0	0
2020	19,964	−13,849	−18,933	0	0	0	0
2021	−12,355	0	0	0	0	0	0
2022	−14,649	0	0	0	0	0	0
2023	−17,087	0	0	0	0	0	0
2024	−19,659	0	0	0	0	0	0
2025	−22,287	0	0	0	0	0	0
2026	−21,570	0	0	0	0	0	0
2027	−24,026	0	0	0	0	0	0
2028	−26,391	0	0	0	0	0	0
2029	−28,576	0	0	0	0	0	0
2030	−30,436	0	0	0	0	0	0

Pension Backloading, Wage Taxes, and Work Disincentives 187

TABLE 7

	1930				1920			
1975	1970	1960	1980	1975	1970	1960	1950
0	835	2,686	0	0	1,178	5,146	7,442
0	562	2,059	0	0	−616	−105	−9,132
0	1,413	3,716	0	0	451	2,175	−5,043
0	1,079	2,710	0	0	−2,739	−2,721	−13,235
2,968	3,053	6,530	0	5,090	658	3,575	−2,995
18,226	26,481	72,527	0	−5,357	−5,328	−8,152	−14,936
5,616	8,227	13,781	0	0	8,151	3,728	831
2,593	3,691	4,118	0	0	2,108	−4,957	−10,017
4,105	5,874	8,553	0	4,176	3,987	−1,882	−6,347
3,745	5,342	5,263	0	5,038	2,968	−3,049	−7,920
3,280	4,726	5,382	0	4,265	2,109	−3,889	−8,984
1,685	2,376	−7,118	0	0	0	0	0
1,389	2,029	−7,356	0	0	0	0	0
683	1,312	−8,127	0	0	0	0	0
−155	419	−8,902	0	0	0	0	0
−1,384	−3,515	−10,152	0	0	0	0	0
3,628	−939	−5,346	0	0	0	0	0
2,855	−1,652	−6,363	0	0	0	0	0
2,041	−2,384	−7,386	0	0	0	0	0
1,187	−3,129	−8,394	0	0	0	0	0
−1,882	−3,874	−9,344	0	0	0	0	0
0	0	0	0	0	0	0	0
0	0	0	0	0	0	0	0
0	0	0	0	0	0	0	0
0	0	0	0	0	0	0	0
0	0	0	0	0	0	0	0
0	0	0	0	0	0	0	0
0	0	0	0	0	0	0	0
0	0	0	0	0	0	0	0
0	0	0	0	0	0	0	0
0	0	0	0	0	0	0	0
0	0	0	0	0	0	0	0
0	0	0	0	0	0	0	0
0	0	0	0	0	0	0	0
0	0	0	0	0	0	0	0
0	0	0	0	0	0	0	0
0	0	0	0	0	0	0	0
0	0	0	0	0	0	0	0
0	0	0	0	0	0	0	0
0	0	0	0	0	0	0	0
0	0	0	0	0	0	0	0
0	0	0	0	0	0	0	0
0	0	0	0	0	0	0	0
0	0	0	0	0	0	0	0

TABLE 8
Wage Earnings by Year of Birth and Year of Hire for Managers

Year Born	1960	1950		1940			1930
Year Hired	1980	1980	1975	1980	1975	1970	1980
1980	20,405	24,053	33,021	27,894	34,020	40,712	31,825
1981	22,852	26,082	34,967	29,403	35,354	41,853	32,739
1982	25,312	28,057	36,807	30,819	36,586	42,898	33,548
1983	27,757	29,965	38,542	32,141	37,720	43,858	34,256
1984	30,615	32,271	40,774	33,869	39,342	45,410	35,390
1985	33,479	34,543	42,948	35,535	40,904	46,913	36,447
1986	36,331	36,774	45,069	37,140	42,409	48,374	37,427
1987	39,155	38,960	47,139	38,685	43,859	49,794	38,331
1988	41,933	41,092	49,158	40,163	45,250	51,168	39,152
1989	44,653	43,166	51,128	41,572	46,580	52,493	39,886
1990	47,309	45,183	53,056	42,913	47,850	53,766	40,530
1991	49,904	47,147	54,951	44,187	49,059	54,987	41,083
1992	52,429	49,052	56,809	45,387	50,198	56,140	41,533
1993	54,889	50,900	58,636	46,509	51,262	57,216	41,873
1994	57,292	52,698	60,438	47,553	52,247	58,206	42,099
1995	59,645	54,444	62,216	48,514	53,142	59,093	42,200
1996	61,954	56,140	63,969	49,382	53,935	59,860	42,166
1997	64,230	57,786	65,695	50,151	54,615	60,487	41,988
1998	66,481	59,380	67,389	50,812	55,166	60,954	41,656
1999	68,717	60,920	69,047	51,353	55,573	61,236	41,161
2000	70,946	62,398	70,655	51,760	55,816	61,307	40,493
2001	73,178	63,814	72,206	52,023	55,879	61,148	0
2002	75,415	65,151	73,676	52,123	55,739	60,728	0
2003	77,667	66,402	75,052	52,047	55,381	60,028	0
2004	79,931	67,550	76,307	51,779	54,783	59,027	0
2005	82,213	68,581	77,417	51,305	53,931	57,709	0
2006	84,502	69,471	78,349	50,609	52,810	56,063	0
2007	86,796	70,199	79,069	49,678	51,410	54,084	0
2008	89,081	70,739	79,543	48,503	49,727	51,778	0
2009	91,347	71,067	79,735	47,081	47,764	49,160	0
2010	93,567	71,151	79,604	45,408	45,526	46,251	0
2011	95,721	70,965	79,114	0	0	0	0
2012	97,774	70,478	78,230	0	0	0	0
2013	99,694	69,665	76,922	0	0	0	0
2014	101,438	68,503	75,168	0	0	0	0
2015	102,959	66,974	72,952	0	0	0	0
2016	104,202	65,062	70,267	0	0	0	0
2017	105,115	62,766	67,124	0	0	0	0
2018	105,638	60,090	63,546	0	0	0	0
2019	105,712	57,051	59,572	0	0	0	0
2020	105,277	53,675	55,254	0	0	0	0
2021	104,279	0	0	0	0	0	0
2022	102,671	0	0	0	0	0	0
2023	100,415	0	0	0	0	0	0
2024	97,484	0	0	0	0	0	0
2025	93,875	0	0	0	0	0	0
2026	89,598	0	0	0	0	0	0
2027	84,690	0	0	0	0	0	0
2028	79,209	0	0	0	0	0	0
2029	73,239	0	0	0	0	0	0
2030	66,886	0	0	0	0	0	0

TABLE 8

	1930				1920			
1975	1970	1960	1980	1975	1970	1960	1950
34,945	38,666	48,446	35,723	35,788	36,519	40,186	47,598
35,666	39,226	48,813	36,006	35,902	36,470	39,794	46,774
36,289	39,693	49,098	36,188	35,919	36,323	39,280	45,765
36,819	40,074	49,300	36,276	35,845	36,080	38,642	44,568
37,818	40,977	50,156	36,819	36,215	36,277	38,446	43,828
38,741	41,803	50,919	37,271	36,488	36,362	38,092	42,847
39,588	42,551	51,579	37,632	36,660	36,333	37,574	41,624
40,358	43,216	52,122	37,900	36,728	36,181	36,885	40,157
41,042	43,785	52,524	38,066	36,679	35,895	36,014	38,445
41,633	44,249	52,765	38,124	36,507	35,467	34,956	36,499
42,127	44,599	52,826	38,067	36,205	34,891	33,713	34,339
42,517	44,827	52,690	0	0	0	0	0
42,790	44,914	52,329	0	0	0	0	0
42,935	44,847	51,724	0	0	0	0	0
42,946	44,616	50,861	0	0	0	0	0
42,809	44,207	49,725	0	0	0	0	0
42,513	43,607	48,307	0	0	0	0	0
42,048	42,805	46,602	0	0	0	0	0
41,403	41,794	44,615	0	0	0	0	0
40,570	40,568	42,359	0	0	0	0	0
39,542	39,125	39,852	0	0	0	0	0
0	0	0	0	0	0	0	0
0	0	0	0	0	0	0	0
0	0	0	0	0	0	0	0
0	0	0	0	0	0	0	0
0	0	0	0	0	0	0	0
0	0	0	0	0	0	0	0
0	0	0	0	0	0	0	0
0	0	0	0	0	0	0	0
0	0	0	0	0	0	0	0
0	0	0	0	0	0	0	0
0	0	0	0	0	0	0	0
0	0	0	0	0	0	0	0
0	0	0	0	0	0	0	0
0	0	0	0	0	0	0	0
0	0	0	0	0	0	0	0
0	0	0	0	0	0	0	0
0	0	0	0	0	0	0	0
0	0	0	0	0	0	0	0
0	0	0	0	0	0	0	0
0	0	0	0	0	0	0	0
0	0	0	0	0	0	0	0
0	0	0	0	0	0	0	0

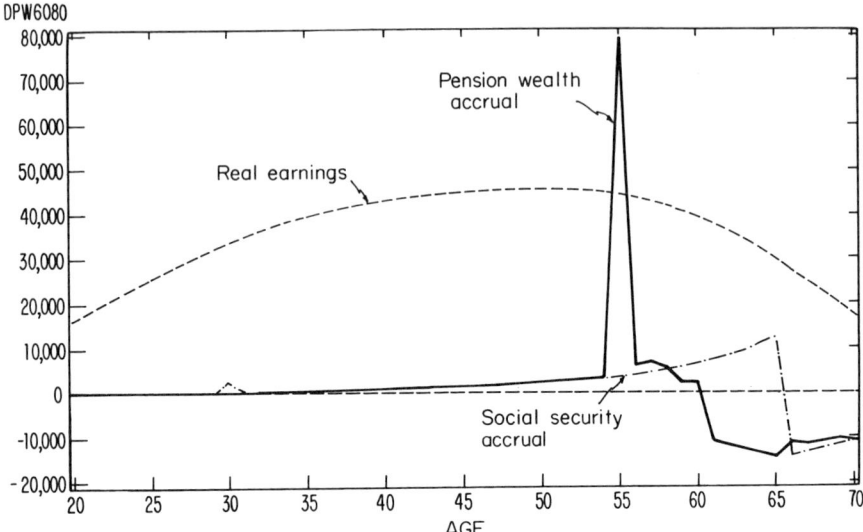

FIGURE 7. *Pension wealth accrual, SS accrual and wage earnings for salesmen born in 1960 and hired in 1980, in real 1985 dollars.*

sharp increase in departure rates at 62 when Social Security benefits are first available. The increase at 62 is also noticeable for employees with less than ten years of service and not yet vested in the firm's pension plan. They can take Social Security benefits, of course.

Finally, there is a very sharp increase in the departure rate at age 65. For many workers the total reward for working after age 65 is close to zero, due to negative pension and Social Security accruals. It is important to keep in mind that the large departure rates before 65 mean that most employees have left well before that age. Thus high annual departure rates at 65 indicate only that a large proportion of the few that continue working until 65 retire then. This point is highlighted in Table 10, which presents the cumulative fraction remaining with the firm from age 50 to each specified age.

Note first that departure rates of employees who have been in the firm for only eight to ten years and are not yet vested are very low at every age, as emphasized above. And again, the increase in the departure rates at 55, 60, 62, and 65 stands out. Based on the 1981 and 1983 departure rates, only 48 percent of those employed at 50 would still be employed at 60, and then 17 percent of these would leave. Only 10 percent would remain until age 65 and then about 50 percent of these would leave.

TABLE 9
Departure Rates, by Age and Years of Service, of All Employee Groups (percent)

Age	≤5	6–9	10	11–15	16–20	21–23	24	25	26	27	28	29	30	31+
40	15	8	5	7	4	3	0							
41	14	9	5	7	5	5	3	5						
42	14	10	8	8	4	2	2	2	0	0				
43	15	7	6	5	4	4	4	3	2	0	0	0		
44	13	8	5	7	3	2	3	1	1	1	0	0	0	
45	11	7	5	6	6	4	3	1	4	2	3	5	0	.5
46	12	9	3	5	3	4	4	1	0	5	2	2	0	0
47	14	8	8	5	4	3	3	4	4	4	0	4	2	0
48	12	7	5	6	4	4	2	5	1	2	4	2	3	2
49	14	9	4	7	4	3	5	1	1	1	1	2	0	0
50	14	8	4	6	4	3	3	2	2	1	1	3	2	3
51	14	9	3	5	3	3	5	2	3	4	2	2	2	5
52	11	7	5	6	4	4	2	4	2	4	1	3	6	6
53	12	7	4	7	4	3	3	3	3	2	3	3	3	3
54	11	7	4	6	4	2	4	2	2	3	1	0	1	3
55	9	5	4	11	9	11	13	10	13	11	12	7	9	9
56	11	6	6	12	11	12	7	8	11	11	12	16	14	12
57	12	10	1	11	8	9	10	8	9	9	3	14	11	11
58	13	10	2	8	8	12	13	11	13	15	9	10	13	12
59	7	10	2	17	8	11	17	14	13	14	9	10	12	15
60	9	9	3	15	12	19	16	17	20	16	20	15	19	26
61	9	7	2	16	17	15	19	12	25	16	23	21	24	30
62	11	15	7	27	34	37	34	33	38	40	42	34	30	41
63	14	18	4	33	35	37	43	35	43	41	62	33	47	40
64	5	8	3	36	33	34	18	32	26	27	42	53	41	34
65	12	35	45	57	52	54	44	55	57	70	50	54	69	59
66	26	17	25	16	16	43	50	16	20	25	38	33	9	24
67	13	28	18	32	17	29	0	14	21	0	13	33	50	21
68	13	50	50	15	25	11	0	50	0	29	0	0	0	12

The data also show the effect of a special early retirement incentive that was in effect in 1982 only. The incentive program provided a bonus to employees who were eligible for early retirement in 1982; that is, those who were vested and were 55 years old or older. The bonus was equivalent to three months salary for 55-year-old employees and increased to twelve

TABLE 10
Cumulative and Yearly Departure Rates by Calendar Year, Years of Services, and Age

Age	YDR[a] (8–10 YOS[b]) 1980	YDR (11+ YOS) 1981	YDR (11+ YOS) 1982	YDR (11+ YOS) 1983	Cumulative Fraction Staying in Firm (11+ YOS) 1981	Cumulative Fraction Staying in Firm (11+ YOS) 1982	Cumulative Fraction Staying in Firm (11+ YOS) 1983
50	7				97	97	97
51	9	3			94	94	94
52	3	5	5		89	89	89
53	0	4	4		85	86	86
54	4	3	4	2	83	83	84
55	5	11	12	10	74	73	75
56	4	12	14	10	66	63	68
57	2	9	12	11	60	56	61
58	5	10	14	12	54	48	54
59	2	11	20	10	48	38	48
60	4	17	29	17	40	27	40
61	0	17	32	18	33	18	33
62	8	36	48	31	21	10	23
63	14	37	54	37	13	5	14
64		29	49	26	10	2	11
65			58	45	5	1	6
66							

[a] YDR = yearly departure rates.
[b] YOS = years of service.

months salary for 60-year-olds. At age 65, the bonus was twelve months salary for employees with twenty or fewer years of service and declined to six months salary for those with thirty to thirty-nine years of service.

It is clear that the effect of the incentive was large. The departure rates for 1981 and for 1983 are virtually identical. But the rates were much higher in 1982. For example, the departure rate for 60-year-olds was 17 percent in 1981 and in 1983, but 32 percent in 1982. For those aged 63, the departure rate was 37 percent in 1981 and in 1983, but 54 percent in 1982. Of those employed at age 50, 40 percent would still have been employed after age 60 based on the 1981 and 1983 departure rates. Only 27 percent would remain after age 60 based on the 1982 rates.

A great deal of effort has been devoted to estimating the effect of Social Security provisions on labor force participation. In particular, Hausman and Wise (1985), Burtless (1986), and Boskin and Hurd (1984) have attempted to estimate the effect on labor force participation of the increases in Social Security benefits during the early 1970s. It would appear from the results here that the effects of these across-the-board increases in Social Security benefits are likely to be small relative to the effects of the private pension provisions. For example, it seems clear that shifting the age of early retirement in the firm plan from 55 to 60 would have a very dramatic effect on departure rates. Leaving the early retirement age at 55, but eliminating negative pension and Social Security accruals, thereafter, would apparently also have a substantial effect on retirement rates.

7. SUMMARY AND CONCLUSIONS

Most defined benefit plans are strongly backloaded, notwithstanding ERISA legislation aimed at limiting it. For a sizable fraction of defined benefit plans, the special shape of pension accrual profiles produced significant incentives to remain with one's current employer before early retirement. After the age of normal retirement, and often after early retirement, pension accrual profiles typically provide substantial incentives to leave employment. They impose a large implicit tax on employment. These retirement incentives appear large when compared, for example, with the retirement incentives arising under Social Security. Hence, the structure of private pensions may be contributing substantially to the very high rates of early retirement currently observed in the United States.

Under the contract view of labor markets, pension accrual profiles might be thought of as carrot-stick incentives to continue working diligently to some age and to retire at a subsequent age. This presumes that pension accrual profiles are well understood by both employers and workers. In our view this is unlikely. The great complexity of pension provisions makes it quite difficult for either employers or workers, in the absence of assistance from actuaries, to calculate correctly their accrued pension benefits. A few firms, including the large Firm examined here, provide accrual information annually to their workers, but most, apparently, do not. It also appears that many firms with access to actuaries do not have their actuaries calculate worker-specific accrual.

It is important to understand the effects of pension plan provisions on the labor force participation of older workers. But the contract view of the labor market also makes it clear that evaluation of pension accrual is best considered in conjunction with age-wage compensation profiles. If, for example, legislation were to prevent the reduction in the compensation of older workers through pension plan provisions, such reduction might be sought through reduction of wage and salary earnings, to conform to age-productivity profiles. In this case, what constitutes age discrimination and the potential effects of age discrimination legislation must also be considered. A partial view of the whole may yield decisions with unforeseen and unintended consequences. Pension plan provisions may provide a graceful way of making adjustments in a firm's labor force, and, in particular, of releasing older workers from the labor force. On the other hand, the decision to continue work at older ages is not, now, a neutral one. In the words of tax analysts, the playing field is far from flat. Should individual preferences for work versus retirement be constrained by the implicit wage-tax structure of pension plans?

The backloading of pension accrual in the presence of limited worker and employer understanding of such backloading raises a variety of important questions. Do workers over- or undervalue their accrued vested pension benefits? Do workers over- or undersave because they under- or overvalue their pensions? Are workers who leave highly backloaded firms prior to the age of early retirement, at which age accrual is often very substantial, aware of the often substantial pension costs of their actions? Is accrual backloading raising the economic costs of early disability, because workers who become disabled prior to the age of early retirement receive less generous pensions than those who remain through early retirement? Should employers be required to provide workers with annual statements detailing accrued vested benefits as well as the time path of future projected pension accrual? These and related questions may need to be asked by employers, workers, and the United States Congress.

REFERENCES

Aaron, Henry J. 1982. *Economic effects of Social Security*. Washington, D.C.: Brookings Institution.

Becker, Gary, and George Shafer. 1974. Law enforcement, malefeasance and the compensation enforcers. *Journal of Legal Studies*.

Blinder, Alan. 1982. Private pensions and public pensions: Theory and fact. NBER Working Paper no. 902.

Blinder, Alan, and Roger Gordon. 1980. Market wages, reservation wages and retirement. *Journal of Public Economics* 14: 277–308.

Blinder, Alan, Roger Gordon, and Donald Wise. 1980. Reconsidering the work disincentive effects of social security. *National Tax Journal* 33: 431–42.

———. 1981. Life cycle savings and bequests: Cross-sectional estimates of the life cycle model. NBER Working Paper no. 619.

Boskin, Michael. 1977. Social Security and retirement decisions. *Economic Inquiry* 15: 1–25.

Boskin, Michael, and Michael Hurd. 1978. The effect of Social Security on early retirement. *Journal of Public Economics* 10: 361–77.

Bulow, J. 1979. Analysis of pension funding under ERISA. NBER Working Paper no. 402.

Bureau of Labor Statistics. Selected Issues. Employment and earnings. Washington, D.C.: U.S. Government Printing Office.

Burkhauser, Richard V. 1977. An asset maximization approach to early Social Security acceptance. Discussion Paper 463-77, Institute for Research on Poverty. Madison: University of Wisconsin.

Burkhauser, Richard V., and John A. Turner. 1978. A time-series analysis on Social Security and its effect on the market work of men at younger ages. *Journal of Political Economy*.

———. 1981. Can twenty-five million Americans be wrong?—A response to Blinder, Gordon and Wise. *National Tax Journal* 34: 467–72.

Burtless, Gary, and J. Hausman. 1978. "Double dipping": The combined effects of social security and civil service pensions on employee retirement. *Journal of Political Economy* 18: 139–60.

Burtless, Gary, and Robert A. Moffitt. 1984. The effects of Social Security on the labor supply of the aged. In *Retirement and economic behavior*, eds. Henry Aaron and Gary Burtless. Washington, D.C.: Brookings Institution.

———. 1986. Social Security, the earnings test, and the age at retirement. *Public Finance Quarterly* 14: 3–27.

Campbell, C. D., and R. G. Campbell. 1976. Conflicting views on the effect of old-age and survivors' insurance on retirement. *Economic Inquiry* 14: 369–88.

Clark, Robert L., and Stephen A. Gohmann. 1982. Retirement and the acceptance of Social Security benefits. Raleigh: North Carolina State University, mimeo.

Crawford, V., and D. Lilien. 1981. Social Security and the retirement decision. *Quarterly Journal of Economics* 96: 509–29.

Diamond, P., and J. Hausman. 1984. The retirement and unemployment behavior of older men. In *Retirement and economic behavior*, eds. H. Aaron and G. Burtless. Washington, D.C.: Brookings Institution.

Fields, Gary, and Olivia Mitchell. Economic determinants of the optimal retirement age: An empirical investigation. *The Journal of Human Resources* 19: 245–62.

———. 1982. The effects of pensions and earnings on retirement: A review essay. In *Research in labor economics*, ed. R. Ehrenberg. 5: 115–56. Greenwich, CT: JAL Press.

———. 1983. Economic incentives to retire: A qualitative choice approach. NBER Working Paper no. 1096.

———. 1984. The economics of retirement behavior. *Journal of labor economics* 2: 84–105.

———. 1985. *Retirement, pensions, and Social Security*. Cambridge, Mass: MIT Press.

Irelan, L. 1976. Retirement history study: Introduction. In *Almost 65: Baseline data from the retirement history study*. U.S. Department of Health, Education and Welfare, Social Security Administration, Office of Research and Statistics. Washington, D.C.: Government Printing Office.

Kotlikoff, Laurence J. 1978. Social Security, time for reform. In *Federal tax reform: Myth or reality*. San Francisco: Institute for Contemporary Studies.

Kotlikoff, Laurence J., and Daniel Smith. 1983. *Pensions in the American economy*. Chicago: University of Chicago Press.

Kotlikoff, Laurence J., and David A. Wise. 1984. Labor compensation and the structure of private pension plans: Evidence for contractual versus spot labor markets. NBER Working Paper no. 1290.

———. 1987. *Pension compensation and retirement incentives: The wage carrot and the pension stick*. W. E. UpJohn Institute for Employment Research.

Lazear, E. P. 1981. Severance pay, pensions, mobility, and the efficiency of work incentives. University of Chicago, mimeo.

———. 1983. Pensions as severance pay. In *Financial aspects of the United States pension system*, eds. Zvi Bodie and John B. Shoven. Chicago: University of Chicago Press.

Parsons, Donald O. 1980. The decline in male labor force participation. *Journal of Political Economy* 88: 117–34.

Pellechio, Anthony J. 1978. The Social Security earnings test, labor supply distortions, and foregone payroll tax revenue. NBER Working Paper no. 272.

Quinn, Joseph P. 1977. Microeconomic determinants of early retirement: A cross-sectional view of white married men. *Journal of Human Resources* 12: 329–46.

Ransom, Roger L., and Richard Sutch. 1986. The labor of older Americans: retirement of men on and off the job, 1870–1937. *The Journal of Economic History* 61.